ONE WOMAN'S WAR

ONE WOMAN'S WAR

Letters Home from the Women's Army Corps 1944-1946

ANNE BOSANKO GREEN
With a Foreword by D'Ann Campbell

Minnesota Historical Society Press • St. Paul • 1989

The advertisement from the *Minneapolis Journal*, August 24,
1944, is from the collections of the Minnesota Historical Society.
All other photographs used in this book are in the author's
possession.

♾ The paper used in this publication meets the minimum
requirements of the American National Standard for
Information Sciences—Permanence for Printed Library
Materials, ANSI Z39.48-1984.

Minnesota Historical Society Press
St. Paul 55101

© 1989 by Anne Bosanko Green
Foreword © 1989 by Minnesota Historical Society
All rights reserved

Printed in the United States of America
10 9 8 7 6 5 4 3 2 1

Library of Congress Cataloging-in-Publication Data
Green, Anne B. (Anne Bosanko), 1924-
    One woman's war : letters home from the Women's Army
  Corps, 1944-46 / Anne B. Green ; foreword by D'Ann Campbell.
        p.   cm.
    ISBN 0-87351-246-4
    1. Green, Anne B. (Anne Bosanko), 1924-
—Correspondence.   2. World War, 1939-1945—Medical care—
United States.   3. World War 1939-1945—Personal narratives,
American.   4. United States. Army. Women's Army Corps—
Biography.   5. Medical assistants—United States—
Correspondence.   I. Title.
D807.U6G74   1989
940.54'8173—dc20   89-13000
                                                    CIP

To my mother, who saved all my letters;

To my daughters Kate and Martha, who
  were the first to read and enjoy them.

Contents

Foreword
COMING OF AGE IN THE WOMEN'S ARMY CORPS
D'Ann Campbell

Historians have been refighting World War II ever since it broke out fifty years ago. Yet only a handful of the tens of thousands of books recognize that women were involved, too. Because war is such a masculine preserve and because historians, whether they celebrate or deplore the war itself, have been mostly fascinated by fighting, there seems to be no place for women. The novels of World War II likewise have avoided the roles women played. The void has been filled, to a limited extent, by Hollywood. A few wartime films have dealt with women in uniform, and to this day movies and television miniseries have an obligatory woman or two in uniform. Only in the last two decades has a vigorous women's history movement given us a clear picture of what civilian women on the home front were like.[1] The women still neglected by historians are those who served in the military. Feminist historians have averted their gaze from anything militaristic. Military historians, perhaps viewing the military as the last bastion of masculinity, have also slighted the topic.[2]

[1] On women on the home front as homemakers, servicemen's wives, factory workers, secretaries, domestic servants, sales clerks, teachers, and nurses, see D'Ann Campbell, *Women at War with America: Private Lives in a Patriotic Era* (Cambridge: Harvard University Press, 1984); William Chafe, *The American Woman: Her Changing Social, Economic, and Political Roles, 1920–1970* (New York: Oxford University Press, 1972); Karen Sue Anderson, *Wartime Women: Sex Roles, Family Relations, and the Status of Women during World War II* (Westport, Conn.: Greenwood, 1981); and Susan M. Hartmann, *The Home Front and Beyond: American Women in the 1940s* (Boston: Twayne, 1982).
[2] By far the best history of the WAC is Mattie E. Treadwell, *United States Army in World War II: Special Studies — The Women's Army Corps* (Washington, D.C.: Government Printing Office, 1954). See also Campbell, *Women at War with America*, chapters 1–2;

ix

ONE WOMAN'S WAR

   If the military was so masculine, why were women allowed to
serve in the first place? The main reason was that senior command-
ers, like Generals Dwight Eisenhower and George Marshall, were
highly impressed with the performance of the British and Canadian women in uniform in England. They typed, filed, telephoned,
and chauffeured with skill and enthusiasm. Best of all they released
able-bodied men who could be sent into combat units instead of
being stuck in office jobs. The generals wanted a million or more
women to volunteer. Civilians were no substitute for subordinates
who could be ordered to work long hours in emergencies, to move
from site to site as needed, to follow every order, and who would
stay on the job as long as the Pentagon desired. Above all they did
clerical work that in civilian life was normally done by women. To
have men do that work was a waste of combat potential. Despite
doubts from traditionalists, the brass got its way. On May 15, 1942,
President Franklin D. Roosevelt signed legislation creating the
Women's Army Auxiliary Corps (WAAC), which enlisted women
but grudgingly yielded them only second-class military status. The
officers of the WAAC did not have the authority of "real" (male)
officers, and all Waacs received lesser pay and fewer benefits. The
navy was more egalitarian, and by July 1942 began to accept Waves
(Women Accepted for Voluntary Emergency Service) on the same
basis as male reservists. Soon the Coast Guard and marines set up
their units. The anomalous status of the WAAC was finally rectified
in June 1943 when it became the Women's Army Corps (WAC) with
equal rank and pay. At peak strength 100,000 women served in the

Jeanne Holm, *Women in the Military: An Unfinished Revolution* (Novato, Calif.: Presidio
Press, 1982), chapters 1–9; Dorothy Schaffer, *What Comes of Training Women for War*
(Washington, D.C.: Government Printing Office, 1948); and June A. Willenz, *Women
Veterans: America's Forgotten Heroines* (New York: Continuum, 1984). Interesting
memoirs include Joy Bright Hancock, *Lady in the Navy: A Personal Reminiscence*
(Annapolis: U.S. Naval Institute Press, 1972), a senior Wave; Charity Adams Earley,
One Woman's Army: A Black Officer Remembers the WAC (College Station: Texas A & M
University Press, 1989), by the highest ranking black woman; Georgia B. Watson,
World War II in a Khaki Skirt (Moore Haven, Fla.: Rainbow Books, 1985); Marie
Bennett Alsmeyer, *The Way of the WAVEs: Women in the Navy* (Conway, Ark.: Hamba
Books, 1981); and Sara Ann Allen, ed., *Daughters of Pallas Athene: Cameo Recollections
of Women's Army Corps Veterans* (Kansas City, Mo.: Women's Army Corps Veterans
Assn., 1983). For contemporary accounts, see Elizabeth R. Pollock, *Yes, Ma'am: The
Personal Papers of a WAAC Private* (Philadelphia: J. B. Lippincott Co., 1943); Barbara
A. White, *Lady Leatherneck* (New York: Dodd, Mead and Co., 1945); Joan Angel,
Angel of the Navy: The Story of a WAVE (New York: Hastings House, 1943); Helen Hull
Jacobs, *"By Your Leave, Sir": The Story of a Wave* (New York: Dodd, Mead and Co.,
1943). On the nurses, see Campbell, *Women at War with America*, chapter 2, and Philip
A. Kalisch and Beatrice J. Kalisch, *The Advance of American Nursing* (Boston: Scott
Foresman, 1978), 445–89.

WAAC/WAC, and 170,000 served in the other branches. Counting turnover, women volunteers included 140,000 Waacs/Wacs, 100,000 Waves, 23,000 marines, 13,000 Coast Guard Spars, 60,000 army nurses, and 14,000 navy nurses.

Turning women into soldiers was the most dramatic break with traditional gender roles that occurred in the twentieth century. In many respects World War II was a watershed. To understand the roles women have played and can play in American society, to understand the all-volunteer military, to understand the importance of this issue in the defeat of the Equal Rights Amendment— we must appreciate what happened to women in the military during World War II.[3]

How can we recreate the experiences of women in uniform during the war? The answer includes ransacking the national archives and state and local libraries, conducting oral histories with women veterans, designing and distributing questionnaires, and encouraging veterans to write their memoirs. Many families have carefully preserved the correspondence of World War II. These letters should be donated to local and state historical societies. Some are love letters between a young man and woman that tell us a great deal about romance in a different age. Some are superficial reports of daily routines. It is rare to find a collection of letters that spans an entire war experience. It is rarer still to find letters from someone who reflects on as well as describes what is happening to her. Some collections will prove as rich, as thoughtful, and as perceptive as the Anne Bosanko letters and deserve publication in their own right. All will enrich the collective memory of the nation.[4]

---

[3] The Equal Rights Amendment was defeated primarily because women (and men) were uncertain about whether women should be drafted in wartime and, if so, whether they should serve in combat. Most Americans wanted women to be drafted if men were, but not to be required to serve in combat. Thus most Americans thought a critical exception should be made to the rule of strict equality between men and women—an exception incompatible with an iron-clad constitutional amendment. Unfortunately, very few people pondered just what "combat" means in a nuclear age, and no one turned to the World War II record where women served in "combat" roles in Britain, Germany, and the USSR. Combat usually meant antiaircraft batteries, where the risk of death was high but the risk of capture by the enemy was minimal. The line was drawn at capture, rather than death. Those nations urgently needed all the combatants they could get, a desperate condition never approached by the United States. See Nancy Loring Goldman, ed., *Female Soldiers—Combatants or Noncombatants? Historical and Contemporary Perspectives* (Westport, Conn.: Greenwood, 1982).
[4] For a fascinating collection of servicemen's letters, see Howard H. Peckham and Shirley A. Snyder, eds., *Letters from Fighting Hoosiers* (Bloomington: Indiana University Press, 1948).

Anne Bosanko's letters to her family are artfully written personal chronicles of day-to-day activities. They tell us of growing up in America in the 1940s, they show what family life was like on the inside, and they reveal the workings of the army and the Women's Army Corps. Through these letters we learn about Anne, about her family, about Minnesota and the home front, and about the experiences of so many young adults who found wartime work disruptive and fascinating. It is not surprising that the author eventually became a psychologist. Her letters characterize people and events in a way that is captivating and compelling and often humorous. They reveal the motivations, ambitions, inhibitions, and frustrations of a generation. Anne was typical of four out of five women in uniform who performed women's jobs and were stationed in the United States. They were not under fire; they never dealt with generals or admirals, let alone presidents and prime ministers. Anne worked in a hospital and saw many wounded and crippled soldiers, but she was never near a battlefield. What Anne described in vivid detail were the experiences of the majority of women—and men—who served in uniform during the war. As she looked back from the vantage of 1989 she remarked:

> For millions of Americans who were young in the early forties, the war years were like a mountain-climbing adventure before coming out onto the settled adult plateau of the fifties. We had suddenly left our humdrum lives, our jobs, and our schools and were moved all around the vast United States or across the Atlantic and Pacific oceans to lands we'd never thought we would see. . . . We were learning new skills, meeting new people, eating and drinking exotic substances, and trying out new social roles.

One Woman's War begins on June 19, 1944, when Anne Bosanko wrote to tell her best friend Carrie that she was joining the Women's Army Corps. What other options were available to Anne? She had attended the University of Minnesota for two years but discovered it had been practically transmogrified into a women's college since most of the men were gone. While she was intent on finishing her education eventually, she wanted to contribute to the war effort now. The $50.00 a month salary for a Wac (plus allowances) paled before the $150.00 to $200.00 a month munitions factories paid. Indeed, Anne could have made more money in a war job than her father did by teaching at a small private prep school for boys, but it would have been rare for someone raised in a middle-class academic family to apply for factory work.[5] Furthermore, Anne wanted a piece of the action. When Waves in the navy recruiting office suggested that army women were second rate, Anne reacted against such snobbism and decided to join the WAC. In addition the WAC was the only corps that offered the possibility of overseas service, and it had just started recruiting enlisted women for a medical corps branch. Anne had no realistic expectation of becoming an officer, for most of the women (and men) who became officers had joined in 1942 or 1943.

Surveys taken during the war by the army and questionnaires filled out forty years later permit us to place Anne's background and motivations in perspective.[6] At age twenty and with two years of college, Anne was better educated and a bit younger than three-fourths of the Wacs. About a third of her comrades had well-educated parents and professional or managerial fathers. Like four out of five women in uniform, she was single. Only 3 percent of all Wacs had dropped out of college to enlist; the great majority had spent several years in the civilian work force, holding a wide variety of blue and white collar jobs.

Why did they volunteer for service? The question is especially important because a nationwide slander campaign—as vicious as it was false—slowed recruitment after 1943 and made many women think twice before they signed up.[7] Far fewer enlisted, despite intensive propaganda campaigns glorifying the woman in uniform. The problem was that most men did not want their sisters or girl friends in the army. It supposedly would, on the one hand, force men with safe jobs into combat duty, and on the other feminize the last bastion of masculinity. It would desex women, and yet make them whores. Forty-five years after the event one veteran filled out

---

[5] Campbell, *Women at War with America*, 101–62; Sherna B. Gluck, *Rosie the Riveter Revisited: Women, the War and Social Change* (Boston: Twayne, 1987).

[6] The questionnaires were collected from a sample of 700 women veterans. See D'Ann Campbell, "Servicewomen of World War Two: Attitudes, Values, and Turning Points," in *Armed Forces and Society* (1990), in press.

[7] The slander campaign painted all women soldiers as sexually promiscuous. Armed forces nurses and Canadian and British servicewomen experienced similar slander campaigns. The Pentagon called in the FBI to see if any of the rumors had any truth in them or if they could have been planted by Nazi agents. The FBI determined that American servicemen were inventing and spreading these rumors.

her questionnaire with lingering bitterness: "I joined the Waves and went to West Coast to be near my childhood sweetheart. While in Boot Camp, he sent a letter, ashamed of me for being in the service (called me a whore), I cried every night of Boot."

Anne Bosanko never faced such intense hostility. She could brush aside any doubts because of her intense patriotism, her relative isolation as a student from "sophisticated" cynicism, and, above all, because of the loving support of her parents. The questionnaires filled out in the 1980s showed that 41 percent of the women had to overcome the opposition of close relatives; only half said their closest male friends were supportive, in contrast to 80 percent of their closest female friends. "My own family didn't like the idea of my dressing like a man and joining the Army, but now they are proud of me," said one respondent who was a thirty-year-old married Waac during the war.

America was a patriotic nation in the 1940s, and patriotic explanations were genuine. Occasional emotional comments were eagerly seized by publicity bureaus: "My husband (brother, fiance) was killed at Pearl Harbor/ Java Sea/ Salerno" or "is a prisoner of war"; "sons are fighting" and "I want to get this war over as quickly as possible." But for the vast majority of women, and for Anne, the patriotic motivation was general, not personalized. "In civilian life I didn't feel I was doing enough. I just felt if I came into the WAAC I would be doing more," was a typical sentiment reported by veterans on their questionnaires. The Marine Corps estimated that one-fourth of its women joined for negative reasons: to escape from a boring job or family difficulty. "I didn't want to live with my aunt any longer" and "I had been working at a desk for 5 years and I thought I would like to get something that would give me a chance to be outdoors more," two Waacs explained in 1943. The Waac who joined because she was "so sick and tired of that typewriter I couldn't stand it any longer" probably erred in joining an army that wanted women to replace the ham-handed male typists who were needed in combat units. About half the marines enlisted because they had loved ones in the service (35 percent) or like Anne were from families with no men to send (6 percent) or wanted revenge because their men had already been killed (4 percent). "There were no boys in our family," a Waac explained. "My sister and I thought we should join since there was no one else to go." Of the remainder, half enlisted for adventure (15 percent) or to benefit themselves.

A Freudian interpretation by one researcher of the motives of eighteen thousand Wacs at Fort Des Moines in 1945 revealed that 35 percent sought to "satisfy their need for masculine gratification." "Ever since I've been a child I've always dressed up in uniforms. I love uniforms. I can imagine myself leading an army. I want to be an officer, and I'm particularly anxious to go overseas," said one respondent. One in six (16 percent) sought justification or expiation of guilt or had a need to sacrifice; 13 percent were escaping monotony or troubles at home. A few sought security (8 percent), enrolled on impulse (6 percent), or had feminist motivations (5 percent). The remaining 16 percent were chalked up to patriotism.[8] Anne Bosanko shared with other women who joined the military the support of her family. The father usually was the key. If he was supportive, a young woman could volunteer for the military. If he was hostile or if a brother was hostile, the young woman seldom joined.

Bosanko's relationship with her parents was close and mutually supportive. Her mother tended to worry if Anne's letters were delayed in the mail; she immediately imagined that her daughter was sick or in danger. Her mother warned her against stringing men along, dating too often, or drinking too much. Anne replied, "Mammy, don't you trust your little Annie? I'm not so little anymore, you know, and downtown El Paso is crawling with MPs who would come to my rescue if I couldn't handle situations, which I know I could." Later she reassured her mother, "you have absolutely no cause to worry. He's too fat to get excited about, so that is purely platonic and I mean really." Despite her anxieties her mother was basically supportive. "My dear, you are seeing Life in the RAW. I feel as if I should be very shocked and maternal and things, but all I can do is laugh at your screwball antics. I think you have plenty of balance and common sense to manage." When her mother admitted that she had been crabby, Anne wrote, "That's silly, Mom. That's your duty, with a silly brat far away from home who needs a crack on the bean." Her mother was proud that Anne was serving for the family. "As a family, I think we were very fortunate that you were the older and Mike did not have to see

[8] Campbell, "Servicewomen of World War Two." For the Fort Des Moines study, see Albert Preston, "The Mental Hygiene Unit in a W.A.C. Training Center," *Mental Hygiene* 30 (July 1946): 368–80. Only 45 percent reported an unbroken, happy home life like Anne's. Preston, a psychiatrist, discovered that 45 percent had a conscious preference for their mother, and 21 percent for their father; 10 percent were hostile to both parents.

service. With you we did not have to worry that you would be wounded or killed."

Like millions of mothers of GIs, Anne's mother made it a high priority to send care packages, filled with Toll House cookies. No daughter of hers would waste away on GI rations! Actually 82 percent of the Wacs gained weight during Basic Training—an average of six pounds, which showed up as one extra inch around the waist. "The diet is heavy and not nearly enough vegetables or salad," Anne wrote home, "I'm turning into a sphere." Anything urgently needed would soon arrive by U.S. Mail—from a suitcase to civilian underwear and pajamas. (Very few Wacs cared to wear the GI underwear designed by the Pentagon.)

Her father was witty as well as supportive in his letters. His shrewd insights into human nature come through clearly. He, too, worried about his daughter but restrained himself from preaching, a role he reserved for his wife. At one point he simply stated that now that Anne was twenty-one, a legal adult, and not doing anything that cost him money, he was prepared to be very support-ive. Yet Anne was just twenty when she first volunteered and began drinking and dating like a soldier. Her father vicariously lived through his daughter's experiences and recalled his own ups and downs nearly thirty years before:

> I know how you felt . . . for your Old Man was in Paris when the last war blew up. Now for a dull reaction and a trying time till you can get out. I have been through that, too, and urge patience and a realization of that fact that all things come to an end and that, rumors to the contrary, you will not spend the rest of your life in uniform, but will be returned to the bosom of your adoring family and the uncertainties of civilian life.

He assured his daughter that her moments of depression and frustration would pass. Their common bond was strengthened by Anne's wartime service.

> Sorry that you are (or were?) still in the dumps, but I have observed during a long, active and, dare I say interesting and not unuseful life (hrump, hrump) that such a condi-tion is not altogether unusual among younger and even more mature adults of both sexes at this particular period

of the ever-changing seasons of nature. Even I have been
known to feel flat in the spring and your honored and
much-beloved mother is quite frequently a pain in the
neck at this season.

But at other times he chastised Anne for giving into self pity;
remembering his own experience in World War I, he counselled a
stiff upper lip:

Take a brace on the fact that the place does not suit you
and remember that you are a soldier in a war and not a
girl on vacation. . . . If you are comfortable and safe, that's
about the maximum you have the right to expect. Most
soldiers are neither, so snap out of the grouch, be a soldier
and make the best of it.

It is amazing how frank Anne was in writing to her parents.
Her letters to her friends provide somewhat more graphic detail
about her love life and drinking sprees but even those episodes
were mentioned to her parents. The Bosankos were a close-knit,
loving, and candid family.

Ever since William Saroyan's 1943 novel, *The Human Comedy*,
and the film starring Mickey Rooney as the telegraph delivery boy,
we think of parents being notified of the death of a son in service.
It went the other way, too, and in June 1946 Corporal Bosanko was
called in to the office and read a telegram from her mother that her
father had died. When family tragedy struck, the army, working
through the Red Cross, would arrange for a compassionate leave.
The depth of mutual support in the Bosanko family revealed itself.
Her mother, only forty-six years old, was able to build a new life for
herself.

Private Bosanko's experiences at Basic Training in Fort Des
Moines, Iowa, were typical of what happened to most young adults
who had not traveled outside their region or even home state and
were suddenly thrown together with people from all possible
backgrounds and ages. Her letters reflect that initial enthusiasm
that comes from beginning a major adventure. "We've started
close-order drill and I'm scared to death of all my Sergeants." At
times one is reminded of a teenager attending summer camp or
even college for the first time. The early letters appeal for cash in
a hurry. While she was usually flat broke before the end of each

month, by the end of her military tenure Bosanko learned to stash
away a few dollars from her pay.[9]

Her gripes about poorly fitting uniforms and tasteless food
were typical: "Boy, am I tough. I can take everything—putrid chow,
no room for my stuff, obnoxious Southerners, pushups, and KP, all
in one week." But these hardships actually represented a rite of
passage into a new role. "I'm really a soldier now. Got three gigs
today—right in the swing of things." Her descriptions of army
lingo and abbreviations were especially apt. "GI: An all-purpose
term (Adjective, noun, verb) for people, things, and events." Thus
she writes later, "We were GIing because of inspection Saturday
morning, and I was eager-beavering into all the musty corners"
(i.e., policing her area).

Letters home dealt chiefly with four themes: the job, recreation
(including dating and drinking), morale, and the new people she
came to know. After two months of training at Beaumont Hospital
in El Paso, Texas, Anne began her real job as a surgical technician,
working in the operating room. She was one of ten thousand Wacs
who were medical or surgical technicians in army hospitals across
the country. Within a year she was promoted to corporal—a fast
move for the WAC—doubtless because of her efficiency in sterilizing every utensil and injecting every patient. "My injection technique isn't too sharp yet but the man with no stomach on whom I
practice is most noble and doesn't complain." Severely wounded
soldiers, after preliminary treatment, were shipped or flown back to
military hospitals. Nurses recall being either very busy, or having
long stretches with only petty routine. Bosanko was fully occupied.
"God, are we busy! Every afternoon I get back to the barracks all
hot and sweating and panting and pooped out." After V-J Day
Bosanko went to Halloran General Hospital in New York to be one
of about five hundred Wacs trained as occupational therapy technicians, working on the physical and psychological rehabilitation of
wounded veterans. She subsequently taught crafts, helped patients
with their projects, and at one point was in charge of a small
weaving department.[10]

---

[9] The first good descriptive history of enlistees' and draftees' wartime experiences is
Lee B. Kennett, *G.I.: The American Soldier in World War II* (New York: Scribner, 1987).
[10] Albert J. Glass and Robert J. Bernucci, eds., *Neuropsychiatry in World War II*
(Washington: Office of the Surgeon General, Dept. of the Army, 1966), 1:661;
Treadwell, *Women's Army Corps*, 340–53.

Anne's basic good humor and outgoing disposition guaranteed good relations with her co-workers, male and female, but the egalitarian Minnesotan in her recoiled at the army's caste system raising officers above enlisted personnel. While the WAC was much more egalitarian than the rest of the army, the distinctions remained troublesome for Anne—and for millions of other enlisted personnel. (The officers, however, seemed to consider the system just about right.)[11] She singled out the more hierarchical WAC officers for special criticism: "The Ma'am is getting more GI every day and is now treating us like Basics. We get it all day in Surgery and then we get it after hours. Our hair style is wrong. They don't like our attitudes. Our clothes aren't right . . . on and on." Bosanko daydreamed the solution: "a. Kick out the Head nurse, b. Change Wardmasters, c. Give the Major a month's leave."

On the whole she enjoyed her medical assistant experience and even considered going back to school to become an operating room nurse. At the end of the war when she was reassigned away from the operating room, morale plummeted. "I told you, didn't I, that Wacs aren't allowed to scrub anymore? I'm mad in a way, but mostly I just don't give a damn. I have become a shameless GB (Goldbrick)."

As a medical assistant Anne was lowest on the totem pole and sometimes treated as a third-class citizen. The doctors and nurses—all officers—had the rank and exuded privilege. The army system not only bothered her, but worse, she began to be much more status conscious. "Another irritating factor is that no one here has ever seen or heard of a WAC before, evidently, and they think we are queer neolithic creatures, or a third sex, or something. Also, the civilian mess hall employees wear our uniforms—the blue ones—so half the doctors and patients think we are kitchen help!"[12] Bosanko's views were generally shared by Wacs assigned as medical assistants. Sixty black Wacs at Lowell General Hospital, Devens, Massachusetts, felt they were given so many menial and demeaning

[11] Samuel A. Stouffer et al., *The American Soldier: Adjustment during Army Life* (Princeton: Princeton University Press, 1949), 1: 396.
[12] Key words like "third sex" and "queer" suggest Bosanko might have been hinting at the widespread—and totally false—rumors that the WAC was a haven for lesbians. In fact the WAC recruitment procedures carefully screened out anyone with either a reputation or a style that suggested lesbianism, and surveillance was continuously maintained. John Costello, *Love Sex and War: Changing Values, 1939–45* (London: Collins, 1985), 93–98; Campbell, *Women at War with America*, 28, 37; Treadwell, *Women's Army Corps*, 625.

tasks that they staged a sit-down demonstration in March 1945. All but four eventually went back to work; those who did not were court-martialed and sentenced to one year of hard labor and a dishonorable discharge, the harshest penalty ever meted out to Wacs. Only after the national black community exploded in protest did the army back down and dismiss the trial on a technicality.[13]

After army life became a matter of routine, off-duty activity became the focus of the letters. "I think I went to two movies, and I knitted and read and wrote letters and sweat the week out." Dating or the lack thereof was a primary focus. "After we ate, we couldn't think of anything to do but go to a movie. Reason: no men, no money, no tickets" or "poor frustrated homely Annie has no S.A. [sex appeal] except by mail." When her mother showed that she was worried about her daughter's dating activities, Anne wrote:

> Don't get excited—Pansy [Anne's nickname] has not degenerated completely, but the man-woman ratio is about 20 to 1 here in El Paso. You get off the bus intending merely to do some shopping and have a malt at the USO when the men descend on you, clamoring to take you to dinner, dances, movies, buy drinks and so on. Of course when they get us back to the WAC area, they start the old closing-in technique, but I'm adept at avoiding such. Victorian Annie, they calls me.

Evaluations of likely dating candidates, especially nonarmy prospects, became an art. "He's the first sailor I've met who isn't a wolf," or "Here we met two unusual Marines—different:

1. Handsome—swoon.
2. Intelligent.
3. Witty, on the cynical side.
4. Not in diapers."

And, finally, "His friend was a cute little Pole (nineteen) who tried to be a junior commando (encircling movements) but he was obviously a novice at the job and I was greatly amused." Bosanko hoped to get an overseas assignment, which never came. Perhaps she was lucky. When the male-female ratio soared to 50–1 or even 100–1, the women were under tremendous psychological pressure

---

[13] Treadwell, *Women's Army Corps*, 345, 346, 349, 598–99; *Time*, April 2, 1945, p. 20, April 16, 1945, p. 24.

to respond to hordes of love-lorn men who could, and did, promise anything.[14]

Bosanko's morale fluctuated with the ups and downs of her working environment and her love life. It ranged from "suffice it to say that I'm happy, healthy, and having mucho fun," to "this is going to be just another 'I'm still alive' letter. Life doesn't drool, it just drizzles." Morale sank lower and lower as the war ended, and Bosanko waited many months to receive her discharge papers. She speculated, "In 1947 I'll be twenty-three, a hell of a time to go back and finish college and try to get started on a profession." As more and more Wacs were brought into her unit with less and less work to do, the crisis worsened. Anne's inner reserves of patriotism were wearing thin because the war was over and there was no compelling reason for her to waste her life away in service doing so little service. "Never have felt more useless, never has life seemed more futile than now." Wacs were released on a point system, with a point for every month each woman had served in the army. Extra points were awarded for overseas duty and for married or pregnant Wacs. Bosanko sighed, "Maybe I could find some guy, marry him, get out, and have the marriage annulled afterwards."

The LRs (latrine rumors) were constantly flying about when individual Wacs would be discharged and when the entire WAC organization would be disbanded. Bosanko assumed, as did many soldiers, that the WAC had been created "for the duration." Only after long debates with testimony by major wartime generals and admirals urging Congress to create peacetime women's units was a bill passed and signed in 1948 by President Harry S. Truman that guaranteed a handful of women a place in both the regular service and the reserves. Women were not to exceed 2 percent of the military and were to serve as a nucleus in case of future wars since months and months had been lost in World War II simply establishing these reserves. But Bosanko, like most women who had served in uniform, did not focus on the fate of the WAC but rather on what she was going to do with her life. Anne constantly planned for her post-WAC years even though she was not sure until the very end exactly when she would be discharged. She wrote for an application and took the admissions exam for the University of Chicago. "I don't want to go back to the U of M and get in the same rut I joined the Army to escape. Besides, if I stayed home I'd want

[14] Glass and Bernucci, *Neuropsychiatry,* 1:455.

to spend all my time working on the farm and I'd never get any studying done."

As a typical hometown booster, Bosanko could not resist filling her letters with cracks about the depressing weather and the mediocrity of America outside Minnesota. Des Moines: "What a dump—nothing to do but spend all our money on liquor." Los Angeles: "I hate L.A.; it's dirty and depressing, filled with bums and aimless people; has no atmosphere at all." New York City: "Never saw the like of the way everyone tears around here. A cop with a great Irish brogue directed us; heard all kinds of weird accents." Sensitive to nuances, she began to compare locations. "I find that experiences seem to match the climate. In insipid, pleasant N[ew] O[rleans], insipid, pleasant amusements. In rugged, wonderful Texas, exciting and wild evenings." And the weather was always a source of comment. "Weather here is foul—raining and putrid but not very cold" or "The weather here has gone berserk" or "Sun every day (see weather)." Memories of Minnesota winters seemed especially bracing and wonderful to the homesick young woman bored to tears in Los Angeles.

The letters never stated it in so many words, yet reading between the lines it is clear that one of the main lessons Bosanko learned from her years in the army was what being a Minnesotan meant. Minneapolis prospered during the war but never became a tumultuous boom town like Detroit or Los Angeles. Home remained a beacon of sanity for Anne: she knew what she had to return to. Minnesotans, like Anne's family, learned to cope with rationing and shortages and engaged as volunteers or as paid employees in war-related activities. But day-to-day life was not significantly altered unless a family member was seriously wounded or killed.[15]

To her father, being a Minnesotan meant owning a farm. The motif of a return to the land runs through the letters, and by 1945 the dream was within his grasp. He purchased a working farm not too far from Minneapolis and planned to resign from his teaching job, focusing his energies on getting a retirement income from

[15] Unfortunately Minnesota still lacks a good war history. The best state history is Mary Watters, *Illinois in the Second World War,* 2 vols. (Springfield: Illinois State Historical Library, 1951–52). On the home front generally, see Richard R. Lingeman, *Don't You Know There's a War On? The American Home Front, 1941–1945* (New York: Putnam, 1970); Campbell, *Women at War with America;* Hartmann, *Home Front.*

running the farm. After the war Anne's mother continued to rent out the farm, visited it rarely, and finally sold it in 1951.

It was Anne who learned what being a Minnesotan was really about. By traveling across the country she saw that other Americans were different. She lived in Hollywood and was not swept away by the glamour. She lived in New York and was not dazzled. She learned about other styles of life and thereby better understood her own people and her own values. It was not simply that others had adapted to a different climate in El Paso or spoke with a southern drawl in New Orleans. Minnesota was a mind-set, a world view, not a farm nor even a place.[16]

This is history—but is it Minnesota history? These letters are as close to the heart of Minnesota as is Lake Wobegon. It is often remarked that nothing reveals what home is like more than travel away from it. What were families and communities like in Minnesota in 1944–46? A great many of them were like the Bosankos, struggling to express their patriotism, to find fulfillment in a farm, to support their children away at war. Everyone in Minnesota at the time, I would aver, felt that their hopes and fears and dreams of the future were tied up with their sons and daughters who were away at war. For Anne to be a Minnesotan meant patriotism, friendliness, and helpfulness mixed in with a zest for work, a shrewd understanding of people, and an innocence about the darker side of human nature that is as refreshing today as it was naïve then.

Anne, like all the children of Lake Wobegon, was above average. In 1959 when the University of Minnesota began an experimental continuing education program for older women who wanted to upgrade their skills after their children were safely in school all day, Anne was one of the first to volunteer. A touch of math anxiety kept her from following up her service job by becoming a nurse. Law school in 1959 was still beyond the aspirations of women, so Anne selected a program in counselling and psychology. It was reminiscent of the training she had received late in the war and the work she did with hospitalized veterans. She then launched a career as a school psychologist, retiring in 1985 to

---

[16] Annette Atkins, "Minnesota: Left of Center and Out of Place," in *Heartland: Comparative Histories of the Midwestern States,* ed. James H. Madison (Bloomington: Indiana University Press, 1986).

enjoy her family and her leisure. Her wartime letters exhibit the same skills of analyzing people and describing events that make for a first-rate psychologist.

Anne was typical of so many young adults who served in the military during the war and in the process grew into adulthood. She married not a soldier or a patient, but a hometown boy. Anne Bosanko Green settled down to raise three children. As every reader of these letters will expect, Anne remains an activist and hometown booster and has immersed herself in civic activities, such as the League of Women Voters. Like most women veterans, Anne supports the women's movement and favors passage of the Equal Rights Amendment. She worries about the prospect of a future war but feels that both women and men will have to serve if another war should come.

Anne and her age cohort occupy a unique place in American history. Their fathers served in World War I, they were youngsters during the Great Depression, and they came of age during World War II. They married servicemen and often saw their husbands recalled for duty during the Korean War. Their sons came of age and were eligible for the draft during the Vietnam War.

While in these respects they are unique, these veterans can add a broader and deeper perspective to our understanding of what being a young woman, a young American, was like under very trying circumstances. When asked if they would recommend military service to a young woman today, the overwhelming majority of women veterans would definitely advise her to join. When asked if they had it to do all over again, almost all say that they would volunteer in a minute. Anne and her generation gave of themselves, and in so doing they shaped their own lives and have shaped the meaning of what it means to be an American for all the rest of us.

Introduction
THE LETTERS

Some years ago my mother announced that she was cleaning closets and handed me a paper sack that contained all the letters I had written home during my days in the Women's Army Corps in World War II. They were arranged in chronological order and carefully tied up in bundles according to my locations and assignments. I skimmed the first couple of bundles and thought they were amusing but put them away in *my* closet and forgot about them.

Later, when my daughter Kate and I were staying at our cabin in northern Minnesota, I thought it would be fun, while she worked on a novel, to get out my "autobiography" and type the letters so that my family and friends could enjoy them. The letters that follow are exactly as I wrote them, weekly and more than weekly, including slang, cusswords, family joke phrases, inquiries into people's health, and accounts of weekly duties. I omitted a few purely family messages, and I altered many of the names of individuals who might be embarrassed if the letters got beyond the family circle. Misspellings have been corrected, and some punctuation, paragraphing, bracketed annotation, and footnotes have been added to aid the reader.

When you are reading a series of privately written letters, it is something like listening in on a party-line telephone: it is interesting, but you do not know who the characters are. Some background information here may help to tell who was who and what was going on before the action started.

My "little family" to whom the letters were addressed consisted of my father, Paul; my mother, Blanche; and my brother, Michael,

1

who was five years younger than I was—all living in Minneapolis. When the letters start in 1944, my father was the head teacher of French and Spanish at Blake School, a private prep school for boys on the outskirts of Minneapolis, and Michael was a freshman (ninth grade) at the school. One more family member was Midge, a black female cocker spaniel, who was a new puppy when I was in the tenth grade.

My father was born in Leadville, Colorado, at the height of the silver mining boom in 1891, where my grandfather was practicing medicine and probably also hoping to strike it rich on the side. Those were the opulent days of Baby Doe Tabor, when great fortunes were made almost overnight. When Dr. Samuel Arthur Bosanko died of pneumonia following overwork during a diphtheria epidemic in the town, my grandmother, Harriet Newton Bosanko, took her only child, four-year-old Paul, back to the ancestral home in Hartford, Connecticut, where my father was raised as a proper New Englander on the remains of a family inheritance. He went to prep school and to Yale, graduating in 1914. Then he earned a law degree at Yale and was admitted to the Connecticut bar, but he was not what might be called a typical preppie. He always felt himself something of a loner, pursued unusual interests in college (calligraphy, banjo playing, fencing), and was on the radical fringe in his thinking about ethnic and racial minorities, women's rights, and other social issues.

The war in Europe was in full spate when he left law school. He found employment with a Hartford law firm, and when President Woodrow Wilson asked Congress to declare war against Germany in April 1917, Paul immediately tried for acceptance into an officer training program. He was rejected on the grounds of poor eyesight, but in September the British army recruiting office in Hartford accepted him as an enlisted man; the Empire was desperate for manpower and would take what it could get.

Paul trained in Canada, went to England, and then in the summer of 1918 to France, where he was behind the front lines as back-up personnel until the end of the war in November. At the time of the armistice, Paul was stationed in Paris in a British army office as a telephone operator because of his facility with French, and he stayed there until he was demobilized in May 1919.

He was enchanted with the city, the people, the food, and the language. My mother told me years later that he had had a thwarted romance with a French girl. When I was a kid there seemed to be an unspoken rule among adults not to talk about "the war" to young people, so I never got a straightforward story about what my father did and where he was stationed. I knew he had been in the British army as a Tommie, and he taught me funny English soldier songs and expressions, but that was all. Now, nearly seventy years later, I read in his diaries of an intense, troubled affair with Claudine that lasted six months until he sailed back to the States to look for employment, with fervent hopes to bring her over from France to be his wife. Why this never happened, the diaries, ending on shipboard that May, do not reveal.

After a hated stint in a stock brokerage firm to which his family had some ties, Paul worked for six months in a college bookstore in New Haven. He was still searching for his career niche when he decided to explore becoming an Episcopal priest. This led in a round-about way to returning to his Colorado birthplace to a divinity school in Greeley in the late winter of 1921.

My mother, who in the family saga was always styled "The Mountain Flower," was a freshman at the teachers' college in Greeley. She met my father in the spring of 1921 while rehearsing for a college production of *The Pirates of Penzance;* she told me she was dazzled by the sophisticated older man from the East. The dazzlement was understandable, since my father was well known for his Celtic charm and gift of gab, which he claimed was due to his Cornish ancestors. Years later when he visited me at boarding school, the women teachers were abuzz for days because "Mr. B." was so charming and funny. After a short courtship, my mother and father were married in August when my father was thirty and my mother was twenty-one. Father gave up his idea of the ministry and started working on a master's degree in French, with the goal of becoming a teacher.

Mother's parents had headed west to Colorado in the 1880s as young people — Grandfather Ephraim Wadleigh from Canada and Grandmother Sarah Anne Webster from Kansas. They met and married in Denver in 1884. Grandfather became a railroad telegrapher and station agent in several small towns in the mountains west of Colorado Springs. Mother, born in 1900, was the youngest of nine children, seven of whom lived to become adults. This family was quite close, especially the four sisters and the youngest brother; the aunts and cousins referred to in my letters are my mother's relatives whom we visited many times in Colorado, Nebraska, and Wisconsin. The three brothers had to leave school after eighth grade to earn a living, but my grandmother insisted on the four girls finishing high school, even if it meant boarding with families forty miles away from Westcliffe, which had no high school. Mother was the only one of her family to have attended college, and she always regretted that it was only for two years.

In 1922 Father finished his master's degree and took a teaching position at the University of Minnesota. I was born two years later, and not long after that, Father started teaching at Blake without completing his doctoral degree at the university where he had done nearly all the work except for taking the oral examinations. He had finally found what he was most happy doing even though a teacher's pay was unbelievably low. My brother was born just before the stock-market crash of 1929.

By the 1940s we had weathered the depression, and there was some financial security from the estate left by my Grandmother Bosanko. In those days my mother was a typical woman of her times, making do and scrimping when the times were tough, caring for her family, and doing church work and women's club activities for outside interest. It never occurred to her or to anyone else that she could get a job in addition to being a housewife. There seemed to be only two choices: a Career (with a capital "C"), which meant being a spinster and probably college educated, or being a wife.

When the United States entered World War II on December 8, 1941, after the Japanese attack on Pearl Harbor in Hawaii, I was in my senior year at St. Mary's Hall (SMH), an Episcopal girls' boarding school in Faribault, a small town about sixty miles south of Minneapolis. The headmistress, Miss Robertson, was an awesome authority figure to the students, but we irreverently called her "Maggie" behind her back. We lived a closely chaperoned and isolated life, with no regular access to newspapers or radios. The only radio listening allowed was in our free time in the common room (the Senior Sit) when we tuned in on such programs as "The Hit Parade" of popular songs on Saturday nights. At that time the top tune for weeks was "Pistol Packin' Mama," sung by Frank Sinatra. Our awareness of the war in Europe was sketchy, but we were kept informed about the war in England because of our church school's close connection with the Church of England. British priests would visit school and tell us vivid stories about the

German bombings and the hardships in England. These accounts inspired us to take up knitting socks and sweaters for British soldiers and to contribute from our allowances to the relief supplies called "Bundles for Britain."

During the winter of 1941–42, my father, who had been ailing for at least a year with what the doctors were calling colitis, was finally diagnosed as having a stomach ulcer and underwent surgery. He regained his strength and weight and was back teaching by the fall of 1942. The next spring he felt good enough to join the State Guard as one of the oldest recruits at age fifty-one. The Minnesota National Guard had been called up for active duty *en masse,* and the State Guard was created, with less stringent age and physical qualifications, for ceremonial duty, crowd control, and possible emergency situations.

After graduation in June 1942 I enrolled in September at the University of Minnesota in the liberal arts program. My freshman and sophomore years there were unique in that the university was in many ways like a women's college. Most able-bodied young men were already in the armed forces, were leaving every week, or were in military units stationed on the campus for various kinds of training. Many of the boys from Shattuck School, the Episcopal military school down the road from St. Mary's, were commissioned directly into the army right after graduation, with only their school military background for Officer's Training.

The result of the lack of men was that women had the chance to run many aspects of campus life besides such traditional women's organizations as sororities and the YWCA. Women staffed the campus newspaper, the *Minnesota Daily,* and the yearbook and took over the Union Board of Governors and other student groups. I was deeply involved in many of these activities. Of course there were still some men around, but the old fraternity-sorority atmosphere of formal dances and parties changed focus to USO mixers at the Union with sailors from the V-12 unit or boys from the army premeteorology or German and Japanese language-school units.

And there was a lot of just plain datelessness. My women friends and I invented a send-up of the college sororities, which most of us had joined in the fall, and on New Year's Eve 1942 eight of us gathered at my house for bridge and illegal beer procured by my father. Borrowing the name of a high school sorority called the Bachelorettes, we decided to be the "Stagnanttes," with our president, the "High Hag," being the one who had gone the longest without a date. A system of fines and fees for the treasury was developed: ten cents if a man said hello; twenty-five cents if someone treated you to a Coke at the Varsity Cafe after class; one dollar for a movie date; five dollars for a fraternity party; and the ultimate fine—twenty-five dollars for getting pregnant. Our meetings were on Friday nights when we were supposed to entertain each other with detailed accounts of any male contacts occurring during the previous week. We had elaborate classes of membership, we made up fake sorority songs ("Hail to the Stagnanttes, the fruits of Youth; Hail to our High Honorable Hag, Ruth; We are the best to be found, forsooth; We won't be seen with a man—that's uncouth"), and we held two rushing events to increase our membership to twelve, which then made for three tables of bridge.

As the war intensified, women rolled bandages weekly at the American Red Cross office in the Union or trained to become nurses' aides. Armed forces recruitment aimed at women—posters and speeches—became more noticeable, and there was pressure to do something specific for the war effort. The pitch was that a woman working at certain "safe" jobs in the services could release a man for active fighting. I think it was a combination of patriotism, idealism, and the urge for adventure that got me seriously considering joining one of the services.

In the spring of 1944 the war news from the Pacific and European theaters had gotten progressively worse, and I really felt that women should not be staying comfortably at home while men were dying on beaches and in deserts. I went around to the recruiting offices of the WAVES (navy for Women Accepted for Voluntary Emergency Service) and the WAC (Women's Army Corps). Some of my sorority sisters had joined the WAVES, and the navy was giving college women a hard sell. Part of their pitch consisted of running down the WAC as somehow lower class and claiming that army women were not as well treated as those in the navy. When I heard this, I thought it was too snobbish, and my nonconformist tendencies impelled me right across the street to the WAC recruiting office. Here I heard about the opportunity to go overseas and the newly formed medical corps branch for enlisted women. At that time only college graduates could be officers, and the only women medical workers were registered nurses.

By summer I had signed up for the "duration plus six," was

There's something about a Wac !

THERE'S something about a Wac...

With her fresh, cool poise, her air of quiet confidence.

Her gallantry and her spirit. Her way of getting things done, quickly and without fuss.

Her pride in her vital Army job. And in the Women's Army Corps...

There's something about a Wac that makes you want to stand up and cheer!

The way the soldiers did — when the Wacs came down the gangplank in Australia.

The way Generals do — with cables that say: "Send more Wacs!"

Receiving radio messages from combat planes

Recording the return of wounded men

Good soldiers...
the WAC
WOMEN'S ARMY CORPS

► FOR FULL INFORMATION about the Women's Army Corps, go to your nearest U.S. Army Recruiting Station. Or mail the coupon below.

U. S. ARMY RECRUITING STATION
1111 Nicollet Avenue—4-E. 2501
Minneapolis 2, Minn.

Please send me, without any obligation on my part, the new illustrated booklet about the Wacs...telling about the jobs they do, how they live, their training, pay, officer selection, etc.

NAME

ADDRESS

CITY_____ PHONE NO.

STATE

Please answer "yes" or "no" to each of the following questions:

Are you between 20 and 50?

Have you any children under 14?

Have you had at least 2 years of high school?

Moving up to new posts behind the front

From the *Minneapolis Journal*, Aug. 24, 1944, p. 4

assigned to take the physical exam at Fort Snelling (just south of Minneapolis) and was due to be sworn in on my twentieth birthday, which was the earliest allowable age for women to enter the army. (The WAC took women up to age fifty. When I first encountered some women in this category I referred to them as "old grandmas," but later on I relaxed my juvenile stance and had some good buddies who were more than twice my age.) My father was gratified that his elder and only available offspring was following in the tradition of army service, and my mother was also proud of me. Mother, Dad, and Mike were there when I was inducted on September 20, 1944, in the WAC recruiting office. Then we all celebrated with an unusual treat for those ration-strict days—a steak dinner at the Covered Wagon, complete with Manhattan cocktails for toasting. Two weeks later (it seemed like a month of waiting) I was on my way to basic training at Fort Des Moines, Iowa, and my correspondence begins.

The tone of my letters is mostly cheerful, with efforts to be funny because we soldiers were supposed to be keeping up the morale of the home front. In reading them today, however, the humor for me is in laughing at my twenty-year-old self: idealistic, selfish, enthusiastic, opinionated, a hometown chauvinist, amazingly frank in telling my parents all (or almost all) about what I was doing. I chuckle at the detailed descriptions of restaurant meals and at the conventions that governed dating and courtship, which by today's standards seem antiquated and quaint. I wonder how I could have complained about the dullness of my routine and then write about a week's social schedule that sounds incredibly strenuous after daily hard physical labor. Both my mother and father wrote to me each week, usually on Sundays, with extra letters sent midweek. They had developed the weekly habit from writing to their parents living far away in Colorado and Connecticut. Their letters were much like mine, with each day's doings chronicled in detail, along with the typical Minnesota concentration on what the weather was like. My mother was a faithful newspaper clipper—items about the university, my sorority, marriages, and engagements—and always told me when she saw any of my friends or when anyone asked after me. She was also a faithful worrier and advice-giver, in the tradition of mothers through the ages. Her letters started, "Dear Annie," and were signed, "Mother."

My father made more of an effort to be philosophical or funny, especially about my young brother with his clarinet lessons and his adolescent friends. Dad liked funny names for the family: I was "Bug," "Pvt. Bug," "Annie," "Darling Daughter," or "Brat." My mother was usually referred to as "Your Maw," my brother was "The Buzzard," and he signed himself "Dad," "Pop," "Pappy," "the old corporal," or "your ancient father." The name "bug" dated from my infant days when I was supposed to have had very big, or "bug," eyes. I have included excerpts from my parents' letters to give a flavor of our family relationships and some details about civilian life during wartime.

I also quote from letters to my oldest and dearest friend, Carrie, which add a different perspective to the family letters. Carrie and I met in kindergarten and were partners in play and mischief until our sixth-grade year when my family moved some miles away, and I went to a different school. We kept up our closeness in spite of the distance and my high-school years being spent out of town. After her first year at the university, Carrie's father entered the navy as an officer and was stationed for a while on the West Coast. Carrie, her mother, and her older sister moved to San Francisco where they found jobs in offices and war plants to be nearby when her father got off duty or returned from tours at sea. Carrie was as much of a letter-saver as my mother and I, and when she moved to California before her unfortunately early death years later, she gave me a packet containing all my letters to her from Girl Scout camp, St. Mary's, and the army. The June 1944 letter to Carrie neatly sets the stage for my transition from college to army life.

Part I
THE WAR

Fort Des Moines

WOMEN'S ARMY CORPS BASIC TRAINING
FORT DES MOINES, IOWA
3 October to 8 December 1944

Minneapolis, Minnesota

June 19, 1944

Dearest Carrie,

Two months whiz by awfully fast, don't they? But then I seem to remember getting a Christmas thank-you letter along towards the end of February, so we are both culprits. Upon reading over your letter I note that your father is overseas. I hope he is still all right. Our father is in the Army now too. (Got you excited, didn't I?) The truth of the matter is that he is a corporal in the State Guard, which is having a two-week session up at Camp Ripley [near Little Falls, Minnesota]. You can calm down now. Mother and I went down to the station to see him off, and put on such a scene (in fun, of course) that I bet people thought he was going at least to France. What were you doing on D-Day [June 6, 1944]? I was sound asleep and took a Humanities test in the morning. Missed any really exciting news. But a friend of mine was up late studying with her radio on and heard the first dispatches. They turned the station over to the news room and the announcer walked around reading the news as it came in, and she could hear the tickers. Also they kept going to London and she heard Churchill and the Belgian Prime Minister and other notables, and heard them broadcasting in French to the French Underground. It was all very exciting. Coming home on the streetcar that day, I was reading a man's paper over his shoulder which inspired me to write a poem:

Allies advance
And push into France;
Summer savings at Grant's . . .
Strike closes down plants . . .
Blake boys give a dance . . .
Go to Krantz for your pants . . .
The newspaper chants,
While the Allies advance
Into France.

I haven't gotten back any grades from exams yet but I know I got an A in Zoology. Happy day. As to English Lit., English History, and Humanities, my fate is in the lap of the Gods. I am letting my mind lie fallow this summer while I work part-time in the [Minneapolis] Star-Journal Want Ad Department and read murder mysteries the rest of the time. Everyone seems to have broken out into a great rash of summer school and nurses' aid this summer, but not me. I ain't so dumb—I know about crop rotation. Spring Quarter my life was very hectic what with being:

AWS (Associated Women Students) Junior Council
     president
Treasurer of Cosmopolitan Club
Secretary of Arts Intermediary Board
Secretary of Commonwealth Party
Member of Sigma Epsilon Sigma, honorary Sophomore
     Women's Society which did committee work for the
     post-war conference

I can't escape dear old activities this summer because I'm in charge of the Big Sisters tea in the fall, which is different this year involving counselors, etc., and has three huge committees and no less than 23 sub-committees. But after the tea is over, I will leave that stuff forever BECAUSE I'm joining the WAC just as soon as I'm 20 which is September 20. It's a really good proposition because when I get out I will get some government subsidy if I go back to school. Even if I don't go back to school I will have a good solid Arts foundation plus invaluable experience. Mom and Dad both approve wholeheartedly. I decided this spring to do it because I felt so useless going to school and being Big Deal On Campus (big sucker on Campus if you ask me,) and I felt that I could do some good in the Army and it certainly will do me some good. In fact, it's a good deal all around and I'm very enthusiastic about the whole thing. Think of the interesting people I'll meet and the places I'll see. I might even get to go abroad, though I'll be satisfied doing anything they give me.

Mother and I are going to Chicago this summer—should be fun. I can visit a sociological architect I know who is running a play center for underprivileged children on his own hook. It's down in the heart of the Italian district. He is really interesting—not a fake intellectual like Sigurd[1] and his little pals. All this guy's friends are in jail because they conscientiously object to C.O. [Conscientious Objector] camps. He would be in jail too but luckily he's 4-F. It's a part of their religion which is sort of like Quakers and sort of not. He's always giving me tracts about being "One with the Universe," but I don't understand them very well.

Well, my dear, when are you coming back, if ever? You aren't going to work for Mr. Schlage all your life, are you? Who knows, maybe I'll be stationed out in San Francisco near you. That would be a truly happy coincidence. Just think if we got together how much we would have to talk about and what fun you could have taking me around. It probably never would happen, but it's nice to think about. Please write a huge letter soon and I'll answer it right away 'cause I'm not busy now.

All my love,
Pansy[2]

P.S.: Please don't write to any of the kids here about my joining the WAC because I want it to be a secret (except from you).

Fort Des Moines, Iowa

October 4, 1944

Company 2 Receiving and Staging Battalion, Army Post Branch, Wednesday morning, crack of dawn (almost) . . .

Dear Family,
What a God-awful night I spent. That train was a horrible local

[1] Sigurd was someone I had dated in college. My mother disapproved of him because he was a lot older than I was.
[2] Pansy, sometimes written Panzy, was short for "Anne-sy-Pansy," a nickname applied to me by my friend Carrie.

that stopped for twenty minutes at least at every station. Bumpy and draughty and sooty. We trailed into Des Moines at 1 a.m.—no sleep at all of course—were bundled into Army trucks and bounced out to the Fort. We had breakfast and were checked in, and got to bed at 3 a.m. At 5:45 we were dragged out and had more mess. The barracks are quite nice and hold about 100 girls I think. Look like horse barns from the outside—only one story and made of red brick. Inside is cream whitewashed and sort of mapley double-deck bunks. SOS! I have no towels or washcloths and they aren't issued. Those dopes at the recruiting office didn't tell us anything right, so I'll probably be writing frantic letters or sending back packages for the next three weeks. You can't write to me for a week, so I'm told, because we don't get in our regular barracks till then. My fellow rookies are sort of dopey but no doubt they'll improve with time. Our Sergeant, called Sergeant Mac, is young and peppy and nice but firm. Good gal. I'm going to try to catch up on my sleep now so goodbye and love and I don't think I'll die.

Later: We've started close-order drill and I'm scared to death of all my Sergeants. They all scream at the tops of their lungs and I can't understand a word they say. Ergo, I do everything wrong and get glared at. Very humiliating. I'm worse than Private Hargrove.[3]

5 October 1944

Thursday

Dear Family,

Well, here I am before dinner in the Day Room sitting at a nice maple desk, drinking a Coke and inhaling a fag [cigarette]. I suppose you'd like a more coherent account of what has cooked and is cooking. My last letter was written about 7 a.m. and I had just found out about no towels and was understandably hysterical. I've been going to bed wet since then and trying to make the best of it. Tried to buy some at the PX but with no success. You can't write or send me anything till next week but then I would like a supply of

---

[3] Pvt. Hargrove was the hero of a comic novel about the life of an army draftee by Marion Hargrove, entitled *See Here, Private Hargrove*. The book was also the basis for a Broadway musical of the same name.

bath towels and washcloths. I'll give you my permanent address before then.

History of Pvt. A.L.B.

Tuesday afternoon: Sat and sat . . . had foul supper at Dyckman Hotel[4] . . . marched to station . . . saw you . . . got on train. Horrible ride down. Day coach, and absolutely the most uncomfortable ride ever taken by me. Worse than trying to sleep on a streetcar. One a.m.: shoved off train and carted to fort. You heard about the rest.

Wednesday morning: Got our clothing issue which I will list for you on the next page.

Time out for mess—ON THE DOUBLE!

Much, much later: On a very wobbly table this time. All the desks are being used.

Clothing issue:

2 Winter jackets
2 Winter shirts
3 Winter skirts
2 Summer jackets (known as blouses)
4 Summer skirts
7 Summer shirts
Khaki underwear pants (rayon—ick)
Woolies (long sleeves)
Shoes, 1 pr., service
Shoes, 1 pr., field (high)
    Shoes are *comfortable*
1 pr. wool gloves (nice)
Purse [commodious, with shoulder strap]
1 pr. dress leather gloves
Wool knit hat (cute)
Fatigue hat
2 Winter hats
2 Summer hats
2 Winter Garrison caps

---

[4] The Dyckman Hotel in Minneapolis on Sixth Street between Hennepin and Nicollet avenues was taken over by the armed forces, as were many hotels during the war years. It held offices and a staging area where groups of inductees were assembled and often given a meal before being transported to another location.

2 Summer Garrison caps (no, I'm not crazy, they aren't
    called overseas caps; they *are* Garrison caps)
Gay little green seersucker fatigue dress with bloomers to
    match (this is what the recruiting office said wasn't
    issued—the dopes)
Khaki wool sweater
Various socks and stockings
Two-piece green striped flannel PJs
Toothbrush
Comb
Everything except TOWELS

We look very bunchy and feeble now but maybe later we will look
nifty like the other gals.

We went into uniform (fatigue) this morning. Damn the
recruiting office—nothing they told us was true. I have to have
more of my hair cut off. Anyhow, we sat around most of the day. At
night we got to go to the PX. Mom, the juke box was playing an old
favorite of yours, "Just a Baby's Prayer at Twilight." I nearly
flipped. You should see the cigarettes. Cartons and cartons piled
up. I'd send you a carton but they let us buy only two at a time. I'll
tell you more about the PX later. It's very gay and buzzing with
people, all looking horribly neat and smooth in their uniforms, of
course. Here is a picture of me at this point: wrinkly lisle [cotton

knit] stockings, huge field shoes, immense field hat. A side view, in
imitation of one of the Sergeants: "Eyes and head straight to the
front! DON'T MOVE. TEN HUT!"

I saluted twice tonight. Boy, am I good. This is really fun and
I love everything once I got over thinking the bawlings-out were
aimed straight at *me*. I had a guilty conscience for hours after I had

a letter returned with the wrong address on it. They screamed my name out over the whole barracks.

Wednesday evening: Fell into bed exhausted and what happened? A fat old group of gals from Chicago came in at 10:30 and woke everybody up. They got the giggles trying to get into the upper bunks and I could have killed them. I'm in a lower as you no doubt guessed. I should go to bed about now—it's 10:00 and bed check is 10:45. Lights out at 9:00 in the barracks, but I'm in the Sit.

Heaps of love and kisses,[5]

[All during the weeks of Basic Training we were measured, fitted, and tailored into our uniforms, various components appearing from week to week. The army went to some lengths to make sure its women enlistees had clothes that fit and looked good, doubtless as a public-relations and recruitment measure.

In the WAC we probably had a wider selection of official clothing than was available to the men, the most familiar being the Class A uniform in a brownish color known as "olive drab" and consisting of a skirt, shirt, tie, and blouse (really a tailored jacket), plus sensible shoes. It was worn for office jobs, formal parades and inspections, and off-post in public. Wacs in cold climates were issued wool overcoats, which were weighty and unwieldy. We all received a raincoat with a zip-out lining called a utility coat. This term later became corrupted into "utily" coat. (I still have mine, which I wear at the lake to walk the dog.) We also had off-duty or "date" dresses, rather nice, tailored in a pinkish-beige wool. The color was a pleasant contrast to the olive drab or khaki of practically everything else we were issued. (The khaki underwear was far more likely to be used as dustcloths than worn by the Wacs.)

The "gay little green seersucker fatigue dress" served us for physical training (PT), for sports such as tennis, and for cleaning chores and KP as well. Later on, we Wacs were issued HBTs (herring-bone twills), which were dark, olive-drab jumpsuits of the sort worn by garage mechanics, and still later, on hospital duty, we wore ill-fitting, cleaning-lady housedresses.

---

[5] Lights out in the main body of the barracks room came before lights out in the bathrooms or biff (latrines) or in the day-room or sit (lounge). Bed check was when the sergeant came around to make sure everyone was actually in her bunk.

One final feature of the complete uniform of men and women alike was the "dogtag." Two were issued so that one could be tied to your toe in case you became a corpse and needed shipment home. The dogtag, measuring about one inch by one and one-half inches and made of metal, had the following stamped on it: name, army serial number, blood type, and religious preference. The last was indicated by C for Catholic, P for Protestant, and J for Jewish. No allowances were made for Muslims, Buddhists, Agnostics, Unitarians, or other "nonmainstream" religions—they were all lumped under P. Dogtags had to be worn on a chain around your neck at all times under your clothes and, when put on after a shower, could be cold. Dogtag booties, small sacks that were slipped over the tags, were worn to keep the tags warm and prevent clanking.]

8 October 1944

Company 5, Third Regiment, APF, Des Moines, Iowa

Sunday

Dearest Family,

The irony of something or other. Yesterday I was finally issued three GI bathtowels and today I get your package of towels. Thanks much anyway and I can use the washcloths. Yesterday I sent off that library book which in my excitement at the station I forgot to give you. There is 30 cents due on it (rental book) and I'll send you a money order if you want. Today being Sunday we have it easy. Sleep till 7:30—two hours extra. Went to RC [Roman Catholic] Mass in the morning with Ruth K. who is very congenial. Wrote letters till mess at 12:30. Got dressed up in my uniform, at last, and went over to the Service Club which is tres deluxe. Library, cafeteria, big game room, dancing, ping pong, phone bar for long distance calls. All decorated very nicely. Mess at 4:30 and write letters in evening. You can write me now; my permanent address will probably reach you soon.

Yesterday we got our first series of shots and vaccinations [smallpox, diphtheria, and tetanus] and last night the whole barracks was groaning and moaning enough to wake the dead, namely me. I can't recognize any of my little pals now that they have their uniforms on. They all look like human beings now instead of convicts. I've found out that there is absolutely no chance of a furlough after my basic and probably not even after my training. Of course, it's mostly in the lap of the Gods but the Gods are usually malignant according to all the gals I've talked to. You must really plan to come down in about a month. We could really have fun. After basic, we go into what is known as Staging, which is much like Receiving—crowded barracks, no room, and much confusion. The kids have to be ready to go out on a moment's notice so they have to be all packed and everything all the time. Some kids have been in Staging six months waiting for their orders. That must be a horrible strain. Our little Company is getting better and better at drilling, and we stood inspection yesterday. It's almost like really being in the Army. But next week I guess the heat really goes on. The sergeants probably won't be as fun and as easy on us. I actually heard one sergeant say, "Group Six up front on the double, *please!*" I'm feeling some reaction from my shots, a kind of tired feeling. Went to a movie again last night to take my mind off my troubles. Wrote to Mrs. Nelson, Mom; I am a good girl. Guess what? Our group has latrine detail. Mom, you will appreciate that fact no doubt. Also the fact that every morning I eat a big steaming bowl of Sturdi-Wheat. I'm going to gain pounds and pounds I know. A couple of days ago we were taken to see a parade and it was very thrilling. Huge numbers of WACs all marching in cadence, and a band, and the Colonel, and stuff. Our Sergeant got a Good Conduct ribbon.

Please, I wish you would ask me lots of questions 'cause it's so hard to remember all the little details of things. The sun has finally come out and we can see what the Post looks like. It was an old cavalry post, since 1903, and nearly all the buildings are red brick with white front porches and many tall elms and oaks and flower beds and a big green parade ground. Of course, it's lovely this time of year with the trees just beginning to turn. Got beer at the PX the other night—what a treat.[6] I felt like a fiend, but "Wot the 'ell, a soldier's got to have her relaxation!"

---

[6] In the 1940s the national age requirement for drinking and voting was generally twenty-one. There was a tacit waiving of this requirement for people in uniform, however, that varied from state to state and from place to place. On army posts the Officers' Clubs served liquor and beer, and the Non-Coms' Clubs and PXs served beer without ID checks. When I was settled in my permanent post, a buddy, who was similar to me in hair, eye color, height, and was just twenty-one, loaned me her ID card. She claimed she never got asked for ID because she looked older, which was considered a good thing in one's early twenties. In the fall of 1945 my main birthday request was for a copy of my birth certificate so I could drink legally.

Goodbye for now and please write soon and lots. Much love and kisses and I miss you all immensely.

15 October 1944

Sunday

Dearest Family,

Sunday at last! Well, I'm still alive after a week of Basic. Boy, am I tough. I can take everything—putrid chow, no room for my stuff, obnoxious Southerners, pushups, and KP, all in one week. Am now prone on my little bunk engaged in pen pushing like mad and trying to relax. I felt pretty low at 5 a.m. on Saturday morning while cleaning out the grease trap over at Number 3 Mess, but my spirits popped up again after a couple of beers and some singing at the PX last night. I got a kick out of your frantic queries as to whether or not I had gotten your letters and what was the right address and towels and stuff. I was right in the middle of the letter which said you were going to send me another package of towels when the mail orderly handed me a package, at which point I gave a loud groan with visions of gigs for my over-stuffed foot-locker dancing through my head. I was much relieved and delighted to find it was [chocolate chip] cookies, and I am now the most popular girl in the barracks (see ad for Toll House Cookies, Inc.). A small amount of extra money would be appreciated since I've decided to send out all my laundry on the advice of a fellow KPer in her sixth week of Basic. Irons are impossible to get hold of, time is nil, and there are only three washtubs for our whole platoon, so you can see the situation I'm in.

We have very little time to ourselves. In the morning we have three 40 minute classes: Physical Training, Drill, and one Indoctrination course. Afternoon finds us with three more classes, then retreat, then mess, then mail call, then a clothes check, a Detail or two, put up hair, take shower and collapse on bunk. Studying for one of the weekly tests might be squeezed in there, too. We are now having stuff like Customs and Usage, Uniform Regulations, What to do on KP, Where we can and can't go in town, What to do on Guard Duty, What the Army says caused the War, Urgings to Go To Church, Military Sanitation (Please Take Baths), and so on. PT (Physical Training) is quite the stuff. We started out with the hardest stuff first for a test and later they will compare notes to see if we have improved. We do push-ups (called full dips); that is, *some* people do them. I can't, to save my soul. I can do only knee-dips and my knees are a lovely shade of indigo. There are also wing-lifts (ouch!), sit-ups (can't touch anything with your hands), squat-thrusts (puff, puff). Imagine KP on top of this *plus* another shot in the arm. I'm getting to be a second Atlas. A violent bull-session is raging around my bunk, so I'll adjourn till later.

Later: People were madly exchanging pictures—they're at that stage now—telling all their life history and all about their three or four husbands. Most of the gals are twenty-five and up and have husbands in the Service. Lots of the people have Army backgrounds. I feel sort of silly because I don't have a reason apparent to them for joining—no brothers or friends in. One girl was married and has been divorced six weeks. Her spouse divorced her for joining up, but has now calmed down and is clamoring for a remarriage. I had interesting conversations with one of the Indian girls in our barracks. She's a Chippewa and was telling about how silly some of the Easterners she's met are about Indians. One of these Indians is named Redelk; the others have Yankee-sounding ones like Beale and Eastman. I feel sort of detached from myself because nobody calls me anything but "Hey, You." They haven't bothered to learn it—my name, I mean. The only time I hear my name is at mail call. Gives me sort of a funny feeling. You better send me those pictures before I forget who I am.

You asked about mess. They are one story, brick buildings with three long rows of tables—beamed ceilings—wood stoves, comme ca. We grab a plate and get it cafeteria style. We have thick white plates and mugs. Silver and paper napkins are on the tables. They're very strict about eating absolutely everything and if we leave anything the Sarge makes us eat it no matter how foul it is, like fat and gristle. We have lots of green vegetables and the menus are varied. Very few Hot Dishes. *Much* better than St. Mary's Hall, anyhow. I'll try and send you some postcards showing views of the Post. Of course you'll see it all when you come down. Gee, that will be swell if I don't get Barracks Police, or CQ or something. I'll probably have to let you know for sure a couple of days before just to make sure I can see you. Maybe next week if you are going to be home I could call you. I'm free after 6:00 and it only costs 75 cents. Let me know. I must set you straight about that furlough business. It absolutely isn't a rumor. Nobody gets them after Basic unless it is definite that transportation can't be gotten for a month or more.

You see, we wait in Staging until our transportation to our next post is arranged, and it normally is from one to ten days. After my Surgical Tech stuff I ought to be eligible, but one never knows. Lots of kids were in thirteen months and more before they even got three-day passes. Of course it depends on the work we do, too. I'm sending you a copy of *Yank*—some of the articles are quite hilarious.[7] Also am including a map of the Post. Ruth K. and I are going to the movies now, so I'll say goodbye. I'll try to get a supply of postcards at the PX tonight and drop you some notes during the week. I miss you more than I can say, dear little family. I don't blow [brag] about you all to the other bags, but I love you all just the same. Kisses and hugs, with a few small tears of homesickness.

Here is that map of the Post, with the PX with Beauty Shop and Arts and Crafts. Down the street is the Service Club, a very nice place. Has a good library, but of course I never get a chance to read. I get sort of sick of the constant noise and *never* being alone, but of course I expected as much. Here is our mess hall, and the orderly room, day room, and supply room. Next is our barracks, in "Boomtown," which is the home of "See Here, Pvt. ALB" on the second floor. All out east and west is pretty rolling, wooded country. I'd like to get off and walk around and see things.

16 October 1944

Monday

Hi Family,

I'm really a soldier now. Got three gigs today—right in the swing of things.

> "Bosanko, A. . . . Shoes out of line
> Wall Locker open
> Unauthorized object on bed(!)"

How do you like dat? Well, I don't have any hard labor yet, but two more gigs and I will. Things is coming along fine and I'm existing.

All my love,

---

[7] *Yank* was a national magazine put out by the armed forces for and about service personnel; it contained cartoons, articles, and news items.

From Dad—Oct. 11, 1944:

Your letters are a delight and take me back to the bygone days when I was a rookie. Armies do not seem to change much except that you are getting a better deal. It does something for you to be part of a first-class outfit, doesn't it? Just wait till you have been in long enough to get the real feel of it, to learn proper Army grousing and know that your outfit is the best damned outfit in the Army. The old Metal Corporal envies you, kid!

Sorry that there is to be no leave, but don't worry: we'll be down for a good weekend even if I have to put another mortgage on the garage. In the meantime we shall hold down the Home Front, look after Civilian Morale and I shall work on my company in the Guard with renewed enthusiasm, knowing that we are both working on the same kind of job. How's about both of us getting together some fine day with three stripes? Heaps of love and things, Pvt. Bug from . . . Your old man.

From Dad—Oct. 16, 1944:

I have finally discovered why your ASN [Army service number] is so very easy for me to remember. "S/Major P. Bosanko, S/385974"; "Pvt. A. Bosanko, A-710974." This must mean something, tho just what I shall let you figure out. Anyhow, it's odd and quaint.

From Dad—Oct. 18, 1944:

Sorry to hear you had been a bad, sloppy WAC! Should be at drill, but my age and service deserve an occasional evening off. Incidentally I got my Good Conduct and Service Ribbon so now I have four and am frequently mistaken for Eisenhower or Patton.

From Mom—Oct. 19, 1944:

We were so glad to have your nice long letter of Sunday with the enclosed map of the Post which was interesting. It surely sounds as if you were working hard and certainly must be toughening up. I'm afraid it would do me in, but then you are a few years younger than I! Cleaning a grease trap at 5 AM sounds rather awful, but I know you survived it. How come you have to work at such an ungodly hour? We were interested in everything you wrote—the girls, the Indians, etc. Do you have any Negro recruits? As always, we appreciate your pictures—they were funny.

I hope you are really getting used to it and not too all in. Basic is bound to be tougher than any other part of the training. I'm going to send another box of cookies. I trust you don't have to give all of them away. We also had your card about "gigs" today—what a gal!

Loads and loads of love,

17 October 1944

Tuesday

Dear Family,

I'm writing this in the biff ducked down under a washbowl to be out of the way of the crowd. Life is fine—no gigs today. Amazing. But I pulled fatigue detail for Thursday, tough bounce. Saturday I'm going to town with a fun personage named Dodack. We plan to sling some vermillion paint around but we will be ladies, don't worry. All of which leads up to a touch for $5.00. We get paid soon, but the five-spot would come in handy. Thanks for the letters. Mike, I will write you soon and send you some postcards.

Goodbye all, I loves you,

22 October 1944

Sunday

Dearest Family,

Gosh it was swell to hear you. I could just see you gathered around the phone in the back hall and Mike hanging on upstairs, a fire in the living room, no doubt, and toasted cheese sandwiches and cocoa. At least that's always what I think of when I'm picturing Sunday night. After I left you, I was walking back to the barracks and I passed the Chapel from whence hymn singing was issuing. So I popped in and they sang "Day is Dying in the West." All of which affected the emotions of little Annie, and I sat and bawled like a sap. I don't know what's happening to me lately—tears roll down on the slightest provocation and I'm really homesick. It's probably just nerves and it doesn't last long. I'm not a Section Eight case, however, so don't worry.[8] The cookies came and thanks much.

[8] Section Eight was a section in the army regulations that referred to discharging people from the service because of mental illness or emotional problems.

They were gone in about fifteen minutes. Mom, you're really popular in the First Platoon.

Friday night in the Army is known as GI night. GI in this case means scrubbing, and I do mean scrub, with a bristly GI brush and hot water in a GI can (very large size empty tin can) and GI soap—horrible brown stuff that's mainly fat and lye and is death on skin. Everyone has what we call KP hands. I use the backs of mine for an emery board, no kidding. You would get a kick out of seeing all us gals on our hands and knees scrubbing away and the whole second floor singing:

Lay that gig sheet down, Sarge
Lay that gig sheet down.
Nasty mean old Sargie,
Lay that gig sheet down.—to the tune of "Pistol Packin' Momma"

We sluice water around like mad and wash the pipes, rafters, bed springs, and polish everything in sight and everything out of sight. Then we fix our foot and wall lockers so that nothing that isn't GI shows. Then we polish our shoes—even the bottoms. THEN we collapse in bed after taking a shower, putting up our hair, pressing clothes, etc.; and the hell of it is that we have shots every Friday afternoon. Maybe they fix it so we can work off some of the soreness scrubbing. "There's a reason for everything in the Army." Next morning we arise at 5:30 and make our beds fancy, with six inches between pillow and top of sheet and a six inch fold of sheet, and bed roll a certain way, and . . . oh, Lord! After that we re-scrub our areas, dress, rush over to mess at 6:30, rush back at 7:15, clean the laundry or whatever, dress in our uniforms, and are ready by 7:45 for inspection. Of course, by this time the dust has settled in the barracks and we do a last minute swishing around. Then comes Inspection when we stand at strict attention for about a half hour while the inspecting party goes around. Pop, you know what a strain that is. After which we have a song fest. This last Saturday, we had a parade for some visiting English dignitaries. It is a very gorgeous sight to see, especially in the fall. The parade ground is bright green and ringed with bright yellow, red, and green trees, and the red brick houses of Officer's Row show between. The sky is blue and the sun is warm and the band plays—it's really fun. Usually we parade on Mondays and Thursdays for Retreat. Family, I will write more tomorrow but I've got a splitting headache and the kids are banging the piano over here in the Day Room. I'll write a longer letter tomorrow.

From Dad—Oct. 25, 1944:

Your Sunday letter just came and was swell. Glad to hear you had a good "bawl" session—do you good. And do I know GI soap, brushes, policing, inspection, GI beds and what have you! Remember, I was the poor NCO this summer. Today I did my bit at the Blood Center.

From Mom—Oct. 26, 1944:

Dearest Annie: We were glad to have your letter which came yesterday. I'm sorry you were homesick—talking to us probably brought it all on! But don't be ashamed of crying; it's a very good outlet for the emotions. A "good cry" really helps sometimes. I hope you are feeling lots happier and I'm sure you are. You are too independent and buoyant to be down for long.

Monday I went to a lecture meeting of the Study Club down at the YW. Dr. [Walter H.] Judd spoke; he has just returned from China and told us about some of the terrific problems China has had in fighting this war.[9] He is a very fascinating speaker and kept us entranced for an hour and a half!

You should see the way we still scrounge around to find enough cigarettes. We have discovered that they generally come in on Tuesday, so beginning then we start putting the pressure on Ray at the grocery, Bertha at System Drug (who, by the way, asks after you frequently), and Art, up where Dad and Mike take the street car. Then by finding an extra pack or two in other stores, we manage to squeeze by for a week! Today I did some more housecleaning, as the weather stays so perfect. Cleaned and aired yours and Mike's closets, aired some curtains, washed windows, etc. I walked up to meet Dad, as I do nearly every day when I'm home. Midge loves to go along. She knows the minute I open the closet door for my coat that a walk is in the wind.

I'm re-reading Sinclair Lewis' Main Street. It's not bad but it's strange to think of the furor it caused when it first came out.[10] Hope you have some good hand lotion for your hands after all that scrubbing. Boy, that

[9] Judd was a Republican congressman from Minneapolis and a postwar leader of the so-called China Lobby in Congress that fiercely opposed any contact with or recognition of the Communist regime in China.

[10] This novel, published in 1920, was notorious for satirizing the people and attitudes of small towns in America.

sounds like hard work—I hope it won't be so hard after Basic. Do you hear from all the "kids?" And Joe? I hope he's writing. Pop is at State Guard and Mike is agonizing over his homework. Lots and lots of love. We miss you a great deal, but are carrying on! Be sure to let us know the probable time off you can have on Saturday and Sunday so we can make our plans.

24 October 1944

Tuesday

Hi people,

Here I am again. Last night I couldn't continue my missive because I had to study for a test on the various stuff we've been having, like Guard Duty, Articles of War, and World History. I didn't study at all but the test was really very simple. The nice thing about the Army tests is that all we find out is whether we pass or fail. No one ever knows whether she was highest or lowest or anything. Of course this doesn't make for much scholastic motivation, but we only have to pass three out of five tests. My little brain is really relaxing.

Now for some answers to questions. I can't tell from now whether or not I'll be pulled for duties, and I won't know till one day before you arrive, according to the Top Kick. With CQ and BP I can trade, but if I pull Guard Duty all is lost because I can't Welsh out. That is posted two days before and if by any wild chance the worst happens, I'll frantically telegraph you. It's a thin chance that I'll get it though, so let's cross our fingers and hope for the best. Now for my weekend schedule: I'm free from 4:30 on Saturday. Have to check in by 11:30 at night. Takes 45 minutes to get back from downtown by streetcar, and less by taxi—really twenty minutes ride and twenty-five minutes walk from entrance to the Post to the barracks. Sunday I'm up at 8 and free from then till 11:30 again. You'll probably have to leave Sunday afternoon so my evening check-in doesn't matter.

Thanks for the picture (mental) of the new living room arrangement. It helps in my visualizations of home. The Service Club is having a competition barn dance, and our Recreation Officer rooked me and some other gals in on doing some sets. We practiced last night and tonight and Wednesday is the gala affair. I fling myself around with such abandon and enthusiasm that my leg

My date or off-duty dress

In front of the Fort Des Moines service club

WAC barracks, Fort Des Moines

In my fatigues and high-top shoes

Anne Bosanko and her little cocker will part company next week when Anne leaves to start her WAC basic training at Fort Des Moines, Iowa. Anne, daughter of Mr. and Mrs. Paul Bosanko, 4119 York avenue south, chose WAC enlistment this fall instead of returning to the University of Minnesota.

From the Minneapolis Times, Sept. 28, 1944, p. 10

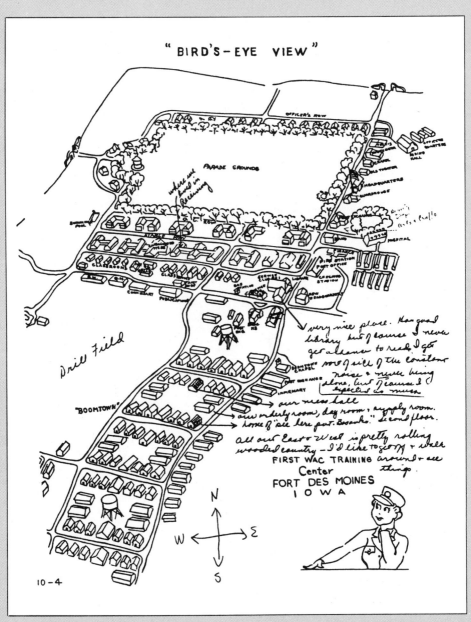

Map of Fort Des Moines

Portrait taken for Mom & Dad

The 154 members of Company 5

The head table at the farewell party

muscles are all strained. I can hardly walk upstairs, poor little miserable me. Life jigs along here in its usual happy rut, and after my wild (!) weekend I sort of appreciate it. Saturday night Jerry Dodack and I had dinner and a cocktail at Babe's—a sort of second-rate Charlie's,[11] but the best Des Moines offers. Then we thought we'd go to a movie, but this dear hick burg's theaters had movies that I saw months ago, like *Double Indemnity,* and *Private Hargrove* and such. So we repaired back to Babe's knowing nowhere else to go and found most of Company Five in the back tap room, where we had fun and spent huge amounts of money. Not having Joseph to buy my drinks really makes a dent in my money bag, and I do mean money bag. I didn't tell you, but all the girls have canvas money satchels that hang around our necks. Here is a picture of GI Jane and her Chest Hardware, with two dog tags, and the money bag. Here is a side view of me with my hair up: "Git that hair off yer collar!" Then on Sunday we were suckers and went into town again. This time the only thing that was open was the USO, which you'll see when you come so I'll not bother to describe it. All the restaurants were closed until later in the day, so we had to grab a snack at the said USO. I played the piano to myself for awhile and we hung around, and Jerry went to sleep, the other kids went to have their pictures taken, and I started playing solitaire, when a sailor came over and offered to beat me at checkers, which he did. This led to Gin rummy and Pitch, and Black Jack (no money involved however) and after awhile he suggested going to the movies. I took Jerry along for protection although he seemed quite respectable. But when we got in, the old octopus routine started. I kept it down to hand-holding by my brute force acquired in PT, but my poor hand is still black and blue from the mauling he gave it. That's why I sounded so pooped on Sunday. Down with all sailors. Never trust a sailor . . . etc.

SOS: Please send at least ten coat hangers *immediately.* They can't be bought at the PX for love nor money and I'm regarded as the plague of the barracks for borrowing them. Please send them as soon as you get this letter. VITAL! But here's a note: Try not to send food and stuff so it will arrive on Friday or Saturday because we have inspection on Saturday, as I told you, and nothing can be

---

[11] Charlie's was considered the premier restaurant in Minneapolis from the 1930s to the 1970s.

around that isn't GI. This package business can be reciprocal, you know. I'll send you cigs, candy bars, chocolate bits (when they have them) and gum, if you like. Just say the word. Something funny happened today which Dad will appreciate. Our platoon had been doing Rear Marches and Oblique pretty well so our Sarge suggested we try some fast drill. But after a few "To the rear, MARCH, to the rear, MARCH, to the rear, MARCH" we were so dizzy and confused that the Sarge compassionately halted us. And lo, as she stood regarding us with her hands on her hips, an amazed smile spread over her face, and she quoth: "I never saw a platoon that could make so many mistakes and still keep covered!" That's all for now, people. Station WAC now signing off for the evening. All my love and a kiss and hug for everybody and a pat for Midge.

[By the third week in Basic Training, I was captivated by army jargon and abbreviations. Using the slang made me feel knowing and "with it," and I knew my dad would understand most of the terms without explanation. However, later generations might find these definitions helpful:

PX: Post Exchange; a general store plus tavern for service people on an army post

Mess/Mess Hall: Army for meals/cafeteria

KP: Kitchen Police; scullery maids

BP: Barracks Police, help the sergeant to enforce Lights Out, monitor cleanliness, and so forth

Police (verb): To clean up or straighten an "area"

CQ: Charge of Quarters; person assigned to be in charge when the sergeant or usual authority was off duty and answer phone, deliver messages, check passes, and so forth

Keep Covered: An order in marching drill routines meaning "Make sure you are in perfect alignment with the person next to you"

GI: An all-purpose term (adjective, noun, verb) for people, things, and events. Originally GI stood for "Government Issue," referring to official uniforms and equipment, but this evolved into a verb and an adjective meaning "according to army rules," as in, "It is GI to GI the barracks with a GI brush on GI night." See army maxim: "There's a right way, a wrong way, and the army way." Also: "If something moves, salute it; if not, clean it." In a further development, GI became the term for the person who did all the cleaning—the nonofficer or enlisted person.

USO: United Service Organization; a wartime volunteer organization that tried to meet some of the social needs of enlisted service people. This group maintained hospitality rooms or booths in train stations and central locations in cities. USOs had toilet facilities, frequently free coffee and doughnuts or an inexpensive snack bar, telephones, and lounges where people could rest or meet friends. Since service people were usually broke, away from home, and in strange places, the USOs were vital to our lives.]

29 October 1944

Sunday Night

Well, here I am again, family. Your correspondent is exhausted. Reason: obvious. It's Sunday—the end of the day of rest. I was really going to rest this week, but Ruth K. persuaded me to go to the Cathedral downtown with her, and that entailed taking a bath after breakfast, and leaping into my clothes and rushing across the parade ground to the street car. It was a beautiful service, though. Good choir, and the church wasn't over-decorated, amazingly enough. The windows were lovely, too. Then we went out to dinner and to Babe's for a nip (tsk!). It's fun to exercise my privilege of buying liquor. Don't worry—Babe's drinks are very anemic. Next on the list was a walk up to the feeble Capitol, where we climbed up thousands of circular stairs to the top of the dome. We could see out over the whole of Des Moines and that, for sure, wasn't much. This is really a burg—absolutely minute.

Last week was really tough. That dance business took up Monday, Tuesday, and Wednesday night. Then we GI'd the barracks Thursday night and had a GI party, namely food—hamburgers and cokes and cookies—and songs which I'll sing for you when you come. Of course, the barracks were dirty by Friday night so we GI'd again. Also, Friday I had a tetanus shot which really did me in. It still aches like mad. Saturday morning inspection and another parade for some more British dignitaries. Curses on the English. Saturday night a bunch of us went to a show on the Post and then I came back and did laundry and fell into bed. Every week gets more and more hurried, but only three more weeks to go. Last Tuesday we had a test on the work we covered, and we have four more tests coming. By now our courses are more difficult: Map Reading (fun), Company Administration, Gases, etc.[12] A couple of days ago we got our Off-duty dresses and mine fits perfectly for a wonder. I'll wear it when you come. We also got our gas masks. I can hardly wait to try it on and scare people. Happy day—I got KP again tomorrow. But that may mean I'll escape other kinds of details over the weekend.[13] I hear that the train gets in about 5:30. If so, I can meet you at the station. Let me hear more about your plans. I've got to write some more letters now, so goodbye and I'll write Tuesday or Wednesday.

All kinds of love,

6 November 1944

Monday

Hi people,

Of course I don't need to say that it was wonderful having you down. To keep me from being too lonesome after the train left, the Finches took me back to their apartment where I sat in comfort, listening to the radio, smoking, sipping cooling drinks, and talking. They really are swell and lots of fun. They talked and talked about their son, Chuck, and about Mary Ann, and finally decided to call her. I got to talk some—the first time since two years ago at the SMH houseparty.[14] Then they took me out and bought me a super

---

[12] We went through a class that gave information about chemicals used in warfare, their effects, and survival of a gas attack and let us practice wearing gas masks while going through a real gas chamber.

[13] Detail, pronounced "*dee*' tail," was a name for a chore and a name for the group of people assigned to do the chore. Another name for these chores was "fatigue." This term was applied to the chore itself ("fatigue detail," "going on fatigue") and to the clothes worn while doing it ("I'm changing into my fatigues").

[14] Mary Ann Finch, a classmate of mine from high school days at St. Mary's Hall, was from Des Moines. Although she was away at college, I got in touch with her parents who were most kind about entertaining me during my brief stay in Des Moines. When my parents were visiting for a weekend, we also got together with the Finches.

gorgeous steak dinner. AHhh. They're taking me and Ruth K. to the Des Moines Club next Saturday.

Love,
Me

8 November 1944

Wednesday

Well, this has been a very eventful week—a sort of "November crisis" as you might say. Company Five has been naughty. We are bad WACs. Tuesday, during the day, the officers made an inspection and found quite a mess in some unidentified platoon (it *couldn't* have been the first platoon) and as a result the whole Company was restricted last night. It was suggested that we do a little scrubbing during the evening, which we did. Then, all of a sudden, at two minutes to eight, the cadre [noncommissioned officers] came upstairs and said, "Formal inspection at eight o'clock! AT EASE!" Here our wall and foot lockers weren't prepared and so on and so on. Lt. Whelan went through this place like a tornado and by a miracle Little Annie was neat and didn't get a gig. Then she hauled the Company into the day room and gave us a bawling-out a la Maggie. It really brought back the good old days at SMH when we got called on the carpet every Thursday night and we kiddies used to scrootch down behind the big armchair to escape Mag's wrathful eye. In this case I was safely ensconced behind the stove. We really got the devil, too, and Whelan made us all feel like heels. Since then we've been GIing every night and every spare minute. We have the floor now so we can eat off it.

Speaking of eating, we had a spread tonight—ice cream, fruit cake, and pork tenderloin sandwiches, and black olives. I gave you some indication of my nice Sunday afternoon with the Finches. It was really swell to relax in a house. Next Saturday ought to be fun, too. The Des Moines Club is like the Minneapolis Club.[15] Exclusive, ain't I? This evening we got our off-duty scarves and gloves—smooth yellow deals—two of each—and of course we had to stand

---

The next weekend Dr. Finch did some "civilian" dental work for me. I had been fearful of having any dental care during Basic. The rumor was that the army never put in any fillings; they simply pulled your teeth if you complained.

[15] These were prestigious private clubs for business and professional men.

in line for hours. I'll be glad when we finally get all of our issue and I bet the Supply Sergeant will be too. About all we have left now is our gold buttons, but one never knows. Today we had our first gas mask drill and we nearly had hysterics at the way we look. Definitely anthropoid or something. We don't look like death's heads, contrary to popular opinion. Tomorrow we have to go through the gas chamber. Hope we don't kick off, but probably no such luck; the drill comes off in the afternoon and sick call isn't until 7:30 p.m. It wouldn't be GI. Well, folksies, I can't think of much more to say except . . . how about some more cookies? Toll House preferred. Love you lots. Say hello to people for me. Much kisses and hugs and a snappy salute. Just remembered: In my top middle desk drawer there should be some envelopes with stuff from the War Department. In one of these is that copy of my interview with Major Bronson and a copy of my Special Orders—a sheet of mimeograph with a list of all the people that were inducted on the 20th. Please send same soon. Thanx. Also, you might send my suitcase along quick-like. If you can't find that envelope in my desk drawer (top middle) look in the other ones because I know it's there somewhere. It's really very important that I have it. Tomorrow night I am a super-numerary for the Guards, which means I run around with coffee and sandwiches and stuff for the kids.[16] Wish I was a Guard . . . damn. Anyway, I won't be able to write and Friday is GI and Saturday is my date with the Finches, so Sunday I'll pen a real letter. Thanks for the *New Yorker.*

12 November 1944

Sunday

Dear Family,

Today was a hell of a day. I went to the dentist and he filled me full of novocain and I'm suffering great after-effects. I feel awful (don't worry). Ruined my whole day. Doubtless I'll recover by tomorrow but now I'm terrible with swollen lips. I'll write coherently tomorrow but tonight . . . ooooh! My suitcase didn't come, what gives? I'm sending home some packages of stuff so I won't be

[16] From lights out to reveille, Wac guards were on post.

so loaded down when I go to Staging. Just unwrap it and put it in my room.

All my love,

12 November 1944

Dearest Carrie,

This is a dirty trick, sending you a postcard, but really, child, I don't have *any* time to write a decent letter. This is the beginning of my sixth week in the Army and I'm not dead yet. In fact I like it, but we are rushed to death in Basic—always scrubbing, drilling, lining up for something: classes, physical training. On weekends we stagger into the bustling metropolis of Des Moines. What a dump—nothing to do but spend all our money on liquor. It's fun on the Post but I wouldn't like to be stationed here cause it's getting cold and rainy now. Been perfect Indian Summer weather before. Pretty countryside. I should be moving out soon and when I get in the field I should have time to give you the gory details, and arguments pro, and stuff. Do drop me a postcard, however, to show me you ain't mad.

Much love,
Pansy

15 November 1944

Wednesday

Dear Family,

Here I am again. A gay social life has prevented my writing sooner. I quickly recovered from my indisposition of Sunday night—hope it didn't upset you to hear about it. Saturday evening Ruth K. and I met Dr. Finch at the Service Club and he drove us in to the apartment where we were greeted with lovely long cooling mixtures of Johnnie Walker. We sat around and talked and then whizzed into the Des Moines Club—a tiny edition of the Minneapolis Club—where I made away with a *beautiful* sirloin, almost too beautiful to eat. Then we pub-hopped and saw some of Des Moines' anemic night life. They really are fun people; I like 'em a lot.

Sunday morning I had to get up and come in to the dentist. He filled that one place with a silver filling—drilled first, of course—for which he nicked me $6.00. How about some remuneration? Could you stand it?

Monday, when I was coming back from the post office, I got caught in a rain and lightning storm and took refuge in the Service Club. There I stumbled on a music appreciation hour and had an interesting conversation about sunsets with a woman in Clerk School. Monday, after the parade, there was a gorgeous one. Many big sculptured clouds, pink-edged, with sun streaming out from behind. Very Rococo and Day-of-Judgment looking, contrasting oddly with the geometric red barracks and bright green lawns. Sort of like a combination of Reubens and Adolf Dehn. Tuesday Ruth K. and I took in a movie and didn't get in till late, and tonight we went to a USO show (lousy imitation vaudeville) and didn't get back very soon. In fact, bed check is in fifteen minutes so I'll have to hurry with this. You know, I am a much afflicted individual. I thought I was getting away from activities and such, and what happens? I get elected to be in charge of the Company party. Oh, well, what is a mere dinner and entertainment for 200 people after a tea for 2,000? Our courses are getting to be very boring—Organization of the Army, Company Administration, Military Sanitation and Supply. I find this Army stuff rather dull and will be glad to be getting on with some medical subjects. LRs fly around like mad as to where we go. Nobody knows definitely about Camp Atterbury, [Indiana,] and how long we will be in Staging, so even if I knew I couldn't tell you. I'm afraid a Delay en Route is kind of a lovely dream.[17] The cadre say that Basics seldom get them going out to their first posts. The suitcase finally came and the cookies muchly admired and appreciated as usual. Mike, thanks for the [Minnesota] Daily and "Fighters Digest."[18] I'll write you Sunday but till then I'll be horribly busy, this being the last week we have classes till late every night. How would Sunday be for a phone call? Yes? "I hear a voice

---

[17] A person moving from one assignment to another was allowed a brief delay or vacation.

[18] The "Fighters Digest," a Saturday feature of the *Minneapolis Daily Times*, contained a four-page "weekly summary of home news and sports for men and women in service."

hummin', bed check is a-comin','" so, goodbye. Will write more gory details on Sunday.

All my love,

Have you had any snow yet? It feels sort of like it here. . . .

19 November 1944
Sunday

1798 Service Unit Headquarters
First Women's Army Corps Training Center
Fort Des Moines, Iowa

Company 5, 3rd Regiment
19 November 1944

Subject: Life and Times of Pvt. Anne L. Bosanko, A710974
To: Family of Pvt. Anne L. Bosanko, A710974

1. Pvt. Bosanko is feeling very well and hopes that her family is also well.
2. Pvt. Bosanko is practicing her military correspondence.
   a. Hence the form of this epistle
   b. Which she learned in Company Administration
   c. Which is very tiring
3. So she, the undersigned, will stop
4. Writing in this manner.

By order of Col. McCoskrie

Anne L. Bosanko
Pvt., WAC

OK, OK, so I ain't GI—it's too much effort. This last week has been very hectic as I intimated and I'm drawing a moderately deep breath today preparing for my gruesome weeks in Staging. I will tell you all I know about my future, which isn't much, so you won't be up in the air about it. But, *please* don't tell *anyone* because they're very strict about this kind of stuff. I know you'll be careful but I just thought I'd mention it. Here's the deal, culled from LRs filtering up from Staging. Camp Atterbury is full up and the next group isn't going till December 10. That's three weeks from today and we go into Staging this Tuesday. However, here's a note of hope. There are a couple of other medical training schools, one in Denver and one in the East somewhere. Now, my orders (which you sent me—thanks) don't have "Assigned to Camp Atterbury" on them. It just says "Assigned to a Medical Installation as Surgical Technician after further training at the Surgical Technician School upon completion of basic training." Sooo, maybe I'll be sent to one of these other schools instead of waiting in Staging for three weeks. There are loads and loads of girls in the Medical Corps coming over every week and they just don't have room for them all in Staging barracks. I'm hoping against hope that I will get sent out to one of those other schools, but of course I haven't heard anything definite yet and won't know until hours before I leave. All correspondence and phone calls are censored in Staging so you won't know if I've gone until you get a letter from a new address. Pray for me that I get sent east or to Denver; Indiana doesn't appeal to me much.

A week ago, I forgot to tell you, we had our White Glove Inspection and came through with Flying Colors! Your little daughter was in the primaries in a cute little posture contest staged by Major Milligan.[19] I didn't get into the finals though. I wrote you about my social week. Thursday I went to a Company basketball game and screamed my lungs hoarser than they were before. When I call tonight you no doubt will notice my deep bass voice.

Last night our entertainment and dinner came off very well . . . muchos fun. I had to sit at the officers' table—it felt like being at head table with Mag. One of the numbers was to that song . . . you, Dad, probably know it:

Bless 'em all, bless 'em all,
The long and the short and the tall.
Bless all the Sergeants we have to obey
Bless all the Corporals who drill us all day.
Cause we're saying Goodbye to them all,

---

[19] This contest was to see who had the best military posture, which consisted of (1) standing straight, (2) eyes straight ahead, (3) chin back, (4) shoulders back, (5) rear tucked in, (6) feet at a forty-five-degree angle, (7) arms back with thumbs along the seam of the trousers (or skirt, as the case may be).

As back to the barracks we crawl.
No ice cream and cookies for flat-footed rookies
So chew up my lads, bless 'em all.

There were three little, short gals and two huge gals in between them—two six-footers and three 4'11"ers. They did a little dance with motions, positively hysterical. There were funny poems and a number from some members of the Third Platoon, "The Goons from the Third Platoon," all dressed up amoosin'. Piano solos and songs and all kinds of stuff like that there. Sgt. Fields sang "I'm Goin' Back to Where I Come From" in her hillbilly accent and convulsed the company. All in all it was a gay party.

This whole last week everybody has been so silly. We're all under such a strain not knowing what's going to happen to us that we let off steam with horseplay. My face still hurts from laughing so much. Pop, did you ever see some training films on Lice and Flies, made in England? They are rare, and I do mean funny. Here are these gory shots of dirty latrines and foul mess halls—flies and lice and stuff, all accompanied by commentary in a veddy, veddy correct British accent: "Nasty little blighters, aren't they?" And then a shot of a fly on a biff; well-modulated voice says, "And now it's time for tea." We were all rolling in the aisles. One of the gals gave me a dog-tag bootie made of blue crocheted silk. It keeps them warm and stops the jingle-jangle-jingle, like so.

Weather here is foul—raining and putrid but not very cold. That letter was from Mu; she's in California, as you could plainly see, and has been spending the year following her husband around. She enclosed $1.00 to send her coat, which I am enclosing. (The dollar, not the coat.) Here's her address. Thanks for the clippings and concert programs. Keep it up, I like to get stuff about ye olde home towne. I've got to go and press some clothes and do various odd jobs, so goodbye and much love. Thanks much for the money; that extra $4.00 will help no end. We got our last tetanus shots Friday. Double dose and they didn't faze me—am I tough. Also, in my PT test, the following results: Push-ups: 1 (hot dog); Sit-ups: 48; Wing-lifts: 84 per one minute; Squat-thrusts: 20 per one-half minute.

23 November 1944

Thursday

Happy Thanksgiving to you,
"   "   "   "

"   "   dear Family,
"   "   to you!

I have just returned from an enchanting one-hour's wait in line at the mess hall and the joyous discovery that there wasn't much left by the time I got there at the end of the line. The hall was fixed up rather quaint-like, though, with little wagons filled with fruit on the tables and nut cups with hard candy, and menus at each place, but that still doesn't calm my not-too-full stomach. Your very welcome fruit cake and cookies will have to fill up the gaps. Curses on mess lines. Today, believe it or not, is a Post holiday—sleep till eight and so on, just like Sunday. Only, of course, I was on mess serving-line detail and had to get up at 6:00 and serve from 6:30 till 9:30. The hungry hordes seemed as though they never would stop pouring in. Mess line serving isn't bad though and a hell of a lot better than KP. It's fun to watch the civvies fresh off the train with their trailing locks, high heels, and mink coats. Of course, I'm an old veteran by now and mentally pat them on the head and greet them with a gruesome cheery smile and a "Happy Thanksgiving!" "Heh, Heh!" I really am cheery, too, in spite of the temporary annoyance regarding Thanksgiving dinner.

Staging is really fun and very comfortable on the whole. I guess I must have changed somehow because, although in Receiving I thought I was going to die on account of the crowded conditions and living out of a suitcase, I feel very cozy here. I repacked my barracks bag today and I'm all ready to leave at a moment's notice, but I have everything to hand and everything is all lovely and happy. Cheer, cheer, cheer. Most of the good kids from Platoon One are near, plus Ruth K. and some other friends from Platoons Two and Three. While waiting for our orders, we go to little orientation courses about how to pack and what to do on the train, and we have drill and PT and stuff, plus various details. The atmosphere here is very exciting with people waiting and packing and yelling around—sort of a continual pre-Christmas vacation feeling. It's also restful, if you can imagine the combination. What I mean is that there isn't so much pressure on us about uniforms (except at our daily morning inspections), sitting on our beds, and various things. I've had lots of time to wash and iron clothes, read, take baths, and stuff. All in all, Staging is quite decent and I don't think that a couple of weeks will kill me.

Of course, the rumor mill is functioning full force. It's rare to watch the kids cluster 'round every time someone says, "Guess what I heard today?" The wildest surmises are floating around and it's fun to think about them even if they aren't true. I found out the reasons for no Delays en Route: we haven't accrued enough furlough time (rate of two days a month). Our Delays come out of furlough time, you see.

Tonight we are having a treat for the small sum of $1.83. We're going into town to hear Marian Anderson.[20] I understand she was out at the Fort today visiting some of the mess halls, but she didn't drop into ours when I was there.

Know what I did? Give myself a two-inch haircut! I look rather like a sacrificial lamb, but I was sick and tired of having my locks bush out everytime it is damp. We've been having much mist and anemic snow, so off came my hair. Today is lovely, though—crisp, clear and sunny with fluffy, drifty white clouds in the sky.

I'm getting sleepier and sleepier so that I can hardly push this pen around so goodbye. All my love and I sure wish I could be with you.

Kisses and hugs,
Pvt. Bug

Enclosed find $1.00 from Mu. Tell any of the Stagnanttes you see, especially E.C., that I'll write as soon as I catch up on my sleep.

29 November 1944

Wednesday

Dearest Family,

Calm down, I'm not gone yet. I've just been too lazy to write which shows you the condition I've degenerated into. All my training has gone for naught, somewhat. The concert Thursday

---

[20] Marian Anderson was a world-famous concert contralto. There was widespread national outrage in the early 1940s when the Daughters of the American Revolution in Washington, D.C., would not allow her to sing with a symphony orchestra on their auditorium stage because she was black.

evening was fine. Anderson was in prime form—sang "Ave Maria" for an encore. At intermission Ruth K. and I decided to go out for a smoke, and not knowing how the Shrine Auditorium (Des Moines' cultural center) ran its schedule, I went up to an aged usher and asked in a dignified tone, "How long is intermission?" to which he replied, "Downstairs and to your left, lady." Everyone within ten feet of us laid back and howled.

Friday the first kids from Company Five shipped out, and since then more and more have gone, and the rest of us meds are rather sad and lonely. Ruth K. left Saturday for Fitzsimons Hospital in Denver (lucky stiff). Dietrich and Dodack have also gone. But I have found a congenial soul in the next bunk who was in my platoon before but whom I didn't know very well. Name: Barbara Braun. Hails from Colorado but never heard of Westcliffe. She didn't get around much, did she?

Saturday: went to a movie and read. Sunday: went to a movie and read. Monday: went downtown in the evening to look over Younkers' [Department Store] Christmas efforts. Not too bad, but not near as gay as Dayton's [Department Store]. I really miss good old Nicollet Avenue and all the greens and lights.[21] Hope I'm not stuck in some grim place for Christmas.

Would you please send me a list of wants. Daddy, send what Mammy wants; Mammy, send what Daddy and Michael want. I may as well say right here that I can't afford a clarinet even if I am getting paid tomorrow. In fact, I don't approve at all of this clarinet business. After all, you know what clarinet players are like and I don't want Mike to be another Sigurd.[22] Of course, I don't mean that seriously—it's too much of an insult to label on anyone.

Tomorrow, Barbara and I are going over to Arts and Crafts to make Christmas cards. Whee . . . gay, mad fun on Post. Staging is getting more and more irritating every day. The left-overs (me and Braun) miss all our pals from Company Five and also we're tired of sitting on our cans or going to lectures that we heard last week. But I grit my teeth and realize that I'll never get a nice rest like this again. We're having formal inspection tomorrow so I must rush now and do my squad duty.

Goodbye and much love,

[21] Nicollet Avenue, the main retail shopping street in downtown Minneapolis, at Christmas time had lighted decorations hung on lampposts and across the streets, and all the store windows had merchandise displays or animated holiday scenes.
[22] See note 1, above; Sigurd played the clarinet.

Here I am again. Just finished madly scrubbing the aisle of our barny barracks. Am very hot and dirty. The snow is snowing all around. It snows on field and tree and parade ground and all looks very pretty and Christmas cardy. Mom, please do procure that iron for me and save it till I get settled. Likewise the snapshots, save them, I mean. For Christmas for GI Annie: Box of homemade cookies and candy and stuff would be marvelous; flannel night-gown with fleurs; writing case; new watch strap; those sock things with felt or leather bottoms for whizzing (not lounging) around the barracks; any purty smells (small), powder, lotions, creams, nail creams [for cuticle removal], and stuff; any bright ideas you can think of. How's that for a suggestion list?

Much love again,

6 December 1944

Wednesday

Dearest Family,

Well, here I am again, still at good old Fort Des Moines. How I love this happy place. Last week I was pretty well disgusted, mainly because I was suffering from the pangs of a cold and fierce headache (which I am over now), but yesterday I got my second wind and snapped out of my depression. Braun and I had hysterics all day, making feeble puns and giggling around, and that sort of cleared the air. I can't say anything about prospects for leaving even if they were good, so be patient and someday you will hear from me with the return address some glamorous place. Please send me letters and stuff here and even if I have gone they will be forwarded and I'll have things waiting for me. Nothing much happens here of interest except rumors and those I can't repeat. We just go on from day to day sort of holding our breaths, clenching our teeth and bearing it all like martyrs. Tomorrow night a party of us is going to *Othello* which ought to relieve the monotony.[23]

Last Sunday I went in to church, then met some kids and had dinner and went to a movie and messed around and didn't get home till late, so no letter written to you. Monday I was feeling foul,

[23] A national touring company was doing Shakespeare's *Othello*, starring Paul Robeson, the famous black actor and singer. Des Moines obviously had a fine selection of cultural events coming through the city.

so had some beer with the kids, and on to the Service Club Library where I got involved in Angela Thirkell's latest, *Marling Hall,* which, by the way, Mom, stinks. It's rather forced and about depressing people and not nearly as funny and spontaneous as her other books. Too bad. Last night Barbie and I went up to Arts and Crafts and made Christmas cards. My evenings, as you can see, are quite human and I enjoy myself, but during the day I feel like a sheep. But such is life. Had a nice letter from Ruth K. who is very impressed with Fitzsimons Hospital which I didn't know was the largest in the world. But the poor gal, who is a graduate med tech with a year of experience besides, is spending her time putting labels on bottles. It seems that there are lots of civilians working there and they won't give up their jobs to WACs. Wotta life — Bergie would gloat, I know.[24]

The weather here has gone berserk. It sleets and melts and rains and slushes and snows and rains and freezes and fogs and frosts and melts and drips and is generally messy, but at least provides some interest for us "Hangovers" as I call us. Sunday everything was covered with a sheet of ice and we had to skate to mess. Monday it rained hard all day, then decided to snow hard. Tuesday morning it was lovely and Christmas cardy. By afternoon everything had melted, and my shoes were like an aquarium lacking the goldfish. Today we awoke to find everything frosted, as though an Art Moderne fiend had sprayed the world with silver paint. Every little twig was covered with white crystals. Added to which was a thick white fog over all. We never know when we stagger out of the barracks at 5:00 G.M.[25] what the world will be like that day. Thank you for the Christmas suggestions. Enclosed find private notes regarding my decisions. By the by, you may cross "watch band" off my list. I pulled a "Father" on you and bought one myself. I saw one Sunday I couldn't resist and at greatly reduced rates and without tax at an Army Store, so bing, it was mine after $1.50 changed hands. Well, family dear, I must bid you "au

---

[24] Bergie was Clara Berghoeffer, my high school science teacher and senior class adviser.

[25] This was family slang for *very* early in the morning, earlier than A.M., if such a thing were possible.

reservoir" if I am to get in on the new Humphrey (ahh) Bogart movie, so goodbye and pray that I leave, but soon.

I miss you hugely,
The Hangover

Thanks for the clippings [from the neighborhood newspaper] and stuff from your party—sounded like a wild time for you-alls.

From Dad—Dec. 9, 1944:
Dearest Private Annie:

Omigoodness! I am pained! Armies seem to be just what they always have been: slow, uncertain, and motivated by forces beyond the mind of mortal to comprehend. Wish I could get hold of the diary of an Egyptian captain during the Fourth Jewish War. Anyway, one learns to cultivate patience, if nothing else, and some time you are bound to be sent somewhere to do something. How well I remember the happy days I spent picking up cigarette butts and paper in Rouen. Have fun when you can and take things as they come and you will live to be a grandmother! . . .

The next evening I came down with the indigoshdangest pain in my right shoulder and managed to sleep about an hour. Next day it was even wuss, like to kill me dead so no work Thursday. This morning I had a date with Dr. Johnson who checked around and said I was in fine shape and that my shoulder was bursitis and was caused by a strain and what had I been doing. I blushingly told him about bayonet drill on Friday and that the piece weighed ten pounds. Then he blew up, told me I was damphool and no commando and told me to lay off drilling with anything but my feet or I could look after my own shoulder. So it looks as tho the old Metal Corporal's drilling days were done. Now I am going to try to sell the CO on letting me stay on with the Guard at some kind of a damn desk job. I'd rather do that than turn civilian. DAMN: I may be 50 plus but I do not like to have to act the part.

WILLIAM BEAUMONT GENERAL HOSPITAL
FORT BLISS, EL PASO, TEXAS
10 December 1944 to 8 February 1945

10 December 1944

Company D, SMDT, WBGH, El Paso, Texas, Sunday

Dearest Family,

Surprise! Surprise! Here is your little daughter in glamorous surroundings and out of Staging at last! I was a very mean girl and played a trick on you. The morning that I wrote you my last letter which sounded very dejected, I had just heard my orders telling that I was going to El Paso. I was dying to tell you, but I didn't dare. The thing was that the orders were read for all the meds to leave that day, and after they finished, they said "Transportation is canceled—but you'll go out soon," and I didn't know whether it would be a week or the day after. As it happened, we left Friday morning and was I glad. Thursday evening we went to *Othello*, which was wonderful, and I dragged to bed at 1:00 and then they woke us up at 4:00 a.m. to get ready to go. It wouldn't have been so bad except that Wednesday morning we got up at 5:00 because they thought the meds were to go out that day, and Thursday morning we got up at 4:30 to GI because in Staging we have inspection on Thursdays. I was really fagged out, believe me. We piled into trucks at 6:00 a.m. and were carted down to the station. I left Des Moines the same way I came in—in trucks, in the dark, and very bleary-eyed. This time it wasn't raining though.

The train was a very old-fashioned Pullman. We occupied four cars and had the same ones the whole trip, though we were shuttled around from engine to engine, and other cars were hooked on and off. We had green plush seats, dark red woodwork and tin washbasins. Not too uncomfortable and it was fun because we were all in a happy group, but I don't see how people traveled in them and kept their dignity or their modesty. The next installment I will describe our trip—three days and two nights—in detail, and the next will give an account of this joint. I'll mail this now so you'll know where I am. Got to fall out for class now, so goodbye.

Yours in ecstasy,

The weather is cool. Sunrise is gorgeous—blue, pink, orange coming up over the mountains! Ahhh. SMDT stands for Surgical, Medical, Dental Technician, and WBGH equals William Beaumont General Hospital.

11 December 1944

Company D, SMDT, WBGH, El Paso, Texas, Monday

Dearest Family,

This is being written in the latrine as per usual. Wow! Am I exhausted. The heat is on but definitely. Basic was never like this. But it's very interesting and no doubt will be more easy once I get the hang of things. We had seven *hours* of classes today and barely escaped having two after supper. For each class we have ten questions to write the answers to and hand in the next day. Took me two hours, not hard, but lengthy.

I'd better gasp out an account of my trip before it's all ancient history. Get out your maps and let's go. Although we got on the train at 6:15 we didn't get started till about 8:30. We chugged on down to Kansas City and didn't get in till 4:00, without having had anything to eat since 4:00 a.m. The scenery was very pretty, nice clean snow and solid farmhouses, rolling hills, typical midwestern country. But in Kansas City it was just like spring. Balmy and fresh air. It was really swell to see tall buildings again. We got off the train and ate in an Army mess hall which was located in the subterranean depths of the station. Then we all piled over to the Service Club a few blocks away where we dispersed, some to take much-desired showers, some to walk up to the Liberty Memorial across from the station on a high hill overlooking the city (guess where I was). It was like a wonderful spring evening instead of December 8. After roaring around over the hill exulting in the view, our little gang from Company Five went back to the station which was very much like the Chicago station, only not quite so huge. All kinds of shops. I bought some Christmas presents. By the way, I bought a swell iron from a girl in Staging who was getting a discharge. Cost me $6.75 because I was bidding against Barbie Braun, who, by the way, is going to Denver. They kind of split us Des Moines gals up. Anyhow, we wandered around the station and saw a big mob of Colored soldiers about to go overseas, an old man with long white hair, a large congregation of bedraggled babies, kiddies, and more bedraggled mothers in the ladies' room, lots of farewells between servicemen and females, a lady Marine with too short skirts and hair on her collar (tsk!), a WAVE in their new overseas-type cap which isn't nearly as natty as ours (organizational pride), and lots and lots of WACs. What a treat—they were us.

After having eaten at 4:00 we had to go back and eat again at 7:00, but we were too full so we made chicken sandwiches and took them back to the train. Before, we were the only ones in the mess hall, but that night there were some sailors (fresh, of course) and a company of PWs [prisoners of war]—Italian, some *very* handsome. We sang songs like mad for the Navy's benefit which was retaliated so enthusiastically and persistently that the Ma'am got rather annoyed, but nothing serious happened. Then we waited and waited in formation for them to hook the train together and we dropped exhaustedly into our berths. Lordy, was it ever cold that night. But we survived and the next morning it was horribly hot, on the train I mean, not outside. We were just south of Wichita by then and chugged along some more till we got to Oklahoma. Main points hit so far: Des Moines, St. Joseph, Mo., Kansas City, Topeka, Emporia, Wichita. During the dull scenery time we sang, played cards, read murder mysteries, slept, giggled, made puns, and generally had a high old time.

In Oklahoma we hit Alva, Waynoka, Woodward and Shattuck. The scenery was very amazing: red dirt, little drifts of snow, very eroded cuttings by the train, scrubby trees and desolate little houses perched at the edges of mesas. That place looked like a bad dream. Von Grob and I were singing "OOOOklahoma" all the way through till everyone in the car was ready to throw things at us. Our train finally got over the Pan Handle, deep in the heart of . . . , via Canadian, Pampa, and Amarillo. Von Grob and I, of course, broke into song again, "The sand of Amarillo keeps a-scratchin' on my pillow . . . take me back to Des Moines." We got off at that dear town about 4:00 and drilled for about a half-hour on the station platform. You should have seen the local yokels gaping. We were pretty good despite the fact that we were half-paralyzed from sitting two days and from the cold, and I do mean twenty above, [and a] wind that howled across the prairie. Then back to the train and on to Clovis, New Mexico, for another dinner in [the] Army mess hall in the station. Forgot to mention that in going through Pampa, Texas, we passed a mammoth field of oil wells and tanks. Very exciting. After dinner we jumped into bed and had a chicken sandwich, apple, candy, and nut party. We were the nuts—six of us wedged into a lower berth. That night was horribly cold. Von Grob and I could see our breath condensing and my washcloth froze solid.

Next morning we woke up and by consulting the maps we bought in Amarillo we found that we had passed through Vaughn, Belen, Socorro, San Marcial, and were in the wilderness just north of Rincon with the prospect of no food till El Paso (12:30) because the diner had been taken off during the night. They were always doing something queer to our cars. We had the same ones all the way, and one day we'd be riding forward, and the next day backward. It was very confusing. Well, you all know what New Mexico looks like—arid, sage brush, Mexican adobe huts, rounded hilly mountains, real wild and woolly West. We spent the morning running back and forth between windows yelling, "Look! Look! Mountains!" You could sure tell we were all from the Middle West.

As it is now 10:00 and I am suffering from acute and chronic writer's cramp and bleary-eyed (got up at 5:30) and I haven't policed my area (translation: taken a shower) yet, I must say farewell till the next letter wherein I will give geographical notes, local color, statistics, a day in the life of Pvt. Bug, and other notes of interest.

Until then, Muchos amor,

20 December 1944

Wednesday

Dearest Family,

Pant, pant. At last I find a spare moment to scribble you a slight note to describe to you the hectic life at WBGH. All week I've been getting the most frantic notes from you, forwarded from Fort Des Moines, written before you heard the joyous news. Then, finally I got a postcard from Dad. "AH," I thought, "I will now hear their reactions . . . they will be excited, no doubt." And I found it to be very phlegmatic. I was disgusted. Doesn't it thrill you to think of me down at the other edge of the USA? It does me. I still can't believe I'm here, especially in the afternoon. To get on with the stuff, I will proceed to make a neat little outline:

1. Weather: Mornings are very cold, about 28 above. Of course, we fall out at 6:00 a.m. so no wonder. Later in the morning it gets up to about 45 and by afternoon it's 70 in the sun. Real nice and springy. In the morning just before we fall out for class there are gorgeous sunrises over the mountains across the valley. The sunsets we don't see very much of, because we're just under the lee of the opposite mountains.

2. Scenery and geography and fauna and flora: Scenery very Western and Texas-y. Sun every day (see weather). Much sand and cactus and sage and a kind of cactus tree. There are some poplars and willows which have dried-up leaves on them, and lots of lawn on the hospital grounds, which will be green in another two months, so they say. The hospital is part way up a mountain looking east and to our left is Logan Heights and the Anti-Aircraft School. Biggs Air Field is to the northeast down in the valley and Fort Bliss is just below us. There are mountains in the east behind Fort Bliss. To our right, or south, is Juarez, Mexico, and southeast is the town of El Paso. The hospital is made up of many different buildings, wards, and what-not scattered around. The classrooms are yellow wood. Hospital is gray stucco, two story. I'll take some pictures so you can get a better idea. As you can see, I'm not in a particularly descriptive mood tonight—too exhausted. The layout is very messed around, not compact like Fort Des Moines. No lawns in the school area—just dusty beige sand. Our shoe shines suffer in consequence. Our barracks are like a "U" with laundry room and bathrooms at the bottom of the U. Our wall lockers are like little

closets and we don't have to have echelon which makes things easier.[26] No fauna to speak of.

Lordy, family dear, I'm just not in the mood for gay letters this evening. Don't get me wrong. I'm having a whee of a time and the classes are fun and interesting. I'll continue with a more jolly description of classes, personnel, friends, and activities on Sunday. In a way, I'm kind of glad I'll be down here for Christmas because it isn't holiday feeling at all. If I were in Des Moines where there was some snow, it would be worse. We will get the day off (Monday) and I'm in a choir that's going to sing in the wards on Thursday evening, Friday evening, Christmas program Saturday afternoon, at the Officers' Club Sunday afternoon, and singing in the wards Sunday evening, so I'm real busy, but that will give some seasonal feeling. Also, all of us Company Five-ers are saving up our presents and are opening them together Sunday or Monday. Goodbye now and expect a real Annie-Bug letter next week. I'll miss you something awful and do miss you now, but I can stand it.

Have a *Merry* Christmas and
much love to you all,

P.S.: Got the package . . . Thanks. Haven't opened it yet. P.P.S.: I couldn't send you very much stuff this year because there's no place to get stuff on the Post and town is eight miles away, for which I'm very sorry and sad. I'll try to get some souvenirs and send 'em on as I get 'em. P.P.P.S.: Very sorry about Dad's arm but I got a laugh out of the story of the confession to the doctor: "Old soldiers never die, they just get bursitis!"

25 December 1944

Monday

Dearest Family,

In case you're wondering where I got the typewriter I must

[26] Most army barracks were a squared U shape, with latrines and utility rooms at the bottom of the U. Each wing contained from thirty to forty people in double bunks, with wall lockers (closets) or footlockers (wooden trunks) for clothing and possessions. "Echelon" meant arranging items in order from tallest to smallest in a neat line. The wall lockers in Basic were actually open shelves with everything exposed for inspection. At the training school in Texas some of the rules of barracks life were relaxed, and later, in some of our field assignments, each Wac had the incredible luxury of a single bunk all to herself.

inform you that I have received the delightful duty of CQ this Christmas a.m. Happy day and stuff like that there. It isn't too bad but I had to get up at 6:30 in order to go to mess. The day is rather grim and gray and not at all like Christmas which is OK with me—if it were I would be awful homesick, but as it is, I'm kind of numb.

Now, to catch up with all the news that you want to hear. I've been very remiss about letters but as you may have gathered we've been busy. School is fun and easy as the dickens. Our classes consist of Anatomy (for me, a simplified review of Zoo[logy]), Nursing, First Aid (this makes the third time I've had that stuff) and Pharmacy. This is quite difficult—full of equivalents, drams, abbreviations. Did you know that OD meant right eye? Or that gtt meant drop? It's all Greek to me as yet, but fun. All our teachers are men which makes class a pleasant pastime to us frustrated gals.

Here's a bird's eye view of My Day:

5:30 Roll out of my top bunk . . . groan
6:00 Reveille—Fall out!
6:00–6:40 Make bed, police area, read, eat orange
6:40 Go to mess. Our mess hall is for both men and gals.
We get whistled at constantly but we don't mind.

The food is really a change from FDM [Fort Des Moines]. The diet is heavy and not nearly enough vegetables or salad. I'm turning into a sphere. Tried on my off-duty dress the other day and nearly burst the seams. For breakfast we have stuff like chipped beef on toast and fried potatoes nearly every morning. After breakfast our platoon (the Third) has classroom detail. We stream over, and Sgt. (Brother) Fox tells us to scram because he doesn't want us messing around in his building. He's tall, forty-ish, gray hair, very laconic and sarcastic, used to be a mortician, and talks out of the side of his mouth. So, exhausted after our hard detail, we stagger back to the barracks and read till we fall out at 8:00 to go to class. We march in formation to an assembly barn where the Surgicals and Meds have lectures together. The X-Rays and Labs are separate. We sit on long wooden benches and chatter till class starts, at which time short, fat and gruff Sgt. Kelly pops out of a little room and roars, "Class, Ten HUT!" The first week we thought that was all he did but we later found out he was cadre. Our first class is usually First Aid with Lt. Moore, who calls us "Miss" and makes us feel like civilian gals again. This First Aid is more detailed: gangrene, reduction of fractures, tetanus treatment, and all about aid stations up at the front, which we won't see but we have to learn about it anyhow. Then we have a ten minute break from 8:40 to 9:00 [*sic*]. During the breaks, Lena Gray (bunk neighbor and friend from Company Five, Second Platoon) and I operate what we call "The Commissary." We go to a little PX near the school buildings and hoard up candy bars and gum which we carry to class in a long box. At the breaks we parcel out the food in exchange for LRs.

Our next class is usually Anatomy with Capt. Sol Dombeck from Brooklyn who talks about "these here arteries and this here gland." We usually have hysterics during his hour. Our next two hours are spent at Lab where we do practical things like Artificial Respiration, put on splints, make up surgical carts, prepare and give hypos to a rubber strip tied to a post (I'm really sharp at that), take blood pressures and give enemas. We split up by squads, and we Three Musketeers are together. There's Lena Gray, tall and skinny; me, middle-sized; and Lilian Howe, short and fat. There are about six cadre men roaming around during Lab hours, only too glad to help take pulses and demonstrate Artificial Respiration. Then there's Sgt. Page: tall, purty, wavy black hair and spaniel eyes; Sgt. Roberts: short and cute and the biggest wolf on the staff. When he counts cadence,[27] he quacks; Sgt. Love: tall and southern accent, and has a cute little baby girl; Sgt. Simmons, who tells dirty jokes to fill out the hour. His cadence is brayed. After two hours of Lab we have lunch. Mess isn't compulsory, you can go or not as you want. After lunch we go over to the PX to stock up our commissary, and then have either Nursing or Pharmacy. Nursing is with Major Halpern, also from Brooklyn, whose lectures are sprinkled with funny cracks. He stages realistic demonstrations of bedmaking, oxygen therapy, enemas, hypos and blood transfusions, with all the fellows in gowns and gloves. After which we have two more lab hours, then an hour of drill or athletics, like tennis or bowling. Then mess, then answer questions for the next day's class. The first week we had classes all day, so we had eighty questions a night and it was definitely rugged. Also in the evening we have Army Orientation for two hours till 8:00. Very dull, but they seem to think we need it.

[27] At the training school we had to march in formation from class to class, and we had frequent drills, mostly in the early morning. The sergeants marched alongside the platoons, gave orders, and counted cadence: "Platoon, TEN HUT! FOR'D HARCH! ONE, two, three, four, ONE, two, three, four," etc.

Last Saturday night I met a farmer from Arkansas and we went off the Post and drank beer.[28] Sunday a bunch of us went hiking up in the mountains. It was just like summer: warm, flies buzzing, little flowers blooming, and birds singing. This last week a bunch of us were in a chorus which was going to sing for the guys in the hospital—I think I told you about that. We had rehearsals every night, getting out of class neatly, then sang Thursday, Friday, Saturday afternoon, and Sunday. In charge of us was the cutest little captain, Capt. Spadino, who is very tiny and dark and funny. The choir got to saying we were going to drool, not to drill! He was a big wolf, too, holding my hand one night as we walked along singing. Then on Saturday afternoon when we were giving out Christmas presents to the officers' children under the big Christmas tree outside, it seemed that Capt. Spadino had quite a brood, and hopes were crushed.

This last Saturday, Lena, Lil, and I went into town just to look around and see what things were like. El Paso is quite interesting looking and full to the brim with Mexicans. Of course, the town is crammed with men. No girl can go into town without running into some congenial personage. It's so queer to be picking up men without a qualm, but when you're in uniform there's a sort of esprit de corps and the fellows are very nice. This night I ran into a big Jewish corporal from Brooklyn named Irving. He was quite a character and covered with hash-marks, overseas stripes, ribbons, and firing medals. He's going to Ack-Ack [Anti-Aircraft Artillery] School over at Ft. Bliss. We went to a Junior Chamber of Commerce dance and drank beer.

Yesterday morning I slept and slept—ahh—and then opened my presents. Family, they were swell. That beautiful bathrobe is the envy of the barracks, to say nothing of my smooth writing case and slippers and nightgown. We all enjoyed the cookies muchly, too. I had everyone gathered around me, watching the great unveiling. Did you get my package in time for Christmas, I hope?

This is, I think, the most incoherent letter I have ever written, but people come streaming in and out asking for passes, and the phone rings. Everything is tres noisy and hustling. Only ten more minutes till my relief comes. Then on to a gay Christmas Dinner at Ye Olde Mess Hall. From now on, I'll try to do better as regards

---

[28] People in the army were frequently referred to by what their civilian occupation had been. This was a soldier from Arkansas who had been a farmer previously.

correspondence. I miss you all so much and all the time I keep thinking of what you'll be doing at such and such time, and here I am in the midst of a desert—Glory Hallelujah!

Just got back from mess where I ate so much turkey I can hardly stand. Goodbye to you all now, and I'll send this off as post haste as the Mail Orderly ever sends anything.

All my love,

26 December 1944

Tuesday

Dear Carrie,

At last, my pet, you receive an honest-to-God letter written on my lovely brown leather writing case that my Dad gave me for Christmas. That sacred holiday wasn't very sacred around here. For one thing, some inspired sap had gay little trees stuck up all around the station—in amongst the cactus and sand—covered with tinsel and red and green bells. Most incongruous and disgusting. Christmas morning I had to get up at 6:30 and be Charge of Quarters in the Orderly Room. Thus I couldn't go to either midnight mass or morning services. My family did send me a swell big package which I opened Sunday in conjunction with a slew of my pals that came down from Fort Des Moines with me. Christmas afternoon, Pvt. G. and I played tennis, and in the evening we went downtown and found some soldiers to take us to dinner. Don't get excited—Pansy has not degenerated completely, but the man-woman ratio is about 20 to 1 here in El Paso. You get off the bus intending merely to do some shopping and have a malt at the USO when the men descend on you, clamoring to take you to dinner, dances, movies, buy drinks and so on. Of course when they get us back to the WAC area, they start the old closing-in technique, but I'm adept at avoiding such. Victorian Annie, they calls me. . . .

Lordy, there's so much to tell you that I hardly know where to begin. Read *See Here, Private Hargrove* for a fairly accurate picture of what our Basic Training was like, with a few small changes, natch, but the slang, routine and stuff much the same. I know, because I read it during my third week of Basic and got a large charge out of it. FDM is a lovely Post. Lots of green lawns (snow-covered by the time we left), red brick buildings with white porches, and very cozy and compact. Absolutely different from William Beaumont General Hospital. Here in our valley I can hardly tell where one Post leaves off and another begins. There's Beaumont, Fort Bliss (big Basic Training center and other schools), Biggs Air Field, and Logan Heights Ack-Ack School all slewed around between our enchanting mountain hills. They change color all day; pink at dawn, then beige, then green, gold at sunset, and blue at twilight. Flora is mainly cactus and sagebrush and the whole aspect is very rugged and beautiful. The hospital has many disconnected buildings of God-awful gray stucco, and yellow wood school barracks, and is half-way up near the foothills. On Sundays we go for hikes. Weather is pleasant; mornings quite chilly, especially at six o'clock reveille, mid-mornings warm and afternoons most sleep-inducingly hot.

As I told you, I'm in the Medical Corps and going to Surgical Technical School. What we're getting is a blitz nurses' course in three months, but so far it isn't too hard. Mostly a review of my Zoology and First Aid stuff I've had so often. All our teachers are men (Officers) and during Lab hours there are slews of non-coms (or cadre, a GI term) who are only too anxious to help with artificial respiration, blood pressure, pulse-taking, and putting on splints— the octopuses! We have one guy who is really a character for Anatomy, Captain Sol Dombeck from Brooklyn, whose accent and profile are in perfect type. He talks about "these here glands" and "this here blood vessel." Then there's Lt. Moore, nice and Yale-man looking who calls us "Miss" and makes us feel like civvies again. We have him for First Aid. Major Halpern we have for Nursing, our most fun course. He's also from Brooklyn, and fills his hour with dirty cracks about enemas and stuff. I'm usually not the shy, prudish type, but once I was honestly embarrassed the time we had to give enemas to men dummies with ten cute Sergeants standing around and making funny cracks. I'm used to it now, even when young Sgt. Roberts paws around in my dress ostensibly searching for my subclavian pressure point.

And then there is the most handsome and witty Captain Spadino who coached our choir that we had last week. He is much big wolf, and Pansy drooled from afar for five days. My salivary glands were exhausted, especially after one evening when we were singing outside the wards and El Capitan came up and held my hand as we walked along singing "Adeste Fideles." Swoon, swoon.

Those glands are now regenerated due to a distressing revelation at the School Christmas Party on Saturday afternoon when Capt. Dombeck (Santa) was presenting gifts to the officers' kids. It seems that our drool-man has quite a brood—four bambinos. Ah—these Italians . . . down with officers . . . give me a Corporal any day. Especially like the big Jew from Brooklyn I met last Saturday, complete with hash-marks, stripes, ribbons, Brooklyn accent (I seem to have a mania for them lately; Capt. Spadino has one, too), and the name of Irving. He was like someone out of a Damon Runyon story, but, withal, a gentleman. There was a certain courtliness with which he asked me to dance: "Wanta sling de body around, Babe?" Yesterday evening, Lena G. and I ran into an Irishman, and I do mean Irish. He was an alien who was most interesting to talk to and not only because of his thick brogue and RAF-tilted hat.[29] We went to a chop suey joint, accompanied by a Polish socialist named Kiersikowski, where Irish struck up an acquaintance with the waiter, since Irish's Chinese laundryman in San Francisco had taught him some Cantonese. Irish persuaded him to show us his Chinese "ready reckoner" (adding machine [abacus]) which is one of those little bead-on-a-wire deals. The Chinese had great fun doing sums and multiplication like 11 x 25 and such, flicking the beads back and forth most adeptly.

El Paso is predominantly Mexican (60%) and on the bus all one can hear, besides GI parlance, is rhythmic Mex chatter. The architecture of all the houses down here is very quaint. Much rock and stucco used; all one-story houses with two-foot eaves and little walls all around the back yards and immense cypress trees in the front yards. I should throw in a bit about Army life in general. It's much like St. Mary's or college dormitory life, only a little more work, like shining shoes, doing laundry, fatigue details, drill, Army Orientation courses after dinner (God-awful dull repetition of what we had in Basic), cleaning the latrine in the morning ("When we begin . . . to clean the latrine . . ."),[30] and scrubbing madly on Friday nights (GI night) for inspections every Saturday morning. Army life is really fun and I love it dearly. Not too exhausting and quite instructive. I'm an expert hypo-slinger by now, to say nothing of bed-maker, biffy-cleaner, and picker-up of cigarette butts, known as

[29] British Royal Air Force men wore their hats toward the back of the head at a jaunty tilt.
[30] A parody of the popular 1940s song, "Begin the Beguine."

"policing the area." It gives me, and all of us, sort of a good feeling to be in uniform and to be in the thick of things you might say. Well, as people are screaming at me to move so they can take a shower (I've moved into the latrine because of lights-out), I must end this epistle which, as I look over it, seems to consist mainly of remarks about men, but after FDM it's quite a novelty to see trousers. Do, now, write me a huge letter concerning your doings, thoughts, and educational career.

All my love,
Pansy

27 December 1944

Wednesday

Just a reassuring mid-week note. It's raining now and the clouds completely obscure the mountains. Pvt. Gray just expressed the wish to go hiking up there and put her hand in a cloud. She has a poetic soul. Aunt Edith mentioned in a Christmas card that she sent me a present; which one was it? William Peck Post[31] sent me a purty blue and black automatic pencil with my name engraved on. EC sent me a subscription to *Time*, and Ruthie gave me a parody of English history called *1066 and All That—*, screamingly funny. Large letter follows this Sunday.

31 December 1944

Sunday

Dearest Family,

How do you like my new stationery? I thought maybe you-all would take the hint of my writing you on notebook paper and send me some better stuff, but the writing case more than makes up for that small lack. I'm going to thank you again for all my wonderful Christmas stuff because I have a feeling my last week's letter was decidedly on the feeble side. This was because I was suffering from a delayed-action hangover from Saturday night's beer drinking with my Brooklyn corporal. The beer down here has a powerful

---

[31] This was the American Legion Post to which my father belonged.

effect on the intestines and my living in an upper bunk doesn't help matters any, if you know what I mean. By Monday afternoon, after three sets of tennis with Pvt. G., I felt much better so we thought we'd go to town and see what was what. In the USO (not very nice here—kind of barny and train stationy) a couple of fellows came up and begged to take us out to dinner and they looked rather decent, so we accepted! One of 'em turned out to be an Irishman—a real one from Ireland with a brogue. He was very interesting to talk to and had evidently had a pretty good education, but he said his pre-Army occupation was being a hobo. His friend was a cute little Pole (nineteen) who tried to be a junior commando (encircling movements) but he was obviously a novice at the job and I was greatly amused. I called him "Sonny" and we got along fine. We went to a chop suey joint where Irish struck up a friendship with our little waiter. Irish got him to show us his Chinese Ready Reckoner on which he did things like 23 x 16 with amazing dexterity and rapid flips of the fingers. Then we went and drank beer and sang songs and had much fun. Time out for Pay Day. This is going to be a rough night for Service people: full purse, plus New Year's Eve, plus 1:00 bed check. And as my bed is in the front of the barracks and in the direct line of traffic, I foresee I shan't get much sleep. Apropos of pay, here is another verse to that well-known song, "Gee, Ma, I Want to Go Home":

> The pay the Army gives you
> They say is mighty fine,
> They give you fifty dollars
> And take back forty-nine . . .
>   And:

> The beds the Army gives you
> They say are mighty fine,
> But how the hell should they know,
> They've never slept in mine . . . [32]

Did I tell you anything about the architecture of the houses around here? They are all one-story affairs made of native stone

[32] The base pay for buck privates was fifty dollars a month, privates first class got fifty-five dollars, and corporals got sixty-six dollars. The pay was in addition to meals, shelter, clothes, and medical care; it was more like a kid's allowance than wages. The phrase "take back forty-nine" referred to withholding for dependents' allowances and war-bond savings.

with little stone walls around the back yards, and high green hedges and immense evergreens and cypresses in the front yards. Another feature is very wide over-hanging eaves to keep out the sun. No one in this country has furnaces. Stores, barracks, houses, and everything are heated with little portable gas stoves. In the stores it seems very quaint and foreign to huddle around one of those heaters and warm your fingers. This week, as I mentioned, we have been waking up to find ourselves in the midst of a cloud. By afternoon it usually lifts so we take off our woollies and overcoats and play tennis and get a sun-tan. Mine is a typical GI one: tan areas on my face, hands, and ankles, and the rest white. Today, Pvt. G. and I rushed around and took many funny snapshots which I'll send on when they're developed. About a nice photograph—I'm still looking for a place to have one taken but so far, no success. I was a sap not to have done it at Des Moines, but I didn't have any money then, but be patient and I'll see what I can do.

Yesterday Pvt. G. and I went shopping and I'm sending you another Christmas box. No wrappings this time, but consider them Christmas presents. We came home early and washed clothes and wrote letters. I owe only about seven now. This case inspires me; besides I like to sit in the latrine and show it off. By the way, nearly every night I get at least three compliments on my bed attire! This week I spent madly writing letters except for Thursday night when there was a dance up at the gym. It felt exactly like a Shattuck dance; looked like the armory, smelled like the armory, and the uniforms of course completed the picture. I had much fun dancing with a rather dull young man who was a good dancer. This evening I plan to take advantage of everyone else's gaiety and stay home to iron shirts. Besides I must observe, in a fitting manner, the sacred Founders' Day of the Stagnanttes. I am with them in spirit and it would be a crime to go out with a man (!) on such an anniversary. I'm next in line for the iron so I will bid you adieu till next time. The newness of the place is wearing off and I'm beginning to get twinges of lonesomeness for my family and gay college days. Your Christmas letter was too good and descriptive, darn it!

P.S.: I'm sending home a $10.00 money order which I wish you'd salt away for me. Then, in case I'm short, I'll have something to fall back on. P.P.S.: A terrible calamity happened to me. My watch fell off again the other day and it's costing me *$7.50!* to have it fixed. Woe is me.

From Mom—Jan. 2, 1945:

I was very much interested to hear all about your classes and work. It sounds very interesting to me, only it is strange to think of your joining the WAC and to all intents and purposes learning to be a nurse! I'm glad you find the courses easy; what a break to have had zoo already and the first aid classes. I can appreciate the light it brings into your young lives to have men around, even though some of them are married wolves. It does seem pretty wild to pick up men indiscriminately but the uniform does make a difference, I suppose. Be careful though! After all you are still just my little Annie and I don't want anything unpleasant to happen to you.

New Year's Day we asked a few people over for eggnogs. Everyone asked kindly after you, and Ellen says she hopes to send you some cookies—only lots of us including Ellen lost a lot of sugar and other coupons in the lovely OPA Christmas present.[33] It seems the Stagnanttes had their annual party at Alta's, loudly bewailing the fact that you weren't here to have it. Poor Alta was in the dog-house for all the goings-on; Ruthie set a coffee cup on the floor and Peg knocked it over on the plain rose rug, a plate and a glass got broken, and then Alta's dad came home and said a three-fourths full bottle of Bourbon was missing! The kiddies had a small amount of their own liquor. Ruthie said it was all pretty sad, but Alta's dad finally found his whiskey!

Pat got her ring and expects to be married in March. Marge told me two news items: (1) The Army meds have all left the U, some to Fitzsimons and some to somewhere in Texas—but you may know all this from Joe. (2) Virginia T. enlisted in the WAC the day she graduated from the U. (3) Pat's brother Bob got home most unexpectedly from two years in the South Pacific and he and Shirley are going to be married January 6. That's about all the news of the moment. Awfully glad you are so happy there and I hope it keeps on being fun.

[From the spring of 1942 to August 1945 my family had to deal with three major kinds of formal rationing: heating fuel oil, gasoline, and certain grocery products, including meat, sugar, cooking fats and oils, and coffee. (There may have been others, but they did not get a mention in my parents' letters.) Many other items were rationed just by their limited availability—such as household appliances, cars, clothes, nylon stockings, camera film, and cigarettes.

[33] The OPA reduced the number of coupons that could be used—an ironic Christmas present.

The rationing system was run by the Office of Price Administration (OPA). Long after the war ended, I found in my mother's desk the remnants of the four War Ration Books in an envelope along with some Civilian Defense/Volunteer Victory Aide material, awards for service to the Red Cross, and the small red-and-white flag with one blue star in the middle that hung in our front-room window to represent a family member in the armed forces. Besides the food ration books there were the fuel ration coupons for the 1944 and 1945 heating seasons.

Heating-fuel rationing made for some real discomfort at our house. Coal furnaces were still widely used, natural gas heating was rare, but oil heating was the modern, up-to-date system and was what we had in our seven-year-old house. The amount allowed for each home was based on the previous season's usage, which in our case was low because of an unusually warm season in 1941–42. The result was, for us, an allowance of sixteen hundred gallons of oil for heat and hot water from July 1 through August of the next year. Our coupon book stated: "The unit coupons for each period become valid on dates announced by OPA. Budget your ration for heat according to newspaper and radio announcements telling what percent of the heating season has passed. If you heat water with fuel oil, save for next summer's use." While I was still living at home, we kept the house at sixty degrees or below and adopted several strategies to keep warm during the cold winters that followed. Between the living room and the front hall of our colonial-style house, my mother constructed and hung heavy homespun drapes to reduce drafts. We kept a coal briquet fire going in the fireplace all winter and essentially did all of our living (except cooking) in the living room. I remember putting a hot water bottle in my bed about one-half hour before bedtime. I would undress in the living room, put on my pajamas and bathrobe, then race upstairs, brush teeth, and dive under the comforter, waiting for the shivers to stop. It was cold enough on our second floor to see your breath during our famous cold waves.

The first restriction to make a real impact on me was gas rationing: no more driving lessons. Gasoline cards came in three levels: "A," "B," and "C." "A" was for normal civilian driving and allowed between five and six gallons per coupon, which were allotted at a rate of roughly one per month. "B" and "C" cards allowed more and were for the use of essential occupations like deliveries, trucking, farming, and medicine. In the forties most people relied on the convenient streetcars and buses to get to work. Grocery stores were dispersed around the city within walking distance, and they made daily deliveries to homes. Milk and other dairy products were routinely delivered to our doors, as were baked goods and bread from the "Bamby Man" of the Bamby Bakery. In my family the car was saved for special use only. My dad and brother took the streetcar out to the city's edge to Blake School. I had a forty-five minute ride each way to the university, using tokens that cost thirty-five cents for five, and my mother's frequent shopping trips to downtown were made on the streetcar. Black market trading in gasoline coupons was doubtless a problem, as well as other deals for food and scarce commodities, but most of us followed the rules and did our part for the home front.

Early in the war recycling was promoted through much propaganda and publicity. Newspapers, metal food cans, aluminum and metal foil, and used cooking grease were brought into the recycling centers. People saved the metal foil from cigarette and tobacco packages and formed it into huge balls. There was a comical sign urging people to remove the ends from metal cans and flatten them that showed two cans with Hirohito's and Hitler's heads and feet sticking out the ends and being stepped on.

My family's first food ration books, one for each family member, were dated May 5, 1942. Series two was dated February 22, 1943, and three and four had no dates. Each series had a different system of coupons, numbers, and symbols that were to be used according to announcements from the OPA. In addition to the books I have a cardboard tube dispensing red or blue "point" tokens that were in use in the spring of 1945, according to my mother's letters. Each book states that "stamps must not be detached except in the presence of the retailer, his employee, or person authorized by him to make delivery." Also printed on the book was a warning: "This book is the property of the United States Government. Persons who violate rationing regulations are subject to $10,000 fine or imprisonment, or both."

Backyard victory gardens were a feature of wartime life in Minnesota to provide vegetables and fruits for current use or for winter canning. I would bet that in the forties a majority of women homemakers put up some food as a regular part of household chores, and with the war this effort intensified. My family had a large vegetable garden in the next-door empty lot every year from 1942 through 1945, and my mother, with dad's and my help, filled enough mason jars to occupy a closet, called a "fruit cellar," in our basement. Here is what was printed on the coupon book for special purchase of sugar for home canning in the summer of 1945:

"WE MUST GET ALONG WITH LESS SUGAR THIS YEAR BECAUSE—

1. Military needs are high. Each soldier actually consumes twice as much sugar a year as the average civilian now receives.
2. Ships which otherwise might be bringing sugar into the United States are hauling supplies to the battle fronts.
3. Manpower is scarce at sugar refineries and shipping ports.
4. Beet sugar production last year was 500,000 tons short, making the stock of sugar smaller for this year.
5. Last year many people over-applied for canning sugar. We used so much sugar that stocks at the beginning of this year were abnormally low.

DO NOT APPLY FOR MORE SUGAR THAN YOU ACTUALLY NEED FOR HOME CANNING—HELP MAKE OUR WAR SHORT SUGAR SUPPLIES LAST ALL YEAR"

A newspaper clipping reads: "Spare Stamp 11 in ration book 4 will be good for 10 pounds of sugar beginning April 1, the Office of Price Administration announced today, United Press reported." Food rationing appeared to be harder on city dwellers than on rural residents, as my father's letters suggest. My mother routinely added cups of oatmeal to ground beef to stretch out the supply for hamburgers and meat loaf. Lots of cheese, eggs, chicken, and fish had to fill the gaps for our red-meat eating society.

Food and gas rationing ended with the Victory Day in August 1945, but that did not mean that civilian goods were instantly available. Meat continued to be scarce for months, as well as nylon stockings and other civilian clothing items. When I was married more than a year after the war was over, the department stores in Minneapolis allowed a bride to buy one pair of nylons if she came in with her marriage license.]

7 January 1945

Sunday

Dearest Family,

I will tell you something to make you jealous. Pvt. G. and I are lying on a blanket outside the barracks with kerchiefs and PT bloomers on, taking sun baths. It's real nice and warm out; the sun is shining (obviously), the birds are singing, the sky is bright blue, and there are lots of pretty silver planes whizzing around. After a while, G. and I are going to have a set of tennis. Oh, for the life of a WAC! This week has rolled along in its usual pattern. This is our next to the last week here. Our final exam is Tuesday and I should be studying Pharmacy, Military Sanitation, Ward Management and Public Property, which I don't know too much about, but it's too nice a day to study and I shall put it off until the morrow. You seem to be having more than your fair share of colds, etc., and I'm right sorry for you. My sinus has absolutely cleared up since I've been here, for which I'm thankful. I hope that Mother's insinuating admonitions about men in her last letter were due to a sinus headache only. Mammy, don't you trust your little Annie? I'm not so little anymore, you know, and downtown El Paso is crawling with MPs who would come to my rescue if I couldn't handle situations, which I know I could. Besides, I don't fall in with just anybody; I'm fussy about the characters who buy me beer. Anyway, you have received my letter about how I spent my New Year's Eve so you ought to feel better. That news about the meds electrified me. Wouldn't it be wonderful if Joseph were sent here? Of course, it would be too good to be true; things like that don't happen in the Army, but it would be nice.

Next week after exams we get a three-day vacation before the next class comes down. I could get a pass but I haven't any place to go, so I shall employ myself playing tennis, reading, and writing letters. Everyone that I sent Christmas cards to has written back five-page letters, so I'm inundated with correspondence. Fanny H. wrote me a nice note with a blanket invitation to camp on her whenever I'm in the East. I sent a Christmas card to Grace S., too, in California, so here I am in Texas with nobody to visit. You know, I had a feeling, when I saw the scenes of downtown El Paso in that postcard thing I sent you, that I'd seen them before. Then it dawned on me—Rachel Katz sent me an El Paso thing just like that and I figured out that she must have been stationed at Beaumont then. How about that?[34]

This letter isn't to be jammed with jolly little anecdotes, mainly because I'm so groggy with the sun that I haven't the energy, and besides, the dirty cracks that our profs tell us in VD class and latrine demonstration class aren't worth repeating. Suffice it to say that I'm happy, healthy, and having muchos fun. I'll see about your Spanish newspaper, Dad, and I'll try to get you some brushes, but I have my doubts. This PX isn't very well stocked. I'm getting homesick again, now that the newness has worn off, isn't that disgusting?

All my love, and some kisses,

P.S.: We broke out the fruit cake today (we'd been saving it) and it met with everyone's enthusiastic approval.

14 January 1945

Sunday

Dearest Family,

What a week it has been! More emotional upheavals, more physical upheavals. Very exhausting, but one thing about the Army is that it's never boring. This confusing week started Monday with tests in the afternoon. They gave us an hour for each subject but I finished in ten minutes because they had read all that day's tests to us under the pretense of highlighting points about the course. The rest of each hour, we read, slept and gossiped. On Tuesday morning we finished up exams. Lt. Morris (weasel-face) pulled a dirty deal on us. He gave us test questions that he'd never discussed in classes and his subjects are the two hardest ones. And, to top it off, we had to finish both in the same hour, because they wanted fourth hour for sick-call. Thus everyone was in very bad humor when we got back to the barracks. Here we discovered that everyone's weekend passes had been canceled because the Ma'am's spies had found out that some gals weren't staying where they said they were. Also, the Sgt. announced that the whole Company was restricted until further notice. What a lovely gripe session we had

---

[34] Rachel Katz, a Russian-Jewish émigrée, had been a student of my father's at the university and was a close family friend. She became a nurse and was in the Army Medical Corps. Rachel appears again in the letters in the summer of 1946.

till dinner. Foul words filled the air and everyone vied in trying to produce the most fitting epithets to apply to Lt. Morris, the Ma'am, and Sgt. Snyder. After lunch we worked off our hate by GIing the auditorium, and later Pvt. G. and I had four sets of tennis, after which we felt pretty good. We went downtown for dinner, which consisted of wonderful steak, French fries, and beer. Then we walked around saluting officers who obviously didn't want to be saluted [because they had their arms around their girl friends] (our favorite sport), played some Ping-Pong at the USO and came home early. On the bus there was a very stinko GI who talked exactly like Professor Carp and who had reached the argumentative stage of alcoholism. He was having a huge discussion with a war worker. "Betcha I know everything about differentials, I betcha," and so on, starting out amicably and soon becoming vindictive and drifting on to the favorite topics of "Why I hate the Army" and "Why the First Sergeant has it in for me." From time to time he would take time out to try and roll a cigarette but he just couldn't seem to make one. All the tobacco kept coming out each end. Gray and I were greatly amused. Wednesday morning we spent GIing the barracks, scrubbing with might and main. I was perched on the edge of the bed clutching a mop in readiness to take over after Gray finished scrubbing, when our dear sergeant came in, glared at me, and said, "Report on KP at 11:15!" She thought I was goldbricking, and here I had KP Friday on the Duty Roster. So I trailed off to KP and got off in the afternoon just in time to change to "A" uniform and go to an orientation course for two hours. By that time, it was 16:00 so I went to sleep and finally roused myself to go to the movies in the evening.

Thursday morning we packed and sat around all morning waiting to move up on the hill to our new quarters. At last we did, and spent the afternoon unpacking. These barracks are old convalescent officers' quarters and as such are separate rooms. Two to a room, with two beds, two foot lockers, two chairs, wall locker, and a little gas stove AND we can arrange our rooms any way we want to. Tres luxurious. Also, the latrine is pine paneled and there is one upstairs and one downstairs, and in each there are three eight-foot-long bathtubs and shower combined. Oh, the fanciness of it all! We are flabbergasted. Thursday evening we went downtown and saw Howe off; she's getting an emergency furlough because her grandma died. Friday morning started the great vacation. Gray

2152   SAN ANTONIO STREET,
LOOKING WEST, EL PASO, TEXAS

③

POPULAR DRY GOODS C
Department Store

GATEWAY
COFFEE SHOP

HOTEL
DEL NORTE

UNITED

Downtown El Paso

ENLISTED MAN'S TEMPORARY PASS

Anne Bosanko .... Pvt. .... A 710274 ....
     (Name)   (Grade)   (Army serial No.)

CO. D ... SMT ... WRGH ... EL PASO ... TEXAS ...
     (Organization)   (Station)

is authorized to be absent—

From 1300 ... 17 Dec. 194 To 1900 ... 17 Dec. 1944

To visit go hiking in fatigue clothes.

Signed .... Isabel M. Baker ....
                            Commanding officer.

*W. D., A. G. O. Form No. 7   (OVER)
   26 June 1943

*This form supersedes W. D., A. G. O. Form No. 7, 8 September 1942,
which may be used until existing stocks are exhausted.

The Surgical Section on its all-day Field Problem

Lining up to get paid

Upper Area at WBGH

In my overcoat

Lena Gray & Lil Howe with me in our HBT's in the Tower Area

and I were on KP so we had to get up, but the rest of the kids got to sleep, and Ma'am relented and gave out some weekend passes and everyone was happy. KP here is three hours during breakfast, then a break, and report on again at 11:00 and then again at 4:00. We were sitting around the mess hall about a quarter to nine, and we decided to go back to the barracks and sleep. No sooner had we poked our noses outside the mess hall when Cpl. Hicks told us to report over at the Assembly Hall. It seemed that Headquarters thought we should have some orientation courses, and so they blew the kids out at 8:00 and said they had five minutes to get dressed. Some had on their pajamas, and no one's hair was combed, and everyone was extremely furious. What a vacation! Goody, goody! They should have scheduled the classes regularly for the morning and given us the afternoons off, and we would have loved them, but no. The next day they blew everyone out at 6:00 just to take reveille, and then they had to do details because the Colonel was coming up to inspect. BUT Gray and I were smart. We'd got passes to go to Carlsbad Caverns and we lit out about 6:00 for the bus station.

The trip there took about four hours and the scenery was gorgeous: mountains, and wonderful views. We saw the highest peak in Texas, 8,750 feet. Some stuff. Carlsbad is about 200 miles from here, so we felt very adventurous. Didn't we go there once? I had a feeling I'd seen it all before. The first hour was fine, but after that it verged on the dull, and the air was musty, and I was horribly tired, and there were lots of gruesome tourists oh-ing and ah-ing all over the place and saying trite remarks. I'm sending you a newspaper which gives the tone of the place very well. Gray and I were gabbing and imitating everybody there and giggling, when suddenly I said, "Let's not talk for ten minutes," which we did, too, believe it or not. After about two minutes, a couple of soldiers who were walking in front of us turned around, and were obviously startled when they saw that we were still there. They probably thought (and hoped) that we'd fallen into one of the "bottomless pits"—three hundred feet deep. When we finally got to the surface via the elevator (at the mere cost of 25 cents per person), we found that the bus wasn't due for an hour and a half. So we waited and waited and got more and more tired and more and more hungry. It came at last, and we started our four hour bouncy journey back, and pulled into El Paso at 10:00, deader than alive. It was a good thing we got to sleep this morning.

I forgot to tell you what happened on KP. We were GIing because of inspection Saturday morning, and I was eager-beavering into all the musty corners. I picked up a GI can which had soap and steel wool in it, and it knocked against the table and fell over. Suddenly, I gave a scream. One of the pieces of soap started to run across the floor. I looked more closely and discovered eight monstrous cockroaches—positively grandfather ones. The mess sergeant was very unconcerned about it however. He was all for putting the can back in the corner, but I badgered him into drowning the horrible things and throwing them out. Here's how big they were—about two inches across. I'm never going to sign my name with the bug sign again! Ugh! Also on KP I had a chance to use some of my Military Sanitation. I made a cat latrine for the mess hall kitty. She makes little poohs in the corner of the hall, so we fixed up a sand-box.

Answers to questions and stuff:

Dad: I can't find you any hairbrushes—velly solly. Also, no Spanish newspapers in evidence, but I'm still working on that. I'm going over to Juarez in a couple of weeks and ought to have success. Is there anything else you-all want me to buy? If so, you'd better send a covering check cause I'm practically broke.

Mom: Yes, I got those pictures taken at Des Moines. I sent them on to Carrie to look at and she's sending them back to me.

Michael: You are a big huge wolf-man. I wonder if I'll know you when I get home!

Everybody: Along about March 10 I *should* get a Delay en Route. This is on the level. The men students get them, and we are supposed to, also.

Dad: We have one more month in El Paso, then a month ending March 10 in some other hospital for on-the-job training, and then we'll be assigned, making three month's training in all. The kids last month went to New Orleans, some to California, and some to Camp Hood, Texas. Our stations may be different though.

Mom: Yes, I got Cousin Frank's check and immediately wrote and thanked him. I'd also sent him a Christmas card before that with a letter on the back.

Today we worked up in the hospital. There have been two mammoth shipments of fellows from the Western Front; some with no dressings changed since the Normandy campaign, really rugged. So the WACs had to volunteer to go up and work on the wards because they were short of help. It was wonderfully interesting and I'm all inspired to go right to work. We made beds, gave baths, gave alcohol rubs, took TPRs, and I worked in the office as a ward clerk. The grades just came out; here's the score for Pvt. B.:

Anatomy	100
First Aid	100
Military San.	100
Arithmetic	100
Pharmacy	99 ⎫ Lt. Moore's course
Ward Management	99 ⎭
Nursing	100
Supply	100

HOORAY! Pvt. G. and I are going to the movies soon so I must end this—and it should hold you till next Sunday. Oh, I must tell you about our private telephone. G. and I are right next to Von Grob and Carpenter, and we have a knot hole in the connecting wall. Very handy for talking through at night and passing food through. This place feels very much like St. Mary's, especially because Gray is a lot like Thale, but lacking in her SA (sex appeal). In that respect, G. and I are much alike. We haven't had a man look at us hardly since the second week we were here. What has this place done to us? Look at the accompanying picture and you'll find out.

Now: Professor Bosanko, who has made an exhaustive study of semantics in the Army, will proceed to give you some examples of queer usages and "slang," some of which you may have heard:

Light the Lamp = Have a cigarette
Willie = Beaumont Hospital
Logging some sack time = Bunk fatigue
Ward 30 = Crazy; psycho-neurotic ward, as in "He's Ward 30."
Cat hole = Little personal latrine used on breaks in the field
Police your hairia = Take out your bobby pins
Police your mouth = Quit swearing
Scoot over = Move over
Take off = Scram, but quick
The Ma'am = Company commander
A Ma'am = Any WAC Officer

People around here talk about "waiting on" someone when they mean "waiting for." Also, everything in the Army is an area: personal area, outside area, upper area, school area, lower area. The kiddies here have an entertaining habit. When a platoon on the march is given "route step" or "rest," everyone yells "Hubba, hubba, hubba, hubba!" The reason for this is that when you're marching at attention, all sorts of witty remarks are bursting to be made, but when "Rest" is given, you can't think of a thing to say, but you've got to say *something* to take advantage of "Rest" so "Hubba, hubba" is the logical answer.

Now Professor Bosanko will give you a list of Army abbreviations in Common Everyday Usage around this Post. It's really something, the amount of alphabet soup the GIs talk. Not all of the ones here are at all new, but I'm listing them to show you what a lot of them there are:

AWOL	=	Absent without leave
MP	=	Military police
NLD	=	Not in line of duty
KP	=	Kitchen police
BP	=	Barracks police, blood pressure, or bed pan
SMDT	=	Surgical, Medical, Dental Training or Surgical, Medical Detachment
PT	=	Physical Training or Physical Therapy
OT	=	Occupational Therapy
TP	=	Toilet paper
HBT	=	Herring bone twill; the green overall things we wear to class
DRO	=	Dining room orderly
PRO	=	Public relations officer
CDD	=	Certified Disability Discharge, otherwise known as Can't Do Duty
LR	=	Latrine rumor
TM	=	Trench mouth
MCC	=	Military customs and courtesy
BS	=	Beaumont shuttlebus
SGO	=	Surgeon General's Office
OCS	=	Officer's Candidate School
AF	=	Athlete's foot
EM	=	Enlisted man
DC	=	Damn civilians
BM	=	Bunkmate (ha, ha, I fooled you)
TPR	=	Temperature, pulse, respiration

B&B	=	Monthly physical (you figure it out)
MO	=	Medical Officer
AR	=	Army Regulations
VD	=	Venereal disease
SMI	=	Safeguarding Military Information
WBGH	=	William Beaumont General Hospital
SOP	=	Standard order of procedure
MAC	=	Medical Administration Corps
IDR	=	Infantry Drill Regulations
GI	=	Government Issue or gastro-intestinal, as in "GI runs" (diarrhea)
AW	=	Articles of War
SIP	=	Seriously ill patient
NP	=	Neuro-psychiatric
WOW	=	Worn out WAC
USO	=	United Service Organization
PX	=	Post Exchange
ASN	=	Army Serial Number
NCO	=	Non compos mentis or non-commissioned officer
EMT	=	Emergency medical tag
AWOL	=	A wolf on the loose
TS	=	Tough situation
CO	=	Commanding Officer
OD	=	Officer of the day, olive drab, off duty, or right eye
EW	=	Enlisted Woman
WDAGO	=	War Department Adjutant General's Office
EB	=	Evil beaver or eager beaver, as in EW wolfing downtown
C&E	=	Clothing and equipment
OG	=	Officer of the Guard
TF	=	Training film
CQ	=	Charge of Quarters
TO	=	Table of Organization
FM	=	Field manual

There are sixty (!) in all and probably lots more at other posts. Well, I'll light the lamp and log some sack time before taking off for the lower area to go to the PX.

> Goodbye and much love, your
> affectionate daughter and sister,
> Anne (*not* Bug)

P.S.: Your last letters sounded as though you were missing me. You must keep up your gay social life and activities (congrats on that Red Cross deal, Mom) and look forward to March (I hope). Please don't let me know your inner feelings because I get sad and brood. I'd rather think of you as being tres social and busy, and Michael's junior Cafe Society whirl, and how the house looks, and stuff. You must keep up my morale!

From Mom—Jan. 17, 1945:

We looked for a letter from you today but none came. We do hope for one tomorrow. Mike opines that you are being transferred but I doubt that. Today I was churchly. Emily drove and took some of the St. John's ladies and me to a talk at the Cathedral, given by the Episcopal Bishop to Japan. He now has charge of all the Nisei and evacuees of the Church. There was a big doings all day in his honor and the Nisei choir from Fort Snelling was to take part in an evening service. They were rehearsing and after tea we went into the Cathedral to hear them. They sang very well—fine bass section. There were about eight or ten Japanese WACs; with so few women's voices it wasn't well balanced but it sounded very good. The Bishop spoke on the brotherhood of man and the hope of eradicating racial prejudice, and said that the Twin Cities had done an outstanding job in taking in the re-located Japanese-Americans.[35]

Emily said that Ginny T. had had, a few days after she enlisted, an offer from the psychology department of a teaching fellowship or something of the sort. She then tried to get out of the WAC, but obviously could not!

---

[35] I was not aware that Minnesota had any evacuees or relocated Japanese Americans. I do remember that there was a Japanese language training unit located at Savage and Fort Snelling, near Minneapolis. Here the Japanese-American soldiers were learning Japanese to use in military intelligence. Many first- and second-generation Japanese-American men, and some women also, enlisted in the army. Some of the men were in a unit that fought heroically in the Italian campaigns and later was the subject of a movie entitled *Gung Ho*.

During my first two years of college (1942–44) when my family would go to John's Place, the only really authentic Chinese restaurant in Minneapolis, we saw the Japanese-American soldiers, who probably felt at home in an Asian atmosphere, eating the somewhat familiar food and manipulating chopsticks and rice bowls with speed and nonchalance.

For more on the Japanese in Minnesota, see Masaharu Ano, "Loyal Linguists: Nisei of World War II Learned Japanese in Minnesota," *Minnesota History* 45 (Fall 1977): 273–87.

17 January 1945

Wednesday

Hello Family,

Your midweek effort of last week inspired me to a similar effort, this being Wednesday. We're back in the old school groove again with classes, squad details, and policing the area. Our teachers are still fellows but different ones. They aren't as amusing as the ones in the lower area. Things are a bit more serious this month and nobody spends much time on funny cracks. Our one "Sir" that has us for General Surgery looks like Mike's friend Dale (amazing), and then one of the cadre bears a striking resemblance to that gruesome slime, Sigurd B. (horrors!). We're deep in ORT (Operating Room Technique), making up surgical cart packs, how to change dressings, put drains in infected wounds, work the autoclave,[36] and we're swamped with the names of all the thousands of forceps, clamps, sutures, scissors, scalpels, needles, hemostats, and other complicated and weird-looking apparatus of the operating room.

This month promises to be more interesting because it's all new to me, and it's more technical. Today we had a torrential rain and hail storm which nearly washed our little encampment away and very nearly drowned Pvt. Bug on her way from Lab to the Assembly Class. This precipitation also streamed through the thinly constructed walls of La Maison Grise et Bosanko, drenching my folio of family portraits. Mom, you now have purple arms. Very becoming, I must say. I forgot to mention that Aunt Edie sent me a snapshot folio which included a picture of Grandpa with an unidentified young male cousin (maybe it's Baird), one of Edie and Kathy, and one of two other people whom I can't figure out— perhaps Alan and Rhea. The last three evenings have been horribly restful. The dear Ma'am has instituted ten o'clock bed check which precludes any nocturnal activities such as the cinema, provender at the PX and so on. We're practically incarcerated way up here on the hill, far from civilization. It takes us twenty minutes to get down to the Post, so I remain in my cell reading the *New Yorker* and *Coronet* [magazine]. Tres intellectual and restful but as this is the third night

---

[36] The autoclave sterilized surgical instruments and equipment at an extremely high temperature under pressure.

so spent, I hanker for bright lights. Luckily, Thursday night is designated as "date night"—we have 11:00 bed check. So the Company Fivers plan big doings.

Two items that I intended to include in my Saturday and Sunday letter have been gnawing at the back of my mind and they suddenly popped out tonight. One was that the night us kids saw Howe off we were afraid we'd miss the train, so we opulently took a taxi. I begged the driver (kidding, of course) to take a different route because it looked as though he were going to take the same way that the bus always takes. After some conversation, he found out we'd never seen more of El Paso than the road from Beaumont to the Plaza, so he took us downtown via the skyline drive, at no extra charge! He said he felt in a "giving" mood. Skyline drive is along the ridge of the mountains above El Paso and, as it was sunset time, we had a marvelous view out over the valley. We also passed through a very nice residential district with green lawns, mammoth cypress trees, and stone and white stucco houses with wrought-iron balconies in the manner of the French Quarter at Nola (GI for New Orleans, La.). The other thing is that the main radio station here is called CRUD (really CROD), and I howl to myself whenever I pass their building. I wish I were home. Our Delay en Route, I learned, is only eight days, if at all. Phooey.

Much love,

22 January 1945

Monday

Dearest Family,

Here another week has passed. Gosh, the time whizzes by. Only about three or four more weeks and I really will be out of here; not that I especially want to leave, but I would like to see some new territory. The end of the last week was a bit boring. Gray and I staggered down to the movies Thursday. Friday was GI night, and Saturday I was on Guard Duty. I haven't been off the Post since I went to Carlsbad a week ago Saturday, and I'm getting in a rut. Most disgusting. Saturday there was a huge wind all day. The old hands say that it is the Texas equivalent of winter. Anyhow, one of the girls got blown right over on her face during mass athletics, and there were numerous tumbleweeds getting in everyone's way. The wind didn't stop at night, either. I thought the guard cabin was going to tip over and that I would end up over in Logan Heights somewhere. It was a very eerie disturbing lonely night, although I did have a good talk with a dietician from New York—my fellow guard. I was glad to get in and have a hot surging bath. Sunday found me sleeping late, lounging around, and hardly getting up enough energy to go down to the Post and see *Keys of the Kingdom,*[37] which was pretty good, but not outstanding.

In the evening we were sitting around in the Day Room eating a cake that Howe brought back from her furlough, and I was beating on the so-called piano, when the CQ came in and said that Capt. Spadino called and wanted someone to take care of his kids. You remember my telling you about him and the chorus at Christmas? Of course, I jumped at the chance (pant, pant), so he came and got me. His three baby boys are real cute. I fed 'em and bottled 'em, and diapered 'em, and read stories, and put them to bed without too much of a battle. It was lots of fun to mess around the house. I policed up the kitchen on my own, and got paid $1.50 (against my will), for three hours of enjoyment. Coming back through the gate we caused a mild scandal—I couldn't bear to disillusion the guards by telling them I was just taking care of his kids.

Today, things were a bit more exciting. The Surgical Section went out all day on a Field Problem. We wore leggings like the men, sang "It's a Long, Long Way to Tipperary," and felt positively Battle of the Argonne.[38] The morning passed quickly setting up Battalion Aid Stations, having Company Aid Men go out and doctor up the victims (I had a fractured jaw and was unconscious—put on a very convincing show, too), carrying the patients back by litter, braving a tear gas attack (real), and giving fake tetanus shots. That little ride nearly gave me heart failure. We were back in the mountains and the terrain is tres rough with many prickly cactus. But I came out all right. Even the bouncy ambulance ride didn't do me in. At noon we ate at the Collecting Station. We had C Rations, of which I will send you a sample. In one can is hash or stew or pork and beans—very good. In the other can is soluble coffee which *really*

---

[37] A film based on the popular novel of the same name by A. J. Cronin.
[38] These are references to uniforms, a song, and a campaign of World War I.

tastes like iodine,[39] sugar, candy, and four biscuits which taste like Dog Nibs. We lay around and sang and mountain-climbed, and got taken for a jeep ride which is more fun than a roller coaster. The guy went sixty miles an hour around curves and up and down hills. Mike would have loved the "Whees" we had. All in all, we didn't learn anything much but it was a swell outing and my face is all sunburned tonight. Mom, I'm mad at you for getting me excited with that LR about the meds. You is mean—but maybe I'll forgive you. That's all the news up to now, so Willie and I will say to you, "Cheerio." This is Station CRUD. At the sound of the gong it will be . . .

Much love and kisses,
Pvt. B.

29 January 1945

Monday

Dear Family,
    This is going to be just another "I'm still alive" letter. Life doesn't drool, it just drizzles. School is getting more and more unbearably dull, but only *one more* week. Next week, guess where I'm going? NEW ORLEANS! I wanted to wait and surprise you after I got there but, on the other hand, you can tell me all the spots to visit and eat in, and we will have only four weekends to cavort in. Gray and I are the only lucky Company Fivers to go there. Most of the Company will be here at Willie or else at Camp (ick) Hood, Texas. Tough bounce, kids! Nola, here we come!
    Saturday night us chums went to our favorite spot to have steak and beer. Just a bunch of chow hounds. That is really quite a charming place. To get to the biffy, one goes through the kitchen and, on the return trip, one detours to watch the jolly Chinese cooks making interesting messes. I then ran into a rather nice fellow whom I had known from the Christmas choir. He went to

[39] A reference to another of many verses in "Gee, Ma, I Want to Go Home":
    The coffee that they give you,
    They say is mighty fine,
    But how the hell should they know,
    It tastes like iodine.

Union College in Schenectady, N.Y., and we went to the President's
Ball and Liberty Hall (pome) and had fun dancing. Gosh, how I do
love to dance.

I've gotten 100 in all of my tests, I had KP Sunday, and Pvt. G.
and I have decorated our room with pictures of babies, apes, dogs,
cats, and Danny Kaye, clipped from *Coronet*—and that's absolutely
all of note to relate to you this Monday eve. What is that about Mu
Marsh and baby? Please elucidate—I've heard nothing about it
from her. Got the excellent cookies today—much thanks. I also get
the *New Yorker* every week, together with "Terry and the Pirates"[40]
and the "Fighters Digest." I always look forward to my long package
but forget to mention it in my letters. My only regret is that the NY
is too short. I usually get it all read during lunch hour. Right now
I'm deep in *The Apostle* which is good, isn't it?[41] Also, for culture, we
have a piano of sorts which I believe I mentioned, and the gal next
door has a radio which she occasionally turns on to some good
music. Boy, do I miss that. When and if I get home I shall run the
phonograph constantly and, no doubt, annoy you all. Ahh—Clair
de Lune, New World Symph, Classical Symph, Trenet, Oklahoma,
Eine Kleine Nactmusik (how is that spelling—I groped but how well
did I grope?). What fun I shall have banging a box that has all the
keys on it. Art here is taken care of by the wonderful sunrises and
sunsets. Texas country is really beautiful. Rugged but right, you
might say if you could remember one of the songs in the Stagnantte
repertoire.

I'm very sorry I rashly mentioned anything about prospects of
the "Schwartz" (Juarez) trip. There just isn't any possibility of our
going now. You see, due to a TM epidemic there, passes are sharply
rationed, more this month than the last, which I didn't foresee, and
they only give out passes to two girls a week out of the whole
Company, and this is our last week. I finally found out where I
could get a Spanish newspaper but the place is down in a very
cruddy section of town and I don't relish going there late at night.
But next Saturday I shall try to buzz down while it's still light and
see what I can do. Likewise with the other item. No promises as to
results but I'll do my best to please. Well, this is absolutely all.
Nothing happens around here and that's the truth. Relaxing but

[40] A nationally syndicated newspaper cartoon strip by Milton Caniff. Terry, the hero,
was in the air force at this time.
[41] A novel by Sholem Asch, published in 1943, of the life of the Apostle Paul.

quiet, which is very conducive to Home Thoughts from Abroad, and bad for morale. Gosh, I'm counting so much on that Delay that if I don't get it I shall pop.

> Much love to you all from Pvt.
> Bug (I've gotten over my
> squeamishness by now)

P.S.: Just remembered; I must explain some of the items I dispatched to you in a package last Saturday. Little tin box contained C Ration coffee powder; Dog biscuit = dog biscuit (what I mean is that this was one of four C Ration cookies); Candy is from C Ration. Mom, are you crazy? You said you liked that picture of me sitting on the rail. Frankly, I think I looked like an Okie after a five-day binge. You-all just don't remember how beautiful your li'l daughter is! Plug, plug. Hope the fags help out your nicotine craving. Mike is a stinker. I haven't gotten a letter from him since just after Christmas, and I sent him a postcard folder, too. I'm mad!

Ja Garde

LA GARDE GENERAL HOSPITAL
NEW ORLEANS, LOUISIANA
9 February to 7 March 1945

9 February 1945

1872 SCU, WAC Detachment, La Garde General Hospital, New Orleans, 12, Louisiana, Friday

Haloo Family,
    Spent the day in Vieux Carre. Ate Jambalaya at Kolbs. Much fun deal. Will write long letter Sunday. Pome from *Yank:*

> Breathes there GI with soul so dead
> Who never to himself hath said,
> "Reveille, hell! I'll stay in bed!"
> . . . and then got up.

11 February 1945

Sunday

Dear Family,
    Well, here I am in Nola on Sunday and the rain is pouring down by the hundreds of CCs and it seems a good time to break down and write after two weeks of silence. My last week at Willie was very gay, with dates. Friday there was a dance for the SMDTs and I went with Cliff, that guy I had been out with the Saturday before. While there I ran into Bill whom I never have gotten around to telling you about. He's a swell fellow from the U of Illinois and we talk the same language. We met at choir practice and discovered that we knew all the same songs, so we had some beer-drinking bouts while I was in the lower area. Anyhow, we fixed

up a farewell beer bust for Saturday. The Friday dance was very gala—free beer and food, believe it or not. Saturday evening Pvt. G., Carp, and I had our last steak at our favorite dive. The little Chinese waiter must have known it was our last night because he gave us a clean tablecloth. Then, while it was still light, we ventured down into the Mexican and Chinese section looking for a newsstand that sold Spanish newspapers. After getting many queer glances, we backed out of that strange neighborhood, and in backing, ran into the place we were looking for. Of course none of them spoke English so we had to barter in sign language and I found myself burbling French phrases which did no good whatever. But I did get some papers and magazines, which I'll send along when I find the post office on this confusing Post.

Then I went to the USO where I met William, who took me to a gruesome cafe on the edge of the Mexican Quarter. No one was in the place but soldiers and one sailor—no women at all, but we were secluded in a booth at the rear so I escaped notice. I'll always remember that night because of the huge wonderful fight between the sailor and two soldiers. Tables tipped over—crushing blows— blood flowing like water. "Haven't had s'much fun since the hog et my little brother!" I jumped up and down on the side-lines and cheered. Then it appeared that the sailor was getting the worst of the deal, so all the fellows took pity on him. Bill and I, being meds, rushed into the fray and carted him off to the kitchen for a little First Aid. The poor guy was so drunk and beat up that he couldn't walk, but I remembered the four-man carry, and we did fine. We held his head under the faucet to wash some of the blood off so we could see just how much damage had been done, and found he had a complete and severe severation of the superior labius. Hmmm . . . OK, a cut upper lip, clear through, wonderfully bloody and gory. We applied pressure to stop the hemorrhage which was kind of hard because he kept passing out in my lap. After much labor he came to and stopped bleeding somewhat, but refused to go to a doctor because he was afraid of the Shore Patrols. So William and I went back to our beer drinking and a half-hour later another fight broke out, worse than the first. It raged all over the whole place and came to a climax right in front of the entrance. This attracted the notice of the law. There were whistles and shouts of "Police!" The sailor heaved himself up and whizzed out the back way and close on his heels thundered the SPs and five MPs. Bill and

I quickly took refuge because he was out on a fake pass and didn't want to tangle with any MPs.[42]

After that, things were comparatively quiet. Sunday afternoon, Cliff and I climbed the nearest mountain in a driving rain. When we got to the top, he proposed and threatened to throw himself over the edge if I didn't marry him, and I threatened to throw him over if he didn't stop talking so silly. That did it; we ate some fruit cake and came down. I can't imagine what got into the guy because I looked just like the Sea Hag. I had twenty minutes to change and meet Bill for dinner and much gay conversation. Monday night I had guard duty; nothing happened. Tuesday we had our finals in Orthopedics, Genito-urinary diseases, and Operative Technique. Don't know what I got for marks and don't care. I'm so glad I'm through going to school. Happy Day—for the first time in fifteen years, no more numbing my seat on hard benches and getting writer's cramp taking down lecture notes. Time out now: I'm going out to see the Johnsons.[43] I'll continue the tale of the trip and first impression of N.O. tomorrow night. This I'll mail now to let you know I'm alive and happy.

Much love,

P.S.: Got your letter of February 5 today. Nice to get a letter so soon after arriving.

---

[42] Soldiers were supposed to be accountable at all times for their whereabouts in wartime. Military rules were rigidly enforced, with passes needed to get off the post and to get back in. MPs (Military Police for the army) and SPs (Navy Shore Patrol) could order you to produce a pass at any time. If you did not have authorization, you could be arrested, taken to your commanding officer, and be dealt some penalty for being AWOL (absent without leave). Soldiers have always been notorious manipulators who circumvent the military system, so fake, forged, and borrowed passes were not unheard of. At field assignments in the States, military rules were much more relaxed. As long as you showed up for work as expected, your permanent pass allowed you to be off-base whenever you wanted—with a few limitations.

[43] Dr. Harry Johnson, a psychology professor at Tulane University, had been a University of Minnesota colleague and good friend of my father's. He and his wife took me under their wing while I was in New Orleans.

12 February 1945

Monday

Halloo, Halloo,

How are you liking my "Urp green" paper? It's all I could get at the PX but I do think it's very appropriate for Louisiana. The rain is still pouring down; evidently Mother Nature objects to La Garde Hospital being reclaimed land from Lake Pontchartrain and is trying to return the Post to its original state. It's kind of unhandy, though, chipping off my night's growth of mold, and my hair is the gay Bohemian style again. Following is a picture of efficient Annie on the Ward. We have horrible blue seersucker uniforms that have even less fit than our PT dresses or HBTs, if such a thing could be. I look like a fugitive from a Women's Detention Home.

I'm really quite a wreck today after my first day of duty. We were awakened at 6:00 a.m. and had only one hour to dress, mess, clean the latrine, police our areas, and blaze a trail to the Ward. I attached a string to the barracks door and unrolled it behind me so I could find my way back at noon. The first thing I did was bathe a fellow that had come out of a gastrectomy two days before. He'd had a tumor and they took out all his stomach except for a couple of inches. He was groaning and gurgling and he was so thin I was scared he'd break, but he didn't. Dad, you think you had a tough time—you should hear what these men have to take. One of 'em has had sixteen operations on his abdomen in four months. He had what is known as a colostomy. That's an opening into the intestine through which bowel movements are made. Sounds gruesome, doesn't it? The man with no stomach is a veritable pincushion. He gets intravenous and plasma all day, plus various blood specimens removed, plus dozens of punctures in his seat for penicillin shots. The most amazing thing about these post-op patients is that they are made to get up right after their ops and walk around. They have to go to the john by themselves, and most of 'em have to bathe themselves and make their own beds. There was another guy whose incision for an appendectomy had popped open about an inch, after they took the sutures out. You can look right down in and see loops of gut, and yet that man is running around to the PX and the barber shop and everything.

Seems to me my last letter ended with the last week at Willie. Bill and I had another farewell beer bust and he said he'd propose if he knew me better—a true gentleman, no less. How do you like that? Two proposals in a week! Not bad, not bad. The trip to NOLA took two nights and a day. Very dull, and we slept the whole time. Friday morning we arrived, very thrilled to be in a big city after two small towns. We dumped our baggage in our temporary barracks— the last class hadn't left yet—had an orientation class, and then were given the day off. We were flabbergasted—this ain't the Army!—until we found that the barracks were filled with PWs who were cleaning the place up. So we whizzed downtown, had lunch at Kolb's as per postcard, and spent the rest of the afternoon enjoying the French Quarter, after paying a visit to the part of the docks that weren't restricted. We were lucky because the first day was really lovely, balmy, and sunny. Now it's just hot—80 degrees and muggy. I'm hotter now than I ever was last summer, but I'm not complaining too much.

Well, you know what the Vieux Carre is like. We had fun just strolling around, popping back into private patios when people left the doors open, sitting in Jackson Square eating Pralines, looking at the live shrimp in the French Market (they looked just like cockroaches in the mess hall—ugh), and we topped off the afternoon with a very good Manhattan at the Court of the Two Sisters. The waiter was swell and brought us matches without our even asking. We were extremely pooped by that time, so staggered back and went to bed early. That was quite a night. These ex-men's barracks that we were encamped in were right next to a neuro-psychotic ward and we had no window shades at all. We had frantic phone calls all evening to duck down, or turn out the lights, or do *something* because the patients were having too much fun hanging out the windows getting an eyeful. Also, the door opens out onto a covered boardwalk which leads to and from the mess hall, so the door was thronged with Detachment men looking in and making cracks. To top it all off, we were awakened in the morning by a husky feminine voice yelling, "Get the hell out of here!" The PWs had returned, but that scared them and wonder of wonders we got to sleep till 10:30 when we had an orientation hour and were told about the training. We are divided into little groups and are switched around every week to different wards and the Op Room. I guess we don't have too much practical experience, but the nurses have us watch while they give shots, intravenous, and dress wounds.

Saturday night we ate at Boussards where I had Oysters

Rockefeller and a shrimp, too. Then, after being tres snazzy, we picked up some sailors and pub-hopped. The Carre at night is very honky-tonk, as you say, but fun when the Navy shows you around. The atmosphere is purely superficial. At "Le Cafe des Artistes" there was a wonderful corny hillbilly band, and at "Le Club Ball" there was a five-piece boogie Negro deal. In the groove but, definitely, Jaxon! Sunday afternoon I went out to Johnsons' who were very fun. They fed me sherry all afternoon and homemade cookies. There was a young PhD there also, and we had a lovely psychological conversation. I'm invited out for Sunday dinner next week. Now it's a quarter to eleven, and I'm very bleary-eyed.

Much love to you,

From Mom—Feb. 17, 1945:

It has been so good to have your two letters from New Orleans and to hear all about your experiences and adventures. I knew you would like it there—the climate is so different. Are the azaleas in bloom now? Also, do you wear summer uniforms there? I should think you would have to, if it's 80 degrees. We were much amused at your account of your last days (or, more important, nights) in El Paso. My dear, you are seeing Life in the Raw. I feel as if I should be very shocked and maternal and things, but all I can do is laugh at your screwball antics. I think you have plenty of balance and common sense to manage. The bar-room brawls must have been very gory and exciting. Two proposals in one week must be some sort of a record for a Stagnantte. Aren't you afraid you'll lose your standing if it should get out? Write as often as you can—we get such a kick out of your letters. And send me a praline sometime.

Lots and lots of love and be good!

From Dad—Feb. 17, 1945:

The gauge on the car has been acting up, so we ran out of gas yesterday and will have to go on foot for a few days till we can catch up. How the poor American Civilian suffers in this fearful war! Your last letters have been most interesting. You certainly managed to have a time for yourself before you left El Paso. And to think that we always tried to bring you up carefully and to shield you from the harsher realities (not to say brutalities) of life!

Glad that you were able to get in touch with the Johnsons and that you found them fun. We have always considered them nice people, tho Harry used to be a bit of a wolf, and Mary has had her moments (tho not with me!). But they are still nice.

From Dad—Feb. 18, 1945:

Well, my darling daughter, here we are again. A sore throat I had been fighting yesterday was giving signs of turning into a cold, so, Lent or no Lent, I refused to go to church with the rest of the family. The throat is better but I still feel a bit groggy and may take tomorrow off and try to kill the bug. (No relation to Pvt. Bug, WAC.) Colds are a proper mess. I do hope that you will be able to get a bit of leave when you are done with NOLA, for we miss you, small Bug, and there are so very many things to say that do not write so well, not that they really need saying, either, for I think that you know them already. Be a good and busy Bug and maybe the Army will let some of you kiddies come home for tea. We count on nothing but taxes here below, but we sure are doing a heap of hoping.

I have just finished doing up the New Yorker *which will go off tomorrow. Would you have time or interest to read the* Atlantic? *I consider that most of its articles are tops and should be glad to send it along. I found that one of the dangers of Army life was that I tended to get into a first-class mental rut and that it was next to impossible to find anything to read which kept me in touch with the world of sane people. This isn't a sales talk—do what you want. Some day this bloody mess will stop and we shall all try to pick up the ways of peace again and make ourselves reasonable and reasoning lives, never an easy job at any time. I trust that you will be able to gather from the new things you see and hear some of the valuable raw materials which will help you in that work. Study and learn people, my dear, and evaluate all other things in terms of them. They may seem queer and dull and, at times, brutal and beyond hope, but they are humanity and ourselves. But enough of lectures in PHILOSOPHY III, Doc Bosko, IV hour, MWF—All our love, dear Bug, have fun, and keep your shades down!*

18 February 1945

Sunday

Dearest Mom and Dad,

Well, here we are again—Sunday evening letter time and Pvt. Bug is very pooped out but will do her best. First, I must thank you for my Valentines—just got 'em this morning. The candy is very good and the hankies are marvelous. I do love hankies, especially the brown one. Where did you manage to get such nice ones? Young-Quinlan's must be running a black market.[44] By now we have moved to a new, or I should say different, barracks. This makes the sixth time I've packed all my worldly goods and carted them around since October third. They took over the other barracks to make wards out of them, and we got kicked out. Our present home is exactly like the one in Upper Area, SMDT, WBGH, EP, and it sure feels queer to look out and see waving palms, lush green grass, and an expanse of blue water instead of the khaki-colored mountains, the desert, and the valley with all its twinkly lights. Personally, I like the latter better! We are one in a room and we have dressers and bed-side tables, my dear! It's too, too excrutiatingly movvelous. To say nothing of a whole wall locker to myself and two shelves. The thing is, though, that I don't have enough stuff to fill up all my nice space.

The past week rushed swiftly by—hope the other ones do the same. I was on a Post-Op Ward. That's right, I wrote you Monday night. Anyhow, none of the other days were much different. In the mornings we rushed around and made beds and such stuff as that, and in the afternoons we rubbed backs and played cards with the patients and gabbed with the ward boys who are ASTP pre-meds.[45] Yesterday I gave a penicillin shot and made it up, and the day before, two.[46] My injection technique isn't too sharp yet but the

[44] Young-Quinlan's (known as "the Y-Q") was an elegant women's clothing store on Nicollet Avenue in Minneapolis.

[45] ASTP stood for Army Special Training Program. Men in these programs were in uniform and were enrolled in various college courses under army auspices. For instance, the army paid for the men's premedical and medical school training during the war in exchange for a certain period of military-based service afterward. These men at La Garde Hospital were in uniform and were probably waiting for a medical school class to open up, meanwhile serving as ward boys.

[46] When writing, I told about the procedure in reverse order. *First* I made up the shot and *then* gave it. The penicillin mixture was combined with sterile water using sterile technique, then it was drawn up into the syringe.

man with no stomach on whom I practice is most noble and doesn't complain. Tuesday evening we took in a movie, and Wednesday evening Jeanne R. from Northwestern U. and I popped over to Tulane for a lecture on "Psychology and the War Effort." The speaker turned out to be Lee, the PhD I met the previous Sunday at Johnsons'. He came over after the lecture, took us around his office and then we all went over to "Uncle Harry's," sat around and discussed Psychoanalysis (which they both disapprove of) and the war political developments (and drank sherry—mustn't leave that out). Much fun. Thursday went to another movie (disgusting, what?) and Friday I stayed home and scrubbed everything in sight, even myself. This barracks hasn't been lived in since last July and so is in pretty foul shape, but little by little we are getting things fixed up. The PWs are working on the barracks next door, turning it into orderly room, supply room and so on. When I work the split shift (four hours on, three off, four on) I sit in my lakeside room and hear German, Portuguese, and Spanish being rattled out from below. Tres cosmopolitan. Perhaps I should insert here the fact that we have about three hundred Brazilian Army patients here, none of whom speak English, so their interpreters live here in the Detachment and that's where the Spanish comes from.

Saturday night, Brad and I went out with some gobs [sailors] we had met. Program was dancing, drinking beer and singing, which is as good a way as any to spend Saturday evening. Today I went to Johnsons' for a very excellent dinner. They really are swell, aren't they? After dinner we lay around, listened to the Symph, and read the Sunday paper. After which Mrs. Johnson and I went— guess where? You're right—to hear good old Beat Me Dmitri and the Minneapolis Symphony.[47] Boy, were they in good form. The horn section was practically perfect and you know that's always been one of their weaknesses. The strings were better than I've ever heard them. Maybe I was just misled by a twinge of homesickness and hunger for good music, but they were really sharp. All of which brings us up to the present minute. I'm so tired I can hardly haul a fag up to my lips and that's bad. Standing up all day and running

[47] Dmitri Mitropolous was the conductor of the Minneapolis Symphony Orchestra and later became the conductor of the New York Philharmonic Orchestra. "Beat Me, Dmitri," suggested by the title of a current popular song, "Beat Me, Daddy, Eight to the Bar," was a boogie-woogie piano and song number dedicated to Mitropolous and the symphony musicians. It was performed for him in 1942 at a Student Union concert by the University of Minnesota Boogie-Woogie Club.

around every night sort of does one in. Added to which it has been over 80 all week. The humidity is worse than a Minnesota heat wave and every damned day it rains and rains and RAINS. Take me back to El Paso. In spite of the lushness, and camillias blooming like mad all over the city, I liked the Beaumont scenery better. There was something thrilling and rugged about it that I miss, and the stars here are so little and pin-pricky. I guess I'm a Western Gal at heart. Enclosed find a check which I never cashed. Hope it doesn't ball up your accounts too much. Got my *New Yorker;* thanks. Only three more weeks, then HOME!!!

From Dad—Feb. 23, 1945:

Idiot child: DAMN! Here I is, propped up in your very comfortable bed into which I crawled on Sunday night and out of whichen I ain't been since. I have had a real touch (with an axe) of the flu. Whatalife! Your Sunday letter came this a.m. and was, as always, very welcome. I had a hunch you would be hearing Dmitri da Grik. Glad he and the boys were in the groove. So it's got to be "Uncle Harry" by now, eh? I told you the man was a wolf! And this phydoodle who, what a coincidence, but isn't life like that, full of the strangest things, just happened to be giving a lecture! Watta you tink? Your mom and me we was borna nexa week? The boy really must have something, in addition to psychology!

My returned cheque is being treated as a relic of the saints. I should think it about the only time on record—in any war—that an army offspring has returned money from home. You are the world's most moral infant. Maybe I better save it as against that coming leave. Being about written out by now, good-night dear Pvt. Bug. Go easy on the boy with no stomach. Remember, he has had a hard life already.

27 February 1945

Tuesday

Cher Papa,

DAMN! also HELL! You think you had troubles with the flu. Well, I am in the hospital and I'm not even sick. Got a little ear infection so the Major thinks I should be put in stir and absorb some sulphadiazene. So here I am, the only woman on the ward (I've got a private room, don't worry) and it's a contagious ward so

In my hospital uniform

*Brad, a fellow
surgical technician*

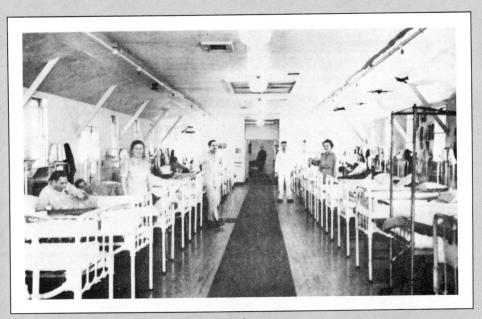

The ward at La Garde General Hospital

Hospital grounds at La Garde

On leave, March 1945

Michael & Midge

Mom with me

Dad in his
State Guard uniform

I can't have any visitors and it's hot as hell and rainy and I haven't anyone to talk to and the nurse is frustrated and hates WACs, and everyone calls me "That WAC" or "Wac-ey" and sneers in the door every time they pass, wondering what the hell I'm doing there. I wonder too, and tomorrow I'm going to raise a stink over at the clinic when I go for treatment. I'm going to demand to be let out or I'll throw two or three fits. I'll probably end up in the NP Section but that, at least, will be a change. As my pal with no stomach used to say when the nurse stuck him with five or six different kinds of needles, and cooed, "Let's try not to complain,"—"I'm not complain-in', I'm just bitchin'!" That's what this is; a bitchin' letter.

First, I must continue my hymn of hate for the nurse. Our battle started yesterday when upon being given five mammoth pills to down, I innocently queried, "What is this, sulpha?" just to make conversation. "It's just some medications that the Major ordered," she snaps out, starting in on the old "patient shouldn't know what he is getting" routine. Of course the Major over at EENT told me I was put in here to get sulpha, and she was present when the ward officer (named Major Ward, believe it or not) told me I would be taking sulpha treatment, but that makes no difference to Lt. Pea Brain. Today the flank attack continues with my pal screaming in, "You made your bed wrong!" It seems I wasn't psychic and didn't divine her particular method for rotating sheets. She then tells me off, but definitely, and rushes cheerfully away to bawl out a suffering colleague of mine who is sweating it out on this ward for a week. The lecture was for not making my bed, which I'm supposed to make, not being crippled—yet. I take a deep breath and try to gather in my staggering forces. The Major whisks by, peeps in, and mutters a "And how are we today?" to which I toss a "Fine, thank you, Sir" after his retreating form. This is known as "making the rounds." "Each patient is individually examined daily by the Ward Officer," it says in the fine print at the bottom of the last page of the La Garde Hospital manual. Then who do I see striding in the door of my cubicle? The Ma'am, this time denounc-ing me for having a filthy, messy room, implying, natch, that it's because I'm just one of those filthy, messy WACs. All I can see wrong is that I have some of my meager possessions laid out in echelon on the bedside table, and that I'm occupying the bed. Ahhh—that is the cardinal sin: a bed patient being in bed, because, you know, that makes wrinkles in the bed clothes, and the Major doesn't like that. What the hell does she think I am, a vacuum? Damn her eyes. Damn every cell and corpuscle in her repulsive, skinny body. There—I will stop my tirade against this so-called nurse. I could go on for hours but that wouldn't leave any room on the paper. It's your turn, man.

Really Dad, your delirious mutterings about my N.O. social activities were in the most shocking taste (at this point I look down my nose in true Mother fashion). First, I must reiterate, though you probably won't believe me, that I didn't know who was going to give that psych lecture. Jeanne dragged me to it; I wanted to go to a movie. Then I should tell you that this PhD is about thirty-five, getting bald, has a lisp, and all he lisps about, besides how he looks down on Psychiatrists, is dishes, and light green blankets, and rose drapes that he and his bride-to-be are storing up for their little nest. And as for this "Uncle Harry" business. If a nice old man, quite fat, with heart trouble and slightly bilious, who sings funny songs and tells all sort of *interesting* stories about you and Mother that I hadn't heard before, who talks all the wonderful homesick talk about faculty meetings and stuff, who lives in a nice old house with lots of books, who gives me free meals and sherry and tickets to symphonies—if such a person, I say, wants to be called "Uncle Harry," why call him "Uncle Harry" I will, all your insinuations to the contrary and so on and so on, burble, burble.

Also, I know that Brazilians speak Portuguese and the Puerto Ricans speak Spanish, but in the usual mad babbling of my letters, I just couldn't manage to put it across. The PWs are quite a source of amusement to me. Yesterday, on my way back to the barracks to gather up my belongings, I passed a slew of them busily painting the upstairs window sills of the next door abode. One of them turned around to look at me and, in turning, dropped his paint brush to the ground. Thus provoked, he yells out, not some German curse, but "Gottdamnshiiiit!" I had a funny feeling last Saturday afternoon when I was lying in my room. The PWs were just outside whanging on the shingles and practically breaking down the all-too-thin walls with each blow, all the while whistling a tantalizing little tune. Here they were, and I was going that evening to see *Faust*, the story of which came from the German Goethe. Incidentally, the production was a trifle sad, put on by a local company, but I should complain; I got in free via the Red Cross.

The Major just *has* to let me up tomorrow—[Vladimir] Horowitz is coming. My week otherwise was a bit dull except for my three days in the Operating Room, but my views of the gory proceedings I will relate when I see you two weeks from today or thereabouts. Here's the deal, and it's pretty well on the level because I saw them written out on the Special Orders in El Paso. We get a Delay en Route of seven days, with probably three day's traveling time. After that we report to Salt Lake City to await orders. Many LRs float around concerning that. Our Special Orders said "To be transferred to Ninth Service Command and assigned." Ninth includes California, Washington, Oregon, Utah, Nevada, and parts of Montana. I'd much rather go East, but that's life. On the other hand, we have a contingent who insists that we are an overseas unit and will be shipping out soon, and backs up their LR with conclusive data. This one is persistent, followed us from El Paso, and there may be something in it, I don't know. But don't let Mom get all hopped up and don't bandy this about. Restricted information, and such. Give all my love to Mom—I know she's real busy with Red Cross, and thank Mike for his rare letter, only don't tell him I thought it was rare. Our term ends the tenth—Saturday, and I should be home Monday or Tuesday, but of that later when I know more about it.

Much love and kisses,

4 March 1945

Sunday

Dearest Family,

Here I am in my inferno of a room—hot is what I mean. I gained some relief by sitting out on the fire escape in my PT pants and a halter, listening to the crickets cricking and the June bugs banging into the screen. There was a faint breeze coming off the lake and it was nice to sit in the dark watching the lights of cars going along the boulevard and the lighthouse blinking on and off, and listening to distant music drifting over from the outdoor theater just outside the Post. The above is to make you the color of this paper (green) with jealousy. I will now continue. Today has been the hottest day since I've been here. I put on a clean, starched shirt and ten minutes later it was wringing with perspiration. But El Army thinks that it is winter everywhere until May, so I groaned, put on my wool blouse, and staggered over to Johnsons' for dinner.

We had a nice cold meat, potato salad, and iced tea repast out on the porch and then lay around in the living room and listened to the Symph. After which Dr. Johnson and I took the dogs for a walk over around the Tulane campus. The azaleas are in full swing now and the bridal wreath is also out, and the city is lush with color and greenery. Everyone's yard has big beds of pansies, nasturtiums, ageratum, wisteria vines, and jonquils, and the sun was out today, for a change, which made it nice.

This last week I spent in the hospital reading and hating the nurse. There were no more open hostilities after the first two days, but there was a feeling of tension and I was happy to leave on Friday. Got out of a whole week's work, too. Good going—I'm getting to be a terrific goldbrick. Ain't it awful? That's what the Deep South does to me. Saturday I spent the day on the porch watching the fellows playing poker. After we made the beds there wasn't a thing to do, though, so we were justified in sitting around. That night Jeanne and I had dinner out in the patio of the Court of the Two Sisters—lovely night it was—and then went to a ballet, free of course. I wouldn't think of *buying* theater tickets now! It was a small troupe, only five people but very good. No scenery; the accent was on lovely costumes and excellent dancing mostly in the traditional vein. They were accompanied by a two-person team for which I would have paid money to hear just by themselves. On our way back, we strolled through the French Quarter via Bourbon Street, watching the drunk sailors and vicariously enjoying the night life. Also vicariously enjoying it all were two New York soldiers who wanted more active participation. We took them up on their polite offer of dancing, and had a nice hour at the Roosevelt Hotel before curfew struck. After which we had spaghetti and a good agreeing session on the Negro race-prejudice problem, and then went home. So ended my last Saturday night in New Orleans.

I find that experiences seem to match the climate. In insipid, pleasant N.O., insipid, pleasant amusements. In rugged, wonderful Texas, exciting and wild evenings. I wonder what kind of life I'll lead in Los Angeles. Let's hope my theory doesn't hold true there—people in California do the most amazing things. All of which is my cagey way of announcing that we finally found out where we are to be stationed. I'm lucky—Birmingham General Hospital on the outskirts of L.A. for me. I could have gone to Walla Walla, Washington, or some forgotten spot in Utah, but I have a little Buck-private Brownie who watches over me. The best part of it is that my buddy, Brad, is from L.A. and knows hundreds of Marines and has relatives with cars and knows lots of good places to go.

Now I'm tres sleepy, and it is as usual at the end of my letters, sack time. I'll wire my exact time of arrival, probably sometime on Monday the twelfth, after I have a confab with the railroad company. Undoubtedly I shall be awful busy so methinks that wire shall be the last communication from me till you see my puss at the station. Oh, how wonderful to be at last coming home. Horray for the cold, frozen North! Kisses for Mom. Kisses for Dad. Kisses for Mike, the Wonderman, the second Harry James. Can you play Chiri-Biri-Bin yet?

All my love,

[Racial segregation in the army and in the South was an issue important to me at the time, and it still is. It is not touched on much in the letters but was discussed with my family when I was home on leave. The family atmosphere had been one where racial or ethnic slurs were explicitly forbidden and where the need for tolerance was frequently discussed at the dinner table. I knew about segregation, of course, but Minnesota had a very small black population, and while there certainly was de facto segregation, I had not seen institutionalized segregation.

Seeing the Jim Crow segregation laws in operation in New Orleans and the Deep South along the Mississippi River was a tremendous shock. "Colored Only" sections on city buses and streetcars and segregated train coaches and train station areas outraged my sense of fairness. There were some minor uproars when I tried to sit in the rear of buses where I would ordinarily sit when at home, causing bus drivers to hustle me away from the black sections. Probably my uniform, my youth, and my northern accent kept me from really serious trouble with the white authorities.

At the university I had become friendly with a few black students through my campus activities, and this was something new for me, having grown up with all-white schools and neighborhoods. In basic training at Fort Des Moines there was a segregated barracks of colored (our 1940s term) Wacs. They had black Wac officers and noncoms, but I do not recall having any classes or mess hall experiences with these girls. My one contact was when I was on guard duty, which was apparently a nonsegregated detail. We spent the boring hours chatting, gossiping, and finding out where each other came from. Fort Des Moines was proud of the black Wac company that had earned more company flags and awards for drilling and marching than any other unit. I never saw black Wacs at any of my assignments after basic. At La Garde Hospital in New Orleans the black enlisted patients were not segregated on the wards and were cared for comfortably by white nurses and corpsmen. Racial segregation in the armed forces was finally ended officially in 1947 by order of President Harry S. Truman.]

7 March 1945

Wednesday

Dearest Family,

Just got Mom's incoherent letter and thought I'd better elucidate a little more on my plans. Now you know where my incoherency comes from—Dad is usually lucid, but Mom and Annie babble. For one thing, railroading is a little uncertain because of the flood. Kids going to Ohio are really worried but I don't know whether the Mississippi will act up or not. So, barring unforeseen events, I will arrive Tuesday morning at 8:00 at the Rock Island Station. If things change, I'll wire you, collect, if you don't mind. I'm going round trip and won't have to report back here till the twenty-second, that's Thursday. The Army then sends me Pullman out to Los Angeles. My ticket is nicking me $32.05, which is a very good deal. Furlough rates are a fine institution.[48] Got to get this in the mail tonight, so goodbye. I'll have eight or nine days at home. If this figuring throws you, don't get in a twit. I'll explain everything when I see you. I have a little deal on in St. Louis which may come through and may not, but I'll for sure wire you verifying my arrival. Don't worry, anyhow!!!!!

Love,

---

[48] The railroads had special low fares for service people going on furlough.

Birmingham

BIRMINGHAM GENERAL HOSPITAL
VAN NUYS, CALIFORNIA
22 March to 17 August 1945

In Transit

22 March 1945

St. Louis, Missouri, Thursday

Hello Family,

9:30 a.m.: Here I am in the vast beautiful Servicemen's Lounge of the vast beautiful Terminal Station in Quaint Old St. Louis, Missouri. Yessiree—great old town. No, I'm not drunk, just very bleary from a night on the Rocket which was filled with kiddies, all ages and all stages of noisiness. Many squalling, tired little two-year-olds. A number of 10-to-13-year-old young men coming home from school for vacation who were much too excited to sleep, so they sat up, conversing in loud tones to anyone who would listen to them, and that wasn't me. Besides the kiddies, there were mothers and grandmothers, but no interesting men. Too bad; had to buy my own provender. My little southern train doesn't pull out till 12:00 so I have to sit around. I don't dare venture more than a block from the station because the neighborhood doesn't look too savory, and besides, the place is crawling with soldiers who are just back from overseas, and who haven't seen women, especially WACs, for months; they are dangerously enthusiastic. I will plop myself down in a corner with my treatise on college education, and the latest

Time, and soon it will be 11:30 and time to go. Will post you when I reach N.O.

Love,

P.S.: Spring isn't much further along here than home. Kind of chilly today, but the sun is shining. No leaves yet.

24 March 1945

Houston, Texas, Saturday

Hello Mom,
   Just as you predicted I forgot to post you from N.O. Hope this makes up. This train is an old thing—just like troop trains. But such is life.

Much love,

25 March 1945

El Paso, Texas, Sunday

Still going strong. Willie looks just the same and that's mighty good.

Love,

25 March 1945

Tucson, Arizona

Sunday evening. Down the primrose path. Lost 45 cents playing poker with the Navy. Just had a Cuba Libre at the Hotel Majestic, but no ill consequences, I trust.

Love,

Van Nuys, California

26 March 1945

Monday

   Arrived OK. Spending the day in Hollywood before reporting in tonight. This place is cold, more so than Minnesota. Fooey on the Chamber of Commerce. The scenery is quite pretty but can't see any ocean, however. Had lunch at Sardi's. Saw Lou Costello of Abbott and Costello at the station this morning. Don't get too much of a kick out of all this, cause I'm so tired. All I want is a bath and rest. Will write a real letter soon.

Love,

From Mom—Mar. 25, 1945:
   It was so good to have you home and it has seemed pretty lonesome the last few days. We are so very proud of you and love you so much. I'm sorry I was irritable and cranky-seeming some of the time you were here, but you know I didn't mean anything by it! It's just my way—you slid so well back into the family picture that I assumed my old motherly, bossy ways.

From Dad—Mar. 25, 1945:
   Well, here I am, sitting in the study for a visit with you and only a few days ago you were here in person. The house certainly seems quiet and empty again. I went to drill Wednesday evening and we had a moderate work-out with riot formations. Friday saw the usual dull faculty meeting with, however, a good chicken dinner. The headmaster went over a batch of post-war building plans and we kicked them around as a lot of compromises and make-shifts (which they are) and didn't please him much. Also, we are to get a $100 increase next year, so go ahead and buy that ermine-lined field jacket you have been wanting! That evening, NCO school and work on the Interior Guard for the Show on the seventh—should be good. We have an ex-marine in the Company now who is good and amusing. We trade war yarns—mine somewhat moldy. Last drill he said that he had been discharged because of ulcers and did I know anything about them! Then we had a real visit and I told him just what to do—go to Fort Snelling and get rid of them!

30 March 1945

1986 SCU, WAC Detachment, Birmingham General Hospital, Van Nuys, California, Friday

Dear Mom and Dad,

I'm a stinker for not having written to you before now. I haven't been busy, but I've been feeling rather depressed and not inspired to write. Things feel very dull somehow; I suppose it's post-vacation let-down or something. Although I'm still having a vacation as far as that goes. Here's the deal: The first Medical WACs to arrive came on Friday. I arrived Monday and nobody worked till Thursday. The Detachment has just started up and there are only about ten hospital technicians and some clerks and a mess sergeant back from overseas. Right now we are living in the nurses' quarters and don't have any detachment organization at all, but they are building barracks, and by summer there should be a big set-up; two hundred hospital technicians, clerks, truck drivers, our own mess hall, PX, Day Room, and stuff. Everything here is in a lull. This used to be a debarkation hospital, and the Surgeon General's Office is changing it over to a regular General Hospital. In the meantime there are only five hundred patients, with five hundred nurses, five hundred detachment men, one thousand civilian employees, and us with nothing to do. I spent yesterday and today reading on the porch. The nurses make all the beds, give baths, take temps, etc., doing all their work and ours, too. Which makes me mad; I feel so useless and bored and tired of sitting around. All of us feel the same way, and we have some fine bitch sessions in the evenings. Another irritating factor is that no one here has ever seen or heard of a WAC before, evidently, and they think we are queer neolithic creatures, or a third sex, or something. Also, the civilian mess hall employees wear our uniforms—the blue ones—so half the doctors and patients think we are kitchen help!

The hospital is mammoth, laid out the same as La Garde but bigger, and it is in the middle of a valley [San Fernando] northwest of Los Angeles. There are quite high mountains all around covered with green vegetation but they're not very spectacular. The weather is much like Minnesota in early spring—cold and rainy with occasional sunshine. The wind howls all the time, too. Ugh! The catch in this dear place is that it is miles away from everything. L.A. is eighteen miles away, Van Nuys about five miles away, Hollywood, ten. Even this wouldn't be too bad—we have Class A passes good till six the next morning, no bedcheck—but the transportation is horrible. There's a bus to Van Nuys that runs only every hour and stops at midnight, and the streetcar from there to town runs only every half hour. We usually can catch rides to town with the personnel or visitors, but getting back is another question. One has to leave town at 9:00 in order to catch the midnight bus. Which is not conducive to evening festivities. I haven't done very much since I got here. All that we did Monday in Hollywood, I wrote you on that postcard. Tuesday, Brad and I went to Hollywood with her brother, a grumpy non-communicative Marine. Dull. Wednesday we trailed out to South L.A. to visit some friends of hers and I was very tired. It took us three hours to get there and three back. Expensive, too. Last night I washed and ironed and mended and read. The books in this Post Library are not too sharp, but I suppose they're OK for the fellows. Mostly best sellers, and ones movies have been made from, not very challenging intellectually. Dad, do send me the *Atlantic*, and *Newsweek* as much as possible, and I would also like *Teacher in America* when you're through with it. Mom, you can send: radio, strollers,[49] blue jeans, hand lotion, white cotton shirt, some homemade cookies.

That's all the news there is, folksies, except (1) we are supposed to get T/5 (Corporal) soon, it says here. (2) We get paid tomorrow—good thing. I have only 55 cents between me and starvation. (3) Tomorrow some of us are going to the Hollywood Canteen. I hear that it's fun. (4) We are considering going to the sunrise Easter Service in the Hollywood Bowl . . . hope I've got enough strength of mind to get up at 4:00 a.m. I miss you all and wish my furlough were thirty days instead of ten. I had such a swell time at home relaxing. It felt so natural; sort of wish I were back. California isn't very exciting, and I miss being with people that speak my language. The men here are very hostile and sarcastic and rather ignorant. But then, there's nothing I can do but bear up.

Love,

P.S.: Give my love to Mike. How did he come out on his exams?

---

[49] Strollers were low-cut leather, moccasin-style shoes, now called loafers.

2 April 1945

Monday

Dear Mom and Dad,

Things are as dull as ever. I don't know what has come over me but life doesn't seem very interesting. Please write me a pep talk to snap me out of this condition because I'm making myself and everyone else unhappy. The kids and the ward boys ask me if I'm sick and the patients ask me why I go around looking like the end of the world but I can't for the life of me say. I have a wonderful job now—in the operating room, and permanently, too. That's always been the thing I wanted to do. There's lots of work and it's interesting and requires some intelligence and effort. Not like taking TPRs or making beds. In a few weeks after they train us a little more, we will be sterile technicians, and can assist the surgeons. Today the nurse showed us where everything is and demonstrated how BGH makes up towel, sheet and gown packs. I suppose the first week or so we'll mostly be learning the set-up and after that we can take over.

Saturday night, Gray, two other kids, and I went into Hollywood by dint of much effort and waiting for buses and streetcars. The bus driver got out at one stop and picked some orange blossoms which have a wonderful sweet smell. At the "Film Capital" (guff, guff) after much wandering around we made our way to the Canteen. It's a barny affair with a stage at one end and a small bar at the side, and was packed with sailors. Walking was like trying to make a beach-head on Iwo Jima. But we finally battled our way to the foodstuffs, where Sidney Greenstreet (sinister type) offered us sandwiches, and Charlie Chan's son gave us milk. Marsha Hunt signed our souvenir postcards, and it was just like in the moom pitchers, thrill, thrill. At this time we bethought ourselves to go to the sunrise service at 4:00 AM and so set about looking for some place to stay. We walked miles and miles up to the hotel section and a fatherly clerk at the Roosevelt referred us to a friend of his who ran a tiny hotel two blocks off the boulevard. Four of us squeezed into a tiny room with twin beds, with no bath, and guess how much? Five bucks. It was a swindle but split four ways it wasn't so bad. We bought some milk and doughnuts to save for breakfast, and proceeded to sleep soundly until 10:30, missing the sunrise service, natch. But it was Easter, so we leaped up and went to church. Gray and I found an Episcopal one on Hollywood Boulevard but it was packed with fancily dressed so-and-so's. The priest was a stuffed shirt who boomed, and jumped the service back and forth from Morning Prayer to Communion, leaving out the Confession in both, so I was completely disgusted. We walked out before the sermon. We spent the afternoon at a movie and that was my Easter Sunday. I missed you all so much. I thought of "wormed eggs"[50] and a nice service at St. John's, and a walk around Lake Harriet in the afternoon. So like a sap I came home and lay around brooding and feeling miserable.

This evening we had a Company meeting and our CO gave us the low-down on ratings, ha, ha. Seems there is no separate TO (Table of Organization) for WACs, and the Ninth Service Command is crowded with ranks coming back from overseas to the Service Forces, and there is no hope whatever. I thought as much and never counted very heavily on a T/5. Such is life. The Army has never increased its allotment for Service Force ratings since 1941 and by now the personnel has *somewhat* increased.[51] The good old Army game. After our meeting which concerned other matters like PT classes, Military Courtesy, orientation classes, laundry, summer uniforms, and such-like, Brad and I went to a corny movie on the post and howled like mad. I feel rather better now. Tell EC if you see her to write me before I go bats from loneliness. I guess this is enough griping for one letter.

Goodbye and much love,

---

[50] "Wormed eggs" was a family term for a dish composed of hot hard-boiled eggs put through a ricer and served on toast. The resulting product looked like little worms.

[51] The army had an unfathomably mysterious system for the allotment of ratings, or ranks, for enlisted personnel (probably for officers, too): so many sergeants (master sergeants, buck sergeants, plain sergeants), corporals, and Pfcs (private, first class) per so many hundred men. Naturally ratings were coveted because of the raise in pay. When people who already had ratings were moved into a unit, that cut down on the possibility for advancement of the people already there. In the Medical Corps there was a relatively new system of designation; a corporal was rated a T/5 (technician, fifth grade). This may have been designed to give the many people who had special training past the buck private, or basic training, level some semblance of appropriate pay. But there sure were a lot of us buck privates and T/5s. There was a raunchy saying, "TS, T/5, T.O.," which translates as, "Too bad, T/5, the Table of Organization has no room to advance you."

From Mom—Apr. 4, 1945:

I had a telephone call from Rachel Katz on Monday night. She was just leaving to go back to Chicago and then New York. She has been given a medical discharge; her heart went back on her during her nursing in England. She said she was going to New York to take a refresher course in Social Work as nursing would be too hard for her now. She was much interested to hear about you, and said she had been at Beaumont for awhile. I told her you had some idea of studying nursing and she said she wished she could have a good talk with you.

From Mom—Apr. 12, 1945:

Last night we went over to church to the post-Easter dinner. We grab all chances for a point-less meal; meat is harder than ever to get, points or no points. However we are not starving. Had a nice fillet of Lake Superior trout for supper tonight with tartar sauce.

8 April 1945

Sunday

Dearest Family,

This is just a quickie to tell you that life is looking somewhat brighter now, although I got positively psycho this last week. Cried myself to sleep two nights, and felt miserable most of the time. But all that is over now, we hope. Gray, Cooper, and I went over to Santa Monica and the beach today, my first view of the Pacific. It was a nasty cold day but we had fun, and as a result of all the unprecedented cold fresh air, I'm very sleepy and just haven't the energy to write. Tomorrow I will toss off a real letter. Got the hankies; they are very handsome and I like 'em lots. Also got the magazines and the envelope with the assorted stuff in.

Till tomorrow, all my love,

From Dad—Apr. 8, 1945:

Sorry that you are (or were?) still in the dumps, but I have observed during a long, active and, dare I say interesting and not unuseful life (hrump, hrump) that such a condition is not altogether unusual among younger and even more mature adults of both sexes at this particular period of the ever-changing seasons of nature. Even I have been known to feel flat in the spring and your honored and much-beloved mother is quite frequently a pain in the neck at this season. The malaise passes and life resumes its normal round in due course, particularly if one's labors are interesting. Plenty of sleep and not too much introspection is recommended by the Old Maestro.

12 April 1945

Thursday

This situation is still not a bed of flowers, but life chugs on somehow. The main blight of my life at the moment is that we are restricted to the Post Sunday and have to be in at 12:00 Saturday evening because of some patients coming in. Blast! Not that there is anything to do on Saturday nights, but it's the idea that gets me. Nothing exciting ever happens around here. Life is very dull. We get up at 6:00, rush like mad to be at work at 7:00. We work on cases all morning and then go to mess. The operations are very interesting; that's the only time I feel alive. Today was my first time to be a sterile technician. That's the one who passes the instruments and stuff. There was another more experienced fellow helping me so I didn't make too many mistakes. After a few more times I oughta be pretty good. After lunch we wash and oil instruments, put up supplies to be sterilized, fold linens and clean up generally. Then fellows come in to be prepped (shaved) for the next day's cases, and we stagger back to the barracks about 4:00. At this time I wash clothes, take a sun bath or read till 7:30 when I and my unhappy companions go to the cinema for a couple of hours of escape from the Bastille . . . shades of SMH, only here I don't have any little chums to play bridge with.

Last Sunday we broke the monotony somewhat by hitchhiking to Santa Monica, as I believe I mentioned. The day was very cold and gray so the view was not inspiring. We shivered along the beach, stared at civilians in nude bathing suits,[52] and then hitched back twenty-five miles to the Post. Fresh air, but not much more. Tuesday, Brad and I went to hear Charles Laughton. He comes out

---

[52] Two-piece swimsuits with bra tops were not common in the States in 1945. We were more used to seeing one-piece, tank-type suits with a little skirt across the front.

every Tuesday to the library and reads aloud. This time he read Swift's "A Modest Proposal" and a long funny bit from *Pickwick Papers* in which Dickens takes lawyers through the mill. Laughton is wonderful, especially at close quarters and with few people present. He's very informal, and intersperses everything with little comments and anecdotes of his own. And that, dear family, completes the history of my week. You can see that nothing happens that could even be enlarged to make an interesting letter. I read in the LA paper about your April storm, but EC assures me that spring has returned and Dad speaks of working in the yard, so evidently it didn't last long. The rains have almost stopped but it is cold and misty much of the time. Last week we could take sun baths but now not even that to look forward to.

I do hope my radio comes soon, also the books. Would you also send my white shorts (bottom bureau drawer, I think) and the snapshot holder Aunt Edith gave me (top middle desk drawer)? Those pictures we took weren't too bad except the one of Mom and me with our mouths flapping. I got the pictures from New Orleans, too. Yes, that was Brad. The fellow was a young boy on Ward 20 who had four operations in a month. He was only nineteen, so we mothered him. I'm glad Midgie is almost all well. I followed her case with much interest, but never got around to mentioning it. Oh yes, just thought of something. Got a note from Grace Symons[53] who very graciously invited me to come to see them anytime I wanted to. Which was very well, but vague, and I never could find my way to their house. Then amazingly, a PFC Denton in our detachment turns out to be a very good friend of Grace's. Denton is an older woman (probably forty-five, heh!), an ex-school teacher and very interesting. She went abroad in 1938 and her experiences of Germany in the early Hitler days make the whole story more real, coming from someone who saw it. But with this Sunday business, I don't know when I can get off to see Mrs. S. Gosh, I'm vague . . . The point about Denton is that Mrs. S. called her and

---

[53] In December my mother had relayed to me a postcard from Grace Symons, a high-school friend of hers who was my honorary godmother. Grace said, with real clairvoyance: "Dear Blanche; I'm thrilled to hear about Anne. Be sure to give her my name and address in case she's sent this way. I know how the young fry feel about 'mother's school friends,' but maybe she'd like someone to know in LA. On the other hand, *maybe* we'd click. We have a livingroom sofa that makes a quite comfortable bed that she'd be *very* welcome to. Love, GS." I had been resisting contacting her in spite of my mother's urging, feeling somewhat shy and not sure of a welcome.

told her to take me under her wing and show me how to find the place. Now it is after 10:00 and *way* past my bed time. I'm usually safe on the sack at 8:00. I got Mike's postcard. Tell him I'll do my best to procure some autographs for him.

> Goodbye and much love from a very Disgusted, Dejected, Down-in-the-Dumps Bug

P.S.: It ain't spring fever, Pappy, dear. It's this horrible place. I sure wish I were home or somewhere else. If I weren't working in Surgery I'd buck for a CDD, no lie. It's too bad this had to happen after six months of gay times.

16 April 1945

Monday

Dear Family,

Another weekend has came and went and life is still drooling along. That seems to be the way I start all my letters, but it's the truth. Thursday I believe I wrote you; also I did my laundry. Friday I listened to my little radio, which came along with the cookies—thanks much. That radio is a great comfort to me. Saturday a bunch of us went in to Hollywood, our usual Saturday evening occupation. At the Hollywood Canteen we saw Roddy McDowall (got his autograph, natch), and many nice looking soldiers and sailors and RCAF [Royal Canadian Air Force] men. I get some pleasure from looking, anyhow. Then we walked up and down Hollywood Boulevard and got home by 12:00. Sunday we were restricted because some patients were coming in, so I slept, read, listened to the radio, and got sun burned. Today, Monday, I settled back into my groove of work. Just got back from a show in the Red Cross Rec Hall. Jose Iturbi came and played Chopin's "Minute Waltz," "The Polanaise," "Clair de Lune," and his own Boogie Woogie arrangement. He is a very charming person. We had very good seats in front on the left where we could see his hands. There was also a patient just back from overseas who hadn't played the piano in two years. He entertained with some very polished Boogie, and the GI band joined in an impromptu jam session. There was much corny joking by other people—that part I didn't like. It was a bit rugged, even for me, but I suppose the fellows like the vulgarity. The patients here are so different from La Garde or Beaumont. Here they all seem to be extremely boorish and coarse, and at the other places they weren't necessarily the refined or intellectual type, but they were good joes on the whole.

News Notes: (1) Tomorrow we are doing a gall bladder operation on Madame Quezon, the wife of the President of the Philippines. (2) There weren't any military ceremonies to commemorate the passing of President Roosevelt here at dear old Birmingdamn Hospital. However, the Post did observe a five-minute interval of silence at 1300.[54] (3) Everybody in Surgery had an April Crisis today. My suggestions for curing the tense atmosphere: (a) Kick out the head nurse. (b) Change Wardmasters. (c) Give the Major a month's leave. That would cure everything. (4) I hate this place. But that's no news.

Much love to you all,
Lonesome Annie

Have you given your paper yet, Mom? If not, good luck. Mike can't have those autographs for good, but he can show 'em around.

From Dad—Apr. 15, 1945:

Reporting a busy but rather dull week most of which has been cold and rainy. On Wednesday when your Maw wrote, I was at drill as usual. It was quite dull, much close-order and elementary stuff for the new men, but hard on the old-timers.

Friday while Mike was on a bender, the old folks took in a movie at the Park—Bogart and "The Look" who strikes me as being a bit too sultry. [This was Lauren Bacall.] Saturday morning saw the usual chores and then I joined the 4th Regiment to parade for and attend the FDR service at the Auditorium. The place was packed and the job quite well done. Though never sold on FDR personally, he was undoubtedly a big man and did much good. I am hoping that with the new administration the balance will swing a bit more to the middle.

[54] President Roosevelt died on Thursday, April 12, 1945. I remember listening over the weekend to my radio, which delivered nothing but gloomy symphonic music and narrations comparing Roosevelt's death to that of Abraham Lincoln on April 14, 1865, almost exactly eighty years before. There were also many quotations from Walt Whitman's "When Lilacs Last in the Dooryard Bloomed." No wonder I was depressed!

The Seversons came in for the evening. We drank Stite[55] and talked about our future farms. I am going to start looking as soon as school closes in June. Most of the empty lots in the neighborhood have been, or are being plowed. Roche has started to dump his sand-heap on my side of the garden. Then we spread it and have it disked in. I hope it works out, but. . . . Roche seems to be a bit fed up with farming and says he will probably sell the lot when building starts again. However, by that time we should have the farm and be thinking of moving out. Just as we have had a change in national administration, we are due for one at Blake before so long and I want to have things lined up for Mike's remaining three years. And time has a painful way of moving fast.

We had your note announcing an improvement in morale, which I figured was about due, but your mother was pained not to have any following letter. Be a good kid and try to keep her en rapport with the situation, as she has a tendency to worry about her offspring when she thinks things are not going 100%. Personally, moods do not upset me unless too long continued and you usually work out of yours in due time. If you haven't time for a letter, drop her a line with fair frequency.

From Mom—Apr. 17, 1945:

Hooray for you—you are a good girl to send us a whole carton of cigs. Once again we were down nearly to bed rock. The day may come when we will really have to quit smoking.

We had your letter at long last yesterday. I'm awfully sorry you were still feeling low. It's too bad the hospital is rather far away from things and that there is not much to do. But I do feel, dearest, that you'll have to make a real effort to cheer up and adjust yourself. This is just one of those situations that you knew ahead of time might arise, and it's too bad. But you will have to try really hard to be cheerful; it has to come from inside, not from outside. You probably are saying to yourself, "But Mother doesn't know what it's like here—she just doesn't understand." I don't know just what the situation is but I do know you and I feel you are too smart to let a few externals get you down. Surely you have resources of the mind and spirit to carry you along. Buck up, honey, it really could be much worse. You maybe can be glad you aren't off on some dreary Pacific island. We love you lots and hate to have you miserable, but you really must try not to give in to an orgy of self-pity.

---

[55] Stite was a trademark name for a smooth beer with a higher than usual alcohol content produced by the Gluek Brewing Company, Minneapolis.

We just came home from having dinner over at the Legion Post. By now even they are requiring one red point apiece for dinner, but that's not as much as buying meat enough for three. I saw in tonight's list of casualties that Jim H. had been wounded. I haven't seen EC or heard from any of the girls for some time so haven't had the news direct. Lots of love, dear—you know I love you even though I have lectured you! How about writing an extra card once in a while even if there is no news and even if you are in the dumps?

Mother

22 April 1945

Sunday

Dearest Family,

Sunday evening is here again: time for my weekly session with pen and this paper which I lifted from Major Hodgeson's office. I'm sure he won't mind because he doesn't know—ain't I wicked? The weeks go by so fast it's hard to realize I've been here a month exactly, but the days are so alike I can't tell one from another. This week I seem to have done a lot of running around in the evening to the neglect of laundry, ironing, sleep, and correspondence. Speaking of which, did I tell you that Bill finally got in touch with me? He's the one I met at Beaumont, the one I was going to meet in St. Louis. I've had a couple of letters since I got here. He's at Camp Crowder, Mo., taking a lot of overseas medical training like Rifle Practice and Bivouac, and then will go to Camp Beale, Cal., which is a POE (Port of Embarkation). At which time I shall beat our wardmaster over the head, get a three-day pass, and go up to San Francisco to bid him fond farewell. He's the one man I know, now that Joseph has thrown me over. Poor frustrated homely Annie has no S.A. except by mail. I guess that is my lot in life, but I shall make a lovely maiden aunt for Mike's kids, you may be sure. He'd better have a slew of 'em too because I love kids. Now to go on with my weekly account.

Monday: Think I wrote you that we went to a Red Cross program which had Jose Iturbi. *Tuesday:* I was in charge of the workroom in Surgery this week which means packaging up all the supplies, keeping the cupboards in order and sterilizing everything. It's kind of fun but takes a long time to finish. After work I went to a music hour they have every day in the library. This was the first day I was able to get off in time. The fellow that runs it is an intellectual squirt who is an ex-concert pianist. In the Army he works for the Reconditioning Service. I promoted myself into his good graces by looking soulful during Mozart's Italian Symph and sprightly during Eine Klein-you-know-what-I-mean. The result is that he agrees to play some of the things I like on days when I can be there. Birmingham has a huge collection of records, singly and in albums. This place gets more gifts of books, records, individual radio earphones for patients, furniture for the ward solariums, all kinds of stuff like that. I guess this is the only thing that the people around here have to be patriotic about. I told you that the Hollywood crowd is fighting over who is going to furnish our Day Room. In the evening I went again to hear Charles Laughton. He read a little snatch of Whitman's "When Lilacs Last in the Dooryard Bloomed" in honor of the President, after which two officers and two patients walked out. Too highbrow for them I guess. Charles made a crack and took it very good naturedly which was noble of him. I would have gotten mad, probably. Then he read GBS's "Arms and the Man," and very good it was. *Wednesday:* Slaved away. Had a Company meeting at 6:00 at which time we had our six-monthly reading of the Articles of War. That legal language never fails to tickle me, while warning me to be a good girl and mind my P's and Q's. Then we all went to see *Two Girls and a Sailor* (swoon) with Van Johnson.

Thursday: The dear old USO got us tickets for the big pension-fund concert of the LA symphony, conducted by Toscanini. They rented the biggest auditorium in LA for it and prepared for a gala crowd. In harmony with the general ballyhoo, the hospital gang was transported in a convoy of snazzy-looking station wagons piloted by the AWVS [Auxiliary Women's Volunteer Service], and accompanied by guess what?—four gaudily uniformed state police on motorcycles, and two MPs also on motorcycles, all with sirens going like mad during the whole trip. We screamed along, brushing aside traffic, going around corners on two wheels, dodging street-cars, going through all stop lights, and looking as though we were rushing to the front with a special message from Eisenhower to Patton. Ah, Hollywood! At the concert we stood in line for hours for our real tickets, and at last got in. The lobby was crammed with people: movie stars, cameramen, and reporters—"Hollywood Goes Cultural." It's amazing what the autograph hounds will go through.

Imagine enduring a Toscanini concert for a signature from Paul Henreid. How do they do it? Again I say, "Ah, Hollywood!" Also I say, "Ah, nuts!" Carmen and I found ourselves seven rows from the front, surrounded by mink coats, tuxedos, orchids, Chanel No. Five, pearl-handled opera glasses, and big fat Brass. I'd rather sit with the proletariat in the balcony. Enclosed find program. I don't think Toscanini could get out of the orchestra quite what he wanted. Anyhow, that's how it looked to me, watching his face and gestures. But the whole thing was pretty good. A most horrible embarrassing thing happened during the second half of the program. I suddenly saw a personage running along the stage in front of the footlights. She ran back and forth doing a sort of fake and feeble ballet dance. Toscanini heard clapping right in the middle of the number, turned around and saw this apparition. Of course, he stopped the music instantly while the audience laughed and clapped and thought it was a huge joke. Finally, two guards came out from the wings and dragged her away, and after a while the well-mannered and polite audience stopped laughing and let the infuriated Toscanini continue with the concert. I bet he never comes to LA again, for which I don't blame him. This personage I immediately took to be a psycho, but it seems that she was hunting publicity, and this inane city gave it to her. Even on Saturday she was still getting full page spreads. She should have been put in the clink and ignored, but no. Still again I say, "Oh, Hollywood," and this time I will add, "Oh, hell." This place disgusts me. You can't even go to a concert to enjoy some good music without their crappy old publicity messing everything up.

Friday: A big bunch of Debarkation patients came in from Luzon and Leyte, and we had a rush of business, working ten and a half hours taking off old smelly casts, changing dressings and putting on new casts. Those poor guys are really in gruesome shape. Very thin, and yellow from taking Atabrine, and banged up with every conceivable kind of wound.[56] Big news: this hospital has

[56] Birmingham General Hospital was a major debarkation hospital for wounded men being shipped in from the Pacific Theater. (In Texas we had patients coming in from the European Theater.) Casualties received temporary hospitalization and treatment in the war zones and then were transferred to the States for further treatment, but there was often a long delay because the transfer was by ship. Men in the Pacific were required to take Atabrine, a medication to prevent malaria. The main side effect was to turn the skin yellow, and many soldiers resisted taking it, preferring to risk getting malaria; frequently they lost the bet and ended up sick with long-lasting and recurring fevers.

been changed to a General Hospital (before it was three-fourths Debark and one-fourth General), so we shall continue to have business. And I'm glad even though it means longer hours. Hemorrhoidectomies are really quite dull. Friday evening I staggered back to the barracks and washed and ironed and fell into bed. *Saturday:* Another heavy schedule of cast-changing, but worked only nine hours. Came down with a huge headache. Miss Snotsky (that's what I call our head nurse) implied that I had a hangover. She always thinks the worst of everyone. I was too tired to go anywhere that evening so lay around. At 8:00 I was routed out by Gray, and we put in an appearance at a dance given for the enlisted personnel by the civilians. They gave us corsages of red, white, and blue flowers. Nice, huh? We watched the various styles of corny dancing, danced ourselves a couple of times, I with an ancient ex-lawyer from Vienna. Then Gray and I ran into a fellow who knew some Company Fivers at Denver, and he had a friend who had part of a bottle of PM [whiskey], so we went outside and helped him demolish it. However, that only made my headache worse, so we decided to head for bed.

Sunday: This morning even after twelve hours of much-needed sleep, my head still ached and my eyes were all puffed out, making me look like a Mongolian idiot, and my nose was very stuffy. I've decided that my sphenoid sinusitis has become frontal sinusitis, like yours, Mom. More damn fun. If this keeps up, I'll probably have to go on sick call. This afternoon I dragged myself into Hollywood (two hour trip) to see Grace Symons as I had promised I would. She works at an information booth for servicemen in Hollywood on Sundays. She's very nice, Mom; we had a Coke over at the drug store; but vague as all get-out. She repeated what she'd said in her letters, "Just drop over any time, I'd love to have you," but people out here don't seem to realize that you can't "just drop over" when it takes three or four hours to get anywhere. If she'd invited me over definitely that would have been OK but as it is, well, skip it. Mary Alice, Dave D.'s girl, also wrote and invited me to just drop in. Maybe all Californians are generously vague (or vaguely generous) by nature. Anyhow, this evening I'm catching up on letters. Did you know that Alta is joining the WAVEs with Sally H., sister Pi Phi and Jim H.'s sister. Also, Bobby W. has joined the WAVEs. Traitors, every one of 'em! Alta writes that Ruthie G. is absolutely outdoing herself, being prominent. (1) She's been asked to do honor work next year and will probably graduate Magna or Summa. (2) She's organized Student Self-government at Holyoke, made it the biggest deal on campus, and got herself elected president. Ah, yes, my prominent friends, E.C. and R.G., the future doctor and lawyer. I knew them when they wore blue jeans and ratty shirts and went on bicycle hikes with the dull Miss B. who is now RN in the Centerville Charity Hospital. Thanks for the *Teacher in America*—haven't gotten to it yet but will in time. Speaking of *Time*, EC gave it to me for Christmas and it just started to come last month. And now, as I am absolutely pooped and have writer's cramp and every other thing, I shall bid you adieu.

All my love,

P.S.: Mom, again I express the hope that your paper went off OK; Dad, elucidate your cryptic remarks concerning Blake's politics; Mike, have you bought any new records? I'm still working on autographs for you. Hope Midgie's ear is fine by now. On reading this over for mistakes, it sounds to me very bitter. Really, it's just my anemic attempt to be gay and humorous.

From Dad—Apr. 22, 1945:

What a very lousy week this has been. Today we have had a combination of cold rain and thunderstorms. Things might be a lot worse, but family morale is not too high. I am glad to hear that the radio and our various packages came through properly. The radio should help in off hours. Take a brace on the fact that the place does not suit you and remember that you are a soldier in a war and not a girl on a vacation. If your work is interesting and of real value, both to you and your country, that's the main thing. If you are comfortable and safe, that's about the maximum you have the right to expect. Most soldiers are neither, so snap out of the grouch, be a soldier and make the best of it. I can remember some fearful holes and jobs I had to put up with in the last war compared to which you are in the seventh heaven of luxury and interest. Look for the good points that every place has and overlook the others. Keep your chin up, Pvt. Bug, be a soldier and make up your mind to have some fun in spite of it all. And piles of love from all four of us—Midge insists on being included—and why not?

From Mom—Apr. 25, 1945:

Saturday evening we were invited to the B's to supper, where we had creamed chipped beef on toast! Funny what we have come to, but no one is starving yet, and I actually did get a chicken for Sunday! I suppose you got the Girl Scout cookies? I didn't have any, as Katie S. could only spare me one box. I'll try to make you some more good homemade ones before long, before I run out of cooking fat.

I've enclosed a note from Carrie and I have sent her your address. I hope you get to see each other before she leaves California. I note your remark about going up to San Francisco to say goodbye to Bill—H-M-M . . . But if you were to, you could see Carrie probably and that would be fun for you both.

29 April 1945

Sunday

Dearest Carrie,

Here at last comes a letter from the biggest, most vile stinker that you know. Mom sent me your sad little note which absolutely broke my leathery heart. I've traveled around quite a lot since El Paso. We were there two months in all, and then a bunch of us went to New Orleans for our third month—till March 10. We had a wonderful time in E.P. If you will dig out that moldy old letter from December and read it, you will get an idea of how we spent our two months. It was all very gay. I met a fellow, also in Surgery Tech., who was a Chi Rho at the U. of Illinois. He and I were soul mates, and had many a discussion of Life, etc., over bottles of 3.2.

I didn't want to leave Texas especially, but looked forward to N.O. and it lived up to my expectations. The weather was hot and muggy, but the flowers were out in full force. The contrast between summer in February in N.O. and reports of blizzes at home made my enjoyment more intense. The famed French Quarter is tres, tres quaint, but awfully rundown and tenement-looking. But I suppose that adds to its charm (unquote from the Hearst-owned N.O. paper). There is one street, Royale, with nothing but antique shops and book shops, and Bourbon Street, appropriately, had one bar after another. During the day, well-dressed matrons could be seen strolling along, picking up bargains (so they thought) in old silver and quaint old jewelry, but at night the armed forces, mostly sailors, took over (also picking up bargains). Typical evening: dinner at Arnaud's or Court of the Two Sisters which is a wonderful outdoors patio with flowers and trees and fountains, and bugs, unfortunately. Dinner consisted of very good, but very hot, Creole food. They drench everything in horseradish. After sitting over our brandy and coffee, listening to soft music and feeling the welcome cool evening breeze wafting through the old willows (I'm outdoing myself, huh?) we would find that it was 8:15 and tear over to the Auditorium for the ballet, an opera, or the Symph, free via the Red Cross. Then after a cultural fling, we would go back to Bourbon Street, pick up some sailors, and make the rounds of the dives— real dives, too, with hot Negro bands and ancient strip-tease gals who were absolutely killing. Along about 1:30, through our alcoholic haze, the grim fact of bed-check would penetrate, and so, hopping a Yellow Dragon (only in N.O. they were red), we would barrel out to the hospital and another Saturday night checked off.

The tenth of March we left for our respective homes. God, it was good to be back after five months. I'd never been away from home that long before. Final week at the U was just starting, but I managed to see everybody; ate at the Dunge,[57] went over to the *Daily* office and saw Harry McC. and Terry C. (remember that goof?), had a fight with Joseph. Very satisfactory vacation, yes indeed. Then the gloom descended on me; I came to LA. But on that I won't dwell. Listen, when are you leaving San Fran for the Middle West? We must have a big old reunion. My Chi Rho friend is being shipped out of the States in about a month, his POE being Camp Beale, and I promised to meet him in S.F., but I don't want to share one three-day pass. It would be too hectic and we couldn't pile up the bull to our heart's content. On the other hand, if you are leaving soon, it will have to do, unless, of course, you could make it down here. At any rate, some sort of meeting *must* be effected.

---

[57] The Dungeon was a popular eating spot in the basement of Dayton's Campus Store on Fourteenth Avenue Southeast near Fourth Street in Dinkytown, as the commercial district on the north side of the University of Minnesota campus was called. The restaurant on the top floor of Dayton's was called The Tent.

Please overlook my shortcomings and answer me quick-like. Give
my regards to your Mom.

All my love,

If this is incoherent, it's because I wrote this just before sack
time, and everyone in the barracks was having a pre-lights-out
fling—much noise and yelling and radios, etc.

30 April 1945

Monday

Dearest Mom and Dad,
    This last week has beat me in, muchos. That little headache I
was telling you about was not sinus-caused, it seems. Monday
morning I went on sick-call and the EENT man looked and tapped
and asked for a smear, which I couldn't give him, and finally sent
me over to X-Ray to discover the hidden source of trouble. On
Tuesday, with the X-Rays showing normal, El Doctor starts insinuating that I'm psycho; "Where do you work? Are you happy? Do
you have any worries?" All the time he's leering at me, rubbing his
hands and mentally booking me up to be psyched. "Case #504:
Nervous in the Service!" But I fooled him. As a last resort he gave
me an eye test, and I have astigmatism. He advised me to wear my
glasses all the time. My aches aren't as bad as they were, but still
kind of nagging. I'm used to it by this time. Maybe my glasses need
some adjusting. Wouldn't I look cute in round steel-rimmed GI's?
"There goes that grim WAC that works in Surgery!" What really is
the matter with me is malnutrition and no vitamins. This mess is
quite the foulest I've ever eaten in. Of course I eat hardly anything
for breakfast because I don't have time, and nothing for dinner
because it makes me ill, but the thing is they don't have any
vegetables or salads. How about sending me some vitamin tablets?
    Calendar of Evening Activities: *Monday:* Accompanied Gee-
Gee, the Blonde Bomber of Beaumont, and Classy Chassis Brad to
Van Nuys' "The Brass Rail" which is tres haute monde and comme
il faut and stuff like that there. This high-class establishment is
patronized almost solely by the members of the armed forces and
by Van Nuys' dregs. The latter are admitted purely for the

entertainment of the regular clientele. After paying for one beer, the GIs took over. Those dopes tell the waitress to "bring those WACs another round of whatever they're drinking." I had six glasses of beer brought me within ten minutes. Don't worry, I gave five of them away. Some sailor gave me a pink drink called a Rosy Joe or something, kind of good. We sang songs, had a good time, and were home at a reasonable hour. *Tuesday:* Bowling with Gray, Cummings, and two Detachment men at Birmingham's swank bowling alleys. They are really very nice; four alleys, nicely decorated interior, coke machine and lots of pool tables. Got some fine points on pool from two ASTPs, Red and Ole, who worked in Surgery last week. Ole is very talented; he can do all sorts of tricks with string, makes designs with a twist of the wrists—very cagey.

Wednesday: I was on emergency call in Surgery and had to stay in. Slept from 5:30 to 11:00, woke up and put up my hair, and hit the sack again. But, my luck, had to get up at 3:30 a.m. to help Daddy (the Major) with some blood transfusions and never got back to bed again. *Thursday:* Dragged myself to that Hepburn-Tracy movie. It wasn't bad, but Katie is getting to look a bit on the haggy side, not nearly as good looking as she used to be. *Friday:* Watched a leg amputation today. The poor guy had gangrene in the upper thigh and also his popliteal artery (behind the knee) had been severed, causing severe hemorrhage. He's had about ten transfusions since he's been here (two weeks). It saved his life, though—the amputation, I mean, but it was ghastly to watch. A kidney in an emesis basin is impersonal and anatomical, but a leg sitting on the floor by the laundry hamper is gruesomely intimate. This evening at Company meeting, the Ma'am informed us that we had to move from Nurses' Quarters to an empty ward. Every month, on the month, I always say. So I packed up my increased pile of stuff, and prepared for the trek.

Saturday: The Move. Groan. We are now in open barracks, after four months of luxury. There's a most obnoxious woman with a radio that she keeps on full blast the whole time, but I suppose I shall be immune to that after a while. I can always retaliate with symphony, which would kill her, no doubt. The bad thing about this ward is, it's immediately next door to the Post theater, and every night there's a constant stream of fellows past the door and outside the windows, so we have to keep the shades pulled all the time. Wonder what the view is like? Brad had a party tonight at her brother's apartment with fellows from her ward. We drank (me, very little—I'm on the wagon except just enough to keep me from being a social blight) and danced, and after a while we piled in their car and went down to Chinatown. It's just a nest of Chop Suey joints, not at all authentic. We rode on Ferris Wheels and Loop-o-Loops at the Shanghai Amusement Park, and then went across the street to Too Lung Far's and had fried shrimp and eggs Foo Yong. What people won't do to their stomachs. G.G. and I stayed at Brad's and came back Sunday afternoon when I slept—ahh. Today is just another day with the notable exception that I am writing letters. Wrote one to Carrie too—I'm a stinker to have put it off for so long.

About San Francisco and Bill: Mom, you have absolutely no cause to worry. He's too fat to get excited about, so this is purely platonic and I mean really. But he is a swell guy and I would like to see him before he goes. So there! EC's mad at me because I haven't written. She claims something odd must be happening to my mail. I enjoy Mike's letters and cards no end. How about that hot date with Suzy? Give with the gore, Michael . . . Haven't been to the Canteen lately, Mike, so I'm kind of low on autographs, but that's the only place I'll get them. I'm not the aggressive hound-type. Say, don't forget the "Fighters Digest"—I missed it last week (and you may quote me). Also (plug) I got the *St. John's Salute,* and believe it or not it's kind of fun to hear what's happening to my old friends from Y.P. Flop [Young People's Fellowship]. Of course, I just skim through the dear Rector's letter in which he describes the basement of the church as the "undercroft" . . . Boom . . . Harrumph! . . . and tells all about how they got evicted from their garage. Maybe the landlord is foreclosing cause Edna won't marry him. More ciggie-butts coming Yorkside plenty soon-like [home to the York Avenue house]. Good old Uncle Sugar. Say Mom, I'm not bitter about Ruthie. What the hell do you think I am? I think it's marvelous about our High Hag. She's going to be a famous woman if she doesn't watch out.

Sack time now, so kisses and hugs all around for Dad, Mom, Mike and Midge.

P.S.: Just haven't had time to read yet, Dad, but will post you when I'm embarked on Barzun [*Teacher in America*]. I can manage the *New Yorker* and *Newsweek,* and I read the *LA Times* (*not* a Hearst paper, thank the Lord) every morning to keep up on the San

Francisco Conferences [planning for the United Nations]. I hope Russia stops being stinky and that nobody else starts anything. That just *has* to come off. Maybe I'm an idealist but if only people would get together, even a little bit, then my kids won't have to be cut up twenty years from now. Wasn't the Mussolini episode dramatic? Just like E. Phillips Oppenheim.[58] Great stuff. Now we want Adolph!

3 May 1945

Thursday

Dearest Family,

Just a mid-week note to let you know I'm still alive although sometimes I doubt it myself. The last three nights and tonight I have spent lying on my little bed valiantly answering letters or rather trying to. I still have a formidable list, but I've checked off Ruthie and Carrie—poor dear; I haven't written her since my second week at Beaumont. Cut my hair tonight. I'm tired of looking so much like a French poodle that I've become notorious among the enlisted personnel of Birmingham. Started *Teacher;* very good but so packed with pertinent remarks that my head swims. I have to read under difficult conditions: radios, laughing, arguments, bad light, uncomfortable bunk, and stuff. But I does my best. Through all my troubles I am sustained by the hope that the war, V-E and V-J, will end soon and then I can go back to being a college girl, which, with all its vicissitudes, suits me better than the rut I am now in. Looking at pancreases and hemorrhoids every day is kind of spoiling my appetite. Down with medicine! Give me literature or give me death! Nothing has happened really. I'm relaxing now with a Lord Peter that I hadn't read before, *Whose Body?*, one of the early ones.[59] Please send some coat hangers. Also, don't stop sending *Newsweek;* I like it. Thanks for the two bucks. Haven't gotten around to sending the cigs yet, but will soon.

Much love and affection,

[58] On April 28, 1945, Mussolini was captured and hanged in a public square by the Italian partisans. E. Phillips Oppenheim wrote international spy thrillers.
[59] Lord Peter Wimsey was the protagonist of the mystery novels by the British writer Dorothy Sayers.

From Mom—May 3, 1945:

Sat. night [April 28] we went to the Westgate Theatre and heard the "Germany has surrendered" rumor there, but of course at the 10 p.m. broadcast found it was not so. Just had your letter this morning and was so glad to get it. I sure will send you some vitamins. It's the bunk that they don't give you a good diet. What the heck are we doing without so many things for, if it isn't so that people in Service can have good food? You better drink more milk and whenever you are out to eat, concentrate on salads and greens. Your account of the amputation sounded gruesome, but that's to be expected in a hospital with battle casualties. I hope the German surrender comes soon. Then bloodshed will stop in Europe at last and some of the men may get rest and relief before they go to the Pacific area. I agree with you on the San Francisco conference. Why are we so afraid of Russia and why can't each nation give a little more?

Mike is fine and I'll urge him to write again soon. He is cultivating a sort of up-swept hairdo in the front—spends much time combing it back. Meanwhile it is growing far too long in the back and by his ears! What an age!

From Dad—May 6, 1945:

Your last letter was good and more in the groove. Sorry to hear about the move, but that's the Army. "Muck the men about a bit, Sergeant!" The war news is so super-good that one can hardly believe it after all these years of waiting. It really looks as though the end were in sight, even though the Japs may take a bit of beating. They can't hold out long alone against what the boys will throw at them, so you may be home again within the next four or five years! Remember, it's "Duration plus 6."

6 May 1945

Sunday

Hello, little Family,

Sunday evening is here again, and I'm perched on the edge of my bunk trying to write a coherent letter through the general conversation, radios, and roaring around. I gotta practice being detached from the mob if I ever expect to get any reading or writing done. My letter of Thursday covered the week pretty well. Friday evening we had a Company meeting. We got jumped on for not cleaning the latrine right, and the Ma'am got sidetracked into telling us the history of her three years in the Army—very interesting. We heard about ratings; maybe we will have a separate TO and then again maybe not. Lots more people have drifted in here, all lousy with stripes, of course. We've about thirty-six in the Company now, and sixty-five are expected within the next two weeks. The spirit of Hollywood, fresh from Fort Oglethorpe.[60] How jolly that will be! Hope some of them are young. Everyone in the Detachment except our little gang from N.O. are old Grammas—very fuss-budgety and impossible to associate with. After a Company meeting, Brad and I were starved, so went in to Van Nuys and had steak and beer and were back early for bed.

Saturday I couldn't bear the thought of staying on the Post, so I called up Grace and said, "I'm a-comin," and she said "OK." I jumped on a streetcar, after first getting a ride to Van Nuys on a jeep—whee!—and she met me at the car line and took me up to their little house. It's on what used to be an alley, but was made into a street. Perched halfway up a hill, with a tiny little terrace behind the house, and a perpendicular backyard. The house was messy but quite comfortable—books and music and papers all over the place. Mr. S. (to be hereinafter known as Dick) is quite a character. I didn't know he was a policeman. He had to leave early on a special detail, but he came back early. He looks like the Englishmen people draw for caricatures—beak of a nose, sardonic mouth drawn down at the corners, little moustache. He's a swell guy, has a dry sense of humor, and very pleasant. When I arrived, I had a sandwich and tea, and then jumped into my PJ's and bathrobe, played the piano, talked to Grace, and then settled down in my studio-couch bed for a good go with Lord Peter. Mr. S. (I mean Dick—I guess I'm too New England to be informal right off the bat) came back after awhile and regaled us with stories of all the drunks he's picked up, while we had tea and Triscuits. Then we started an argument about the relative merits of British and American law. I didn't know too much about it, but we had a lovely argument. They went to bed, and I read real late on my comfy couch. Slept late the next morning and got up to a huge breakfast of wheat cakes, eggs, fried potatoes, and sausages. This was attended by Harriet, a fat, jolly Phy-Ed teacher friend of Grace's. We all sat around and did crossword puzzles till Dick had to go to church to play the organ. Then I had

---

[60] Fort Oglethorpe, Georgia, had a basic training school for Wacs.

a lovely "hot, surging bath" with pine-oil in it. After which I puttered around till about 11:30 when Grace and I left to go out to dinner. She works every Sunday at that Information Booth I told you about from four to ten, so we met her friend who works with her and had a good lunch at the "Gourmet" which is of the same chain as "Le Petit Gourmet" in Chicago. It's about the third meal I've really enjoyed since I hit this place. By then it was time for them to go, so I caught my streetcar and came home to do laundry. Us kiddies went to the show, and now here I am. I forgot to mention that they gave me the key to their house, so I can drop in anytime I want, to sleep and eat, and do everything I want to. Isn't that nice? As you can see, I enjoyed my weekend lots. Now back to the old grind and our eternal battle with the head nurse. We all told the Ma'am about her, though, and something definite is going to be done about her. Criticism about our work is bad enough, but personal slams I won't put up with and neither will the other kids. Sack time now.

All my love,

11 May 1945

Friday

A Special Delivery Letter
> "Oh Mother dear you are so kind;
> A better Mother I could not find."

Dearest Mom,
This will arrive some time after Mother's Day but you know how I am pressed for time during the week. Anyhow, I wanted you to have a special letter all for you. I'd rather call Sunday, but the phones will indubitably be crammed with other GIs calling their Moms, who are more deserving of a call home than I, with a furlough just two months ago. Not that they miss their mothers any more than I do, because nobody could. There's nothing I wish more than for the war to be over so I could come home for good. Then we could do the dishes together, have whistling duets, go shopping, take walks, go to the "moom pichers," talk, and carry on, just the way we did before I left. Of course, letters are the next best thing to seeing and talking to someone, especially this last month

when I was so fractious and ornery and needed advice and snapping out so badly. Sometimes after a letter of giving it to me straight, you add an apology for being crabby. That's silly, Mom. That's your duty, with a silly brat far away from home who needs a crack on the bean. Besides, it sounds so good and home-like to hear you spouting off and getting in a small twit over what I'm doing or what you think I'm doing. Not that I think of you as always crabbing but—heck, you know what I mean. What I mean is I wish I were home and could talk over my problems with you, but my letters of parental advice will have to suffice (pome), and I value them as much if not more than the newsy ones. This isn't the first Mother's Day I've spent away from my Mother, but I hope it's the last for a good long time. I want you to know (you probably do already) that I can't imagine what it would be like to have a different kind of Mom. You are the best there is, and I always feel quite superior when I think of other people's mothers. They are OK in their way, but they can't beat Mommy Mouse.

> All my love,
> Annie

12 May 1945

Saturday

Dearest Carrie,

My God, woman, did your letter ever sound prim and refined. What has happened to my old pal to whom I told my juiciest tidbits? Maybe it's just a reaction to my exuberant vulgarity (can't remember now just what I did write, but it must have been *something* to set you off like that) which sounds worse on paper than in person. I'm really not so much of a loose woman as you might think. I must explain the GI psychology regarding social relationships. It's quite different from that accepted in civil life and often difficult to understand and be sympathetic with. Even my Mom is still skeptical. But this must be expounded in person, or I will leave you in a worse mire of misunderstanding than you are now.

Bad news for us. When I wrote you I was under all kinds of erroneous impressions. The deal on three-day passes is thusly: Only seventy-two hours allowed; can't go further than two hundred and fifty miles from the Post. Damn! It's unthinkable that we can't see each other before you go back to Minnesota. After these years of you flitting around, I finally get somewhere near your section of the country and then to have GI regulations rear their ugly heads is frightfully disgusting and something *must* be done. But God knows what. I do know that a good friend of my Mom's, who is a swell woman living in LA not so far away from here and who is very casual and used to people flitting in and out, would be more than glad to put us both up for a few days (me on a three-day pass). She is a school teacher and is never home during the day, so we'd have the house to ourselves. And I would love to split train fare for you, cause I'm comparatively rich at present. I never have much to spend my money on, anyhow. Now, how about that? Can't you just skip school for a couple of days over a weekend or something. Please consider this deal. We've got to get together. I won't go on much more about my life here (God help my poor self), because I want to get this in the mail soon-like. To reach me, call Birmingham General Hospital in the Van Nuys phone book, and ask for Extension 260 or WAC barracks. I'd love to see your Mom.

Goodbye and muchos love,
Pansy

P.S.: This is not an informational letter, but an arranging one. I really can do much better, you know.

13 May 1945

Sunday

Dearest Family,

Oh hum! I have just finished an immense ironing and am completely pooped. This has been a terrifically exhausting week, emotionally and physically. *Monday:* Nothing special at work—just the same ol' routine. Then in the afternoon things popped. "Sadist-ky," our stinker chief nurse, called us into the Nurses' room and proceeded to give us a one-hour lecture, completely un-called for. First off, she said we couldn't use the Nurses' room except to change into our whites. Since that room was the only place we could smoke in, that really dealt us out. Her reason was that officers and enlisted men (women in this case) could not mix. "I'm *sure* you all come from nice families . . . It's not that we're any *better* than you are . . ." God! Also, she didn't like our work, and so forth and so forth for an hour during which time we didn't say one word, but we thought plenty. That deal clinched things. For the whole eight weeks we'd been there, she'd been picking on us, making slimy personal cracks, and riding, and nagging us till at the end of the day we were wrecks. I never bothered to tell you all this before because it was so petty, but very nerve-wracking. Anyhow, we decided that we were damn well fed-up with the whole business. Besides which, on the wards we would get more time off, would get to see people instead of being cooped up all day.[61]

When we got back to our ward-barracks, we got the jolly news that we were to move again on the morrow, so we spent the evening packing everything up again. Happy day. Also, we had to go over to the new barracks and clean the whole place. What a mess it was. *Tuesday:* V-E Day, May 8: We didn't have to go on duty till the afternoon shift.[62] We spent the morning throwing footlockers and barracks bags and suitcases on and off trucks, and sweeping and arranging footlockers and cleaning the latrine. But we are now officially installed in "Pneumonia Gulch." We have cement floors, lovely draughty ones, and the dear place is heated (?) by two infinitesimal oil stoves. But the footlockers, wall lockers, beds, and bedding are all brand-new, and all of us young kids from La Garde are in a bunch in the back. It's sort of gay, being back in a barracks again, as I said to Dad on Saturday. We spent the evening singing and yelling and having a gay time.

Wednesday: We all went to the Personnel Officer and asked for a transfer to the wards, and he said he'd do it. We told him what the matter was, and he vowed he'd talk to the Major and get it fixed up. None of the kids, fellows and us, can stand it up in Surgery. The

---

[61] My resentment of the army's caste system added to my already strong feminist views on being considered a second-class citizen because of being female. The system, resented by millions of men as well as by women, was quite simply that officers, in addition to being bosses or managers in a work situation, were somehow better educated, nicer, more worthy, more exalted than nonofficers. This ancient aristocrat-versus-peasants arrangement was formalized into a list of army rules restricting any social dealings between officers and enlisted people, whether men or women. It took some time to learn the intricacies of the system, how to deal with it, and how to outwit it.

[62] V-E Day (the end of the fighting in Europe on May 8, 1945) was not a day for a lot of celebrating on the West Coast, probably because of the focus on the Pacific war that, as far as we knew, had no early prospect of being terminated. The hospital authorities did not schedule any special ceremonies, and it was just another work day for us. It was good news, but not really the end of the war.

atmosphere is so horrible and tense that it's impossible to do any
work and still remain sane. Besides Sadist-ky picking on us, she
jumps on the fellows who've been doing that kind of work for about
three years, and know what they're doing. The Major and nurses
are always fighting about sterile technique and draping methods,
and there's always some big argument between the Major and Sgt.
Tony about how he should handle the enlisted personnel, and we're
always being called together and being jumped on for something.
The fellows are all going to ask for transfers, too. You just don't
have any idea how it is to try to work under such conditions—
arguing and bickering and lecturing and nagging constantly. I
really feel as though I were going psycho and so does everyone else
there. What a joint. All of us like the work, but the conditions are
really unbearable. Anyhow, Wednesday night, Baggy and I were so
jubilant over our release from the nut house that we jumped into
our uniforms and went down to Hollywood with a bunch of the
kids. We went to a lot of places, including the Palladium where we
heard Tony Pastor's Orchestra, and also a place where the bar is like
a Merry-Go-Round. You sit on seats and the whole thing goes
round and round. It was so funny to see all the seats filled with
people, all drinking and none of 'em saying a word. All stoned and
sitting at this silly bar revolving slowly around.

   Thursday: Another nerve-wracking day in Surgery. Just the
usual bickering going on still. In the evening I did a big fat washing.
Also, we had Company meeting. The Ma'am is getting more GI
every day and is now treating us like Basics. We got fourteen new
kids just in from Oglethorpe. Why a bunch of adult women can't do
a job that they were trained to do, in peace, and without being
treated like and jawed at like juvenile delinquents in reform school,
I do not know. We get it all day in Surgery and then we get it after
hours. Our hair style is wrong. They don't like our attitudes. Our
clothes aren't right . . . on and on. Everyone in the Detachment is
ready to blow their tops. All you hear in the barracks is Gripe,
Gripe, Gripe first thing in the morning and last thing at night. OH,
Birmingham Jail is quite a place, let me tell you. We were restricted
Thursday to clean up a whole 'nother barracks for the new
kids—this besides Company meeting and my washing!

   Friday: More whoop-de-do in Surgery. Lt. A. told Cooper that
they were going to try and transfer Sadist-ky within two weeks and
to stick it out till then. But now the Major is up on his high horse,

so things are even worse than before. This evening, Cooper, Baggie and I, and Boyko, and Felix, and Chacon all went out to celebrate our victory over Sadist-ky. We drove way up the Valley, pretty scenery when you could see through the fog, to a little joint. No one was there but us, and we sat around drinking beer, playing the slot machines, dancing, and having a gay old time. That was really fun because we didn't have "dates," we were just all in a bunch and all knew each other. *Saturday:* More bitching in Surgery. It was practically unbearable this day. I came to work in the morning, feeling very jolly and eager-beaver, and by afternoon I felt as though I had been put through a wringer. We were restricted because of patients coming in, so I spent the evening writing letters. *Sunday:* Had to get up and go to work at nine. We thought there would be a lot of cast changing to do, but all we had were two appendectomies and a couple of casts. I got off early and ironed and read this afternoon. Just finished *Apartment in Athens* [by Eric Ambler], a queer book: depressing, yet optimistic.

This has turned out to be a griping letter, I'm afraid, but all this trouble is so predominant in my mind that the funny happenings I just can't remember to tell you. And I'm so tense inside (before, I was apathetic, but now it's the other way) that when I do laugh I'm hysterical. Manic-depressive, no doubt. There's a fellow in Surgery named Truitt from South Carolina who can tell the rarest stories about the doctors, and what goes on during operations. He's such a fool, but a clever one. The minute he opens his mouth I start laughing and can't stop. Saturday the Major had us all in a big bunch giving out with the fat lecture, and there was a fly whizzing around him. Finally it settled on his chest. So Truitt walks over to the cabinet, gets a fly swatter, and calmly smacks the Major in the chest, and incidentally kills the fly. All the Major said was "You got him!" looking down and going on with his harangue. Gosh, Dad, it was swell to hear your voice, even though it did sound kind of cracked over the phone. I'm going to call Mom on Father's Day, now! I was so sure you'd all be home because it was right after lunch. Of course I forgot that you were two hours later than us here. Hope you appreciate it, cause they sure soaked me plenty.

The weather continues foul—fog, and it rained this morning. Honestly, I'd rather have rain and snow and stuff interspersed with nice days, than this monotonous putridness. Down with California. My hair is acting worse than it did in N.O. and wearing a turban all day in Surgery doesn't help it, either. Guess what? I finally heard from Carrie; I wrote her directly when I got that sad little note she wrote you. But things look dark. I found out that we can't get passes to go as far as San Francisco. We can only go 250 miles from the Post, and S.F. is 500 miles away. Mom, now you don't have to worry about me seeing William. The only way Carrie and I could see each other is if she could scrape up the dough to come down and Grace would probably put us up for a couple of days. I wrote her last night, and am now waiting to hear. Also got a nice long letter from Mu. She has high hopes that her husband will be discharged soon; he has enough points. I only have eight— thirty-six more to go. My fondest hope is that Japan folds within the next six months, and then we can all go home and forget about the damn Army. My first six months were swell, but this stinks. Don't think it's just me, people. Gals here who have been overseas one and a half years, and have hash marks, and have been all over the US on Army Posts, say that this is the most gruesome place they have ever been, and they're ready to quit. Blah, Blah, Blah.

Love you all lots,

P.S.: I feel well physically now, no more headaches. I wear my glasses faithfully even though I look like a goon.

From Mom — May 8, 1945:

One part of the war is over, thank God. It hardly seems possible that it can be true after so long a time. This morning we heard the President's proclamation; then the air-raid siren downtown started going and many whistles and bells. In a way it was sort of an anti-climax after yesterday (Monday) and the fiasco of the way the news was released. Minneapolis apparently is taking it in the usual self-contained way. Of course I have not been downtown but I doubt people are throwing torn-up telephone books all over the streets. Paul and Michael went out to school and I took the President's advice to "work, work, work"—so I scrubbed the kitchen floor and waxed it, and cleaned up the rest of the house. Dashed over on foot to the grocery before it closed at ten, to get some bread and things. Most of the stores have closed.

The weather has been cold and windy and snow has blown through the air too. What a May!—and after a high of 81 on Sunday. We hung out the flag early and it is whipping madly in the wind. I listened a lot to the radio—lots of brave words have been spoken and I only hope the nations live up to half of them. I wish some sort of surrender could be imposed on Japan without the terrible casualties we are bound to have. I think I'll go to church at 8:00 this evening, and then our friends are coming in to help us open up the bottle Dad bought for this day two or three years ago. Let's hope and pray it won't last too much longer and you can come home, along with millions of others much worse off.

From Dad—May 13, 1945:

Tuesday evening your mother and I went to a service at St. John's which was good, and then the Seversons and Petitclairs came in to have a nip from the bottle I had been saving for the Nazis! Wednesday drill in the evening; I celebrated by asking for my discharge at the end of this month, which I can take, as it will give me two years' service. I have had a lot of fun in the Guard and hope I have done some good, but with the extra summer activities coming on, I shall find it a bit of a load to carry at 50 plus.

I am glad you have gotten lined up with Grace and like her. She used to be an old peach and I am glad she has not changed. The liking seems to be quite mutual, as she wrote all kinds of nice things about you. A place where you can go and relax for a bit is a perfect life-saver and I am glad you have one. I used to miss it so much during the last war. The Nazi flop has been such good news. Now, if only our Big Brains are on the job, I think we can wind up Japan before too long. I hope the Bourbons [extreme right-wing conservatives] in this country and England do not get into the saddle and mess us up with Russia. I have always been afraid of them and with FDR out of the picture they are going to do their best to get in again. However, time will tell and some day Annie Bug will be home again, if only to rush in and out!

22 May 1945

Tuesday

Dearest Family,

This is disgraceful; Tuesday and a letter not off to you yet, but this should make amends. First: the situation in Surgery. Very amazing; things have calmed down no end. Sadist-ky has been very subdued the past week and the Major hasn't started anything, either. Maybe it's just the lull before another storm. I hope not. Of

course, we were very busy all last week and there wasn't much time
to sit around and have petty squabbles. I scrubbed alone on three
cases, and managed quite well. Anyhow I didn't get kicked out for
contaminating stuff, and Captain C. called me "Honey"; he does
that to everyone, but it shows when he's in a good mood.

This last week has also been very gay and social. Monday and
Tuesday I stayed home and read and did laundry. Tuesday evening
I was on call in Surgery and so got Wednesday afternoon off. On
the spur of the moment, I decided to pop over to Grace's and play
the piano and mess around, because I didn't think anyone would be
home. Dick was, though; he'd just gotten back from policing. I must
explain that he is in the Volunteer Reserve Corps which has been
filling in the places of the men in service. It's a full-time job, and
he's a regular policeman, but it's not a permanent thing. There was
a gruesome murder a couple of weeks ago here in LA—matricide—
and Dick was one of the two officers who went to investigate. He
told me all about it. Gore, Gore. I played the piano while he took a
bath, and I listened while he gave a lesson to a little girl, and then
we played duets till Grace got home. Her mother was with her, very
pleasant old lady. We had a good Scrap supper for which I made a
fancy salad. They are all so swell to me, just as if I were their own
daughter. Did I tell you that they're giving me a little back room to
use for my own? Dick is all full of plans to move the ice box so there
will be more space, and he's going to rig up a closet so I can keep
stuff there. At the end of this epistle I will list some stuff I wish
you'd send out. Also, Dick dug out his motorcycle boots and gave
them to me for riding boots. They're very swish black leather ones.
But guess what we found down in the toe? The remains of a bottle
of Puerto Rican rum one of Grace's friends had brought back last
summer. So we celebrated with Cuba Libres before supper. Tuesday
evening the Danny Kaye Show with Harry James was broadcast
from the Rec Hall.

Time out for mail call, and just got your letter saying you heard
the show. It wasn't funny and I agree with you—the only reason we
laughed was that Kaye made funny faces, and the prop men went
through such antics to get applause, that it was sort of amusing.
The half-hour before they went on the air was much better. Harry
James played lots and the famous trumpet practically blasted us out
the back wall. Friday I went to the movies when I should have
ironed. That day I got another letter from Mary Alice, a Kappa

[Kappa Gamma] from the U of M who goes with Dave D., inviting me over for the weekend. There are four kids that have a jolly little house about four miles south of Hollywood. So Saturday I got on a bus, and whizzed over. We had supper, and then sat around, played bridge, and gabbed about people from the U, most of whom I didn't know. These gals are very smooth deals and knew many men and gals that just weren't in my realm. I was an eager beaver, and not a big smoothie. Sunday we went over to Beverly Hills, rented bikes, and rode all over the residential section. Lovely big homes, prettier than Rolling Green [a subdivision of Edina, a Minneapolis suburb], because the section is built up on the mountains, on the other side of which is Van Nuys and the Valley. Beverly Hills is a tres exclusive "area," very much the way I imagined Hollywood should be. Lots of snazzy little shops, and big ones like Bullock's Wilshire, Haggarty's, Sak's Fifth Avenue, I. Magnin, etc. Many gay [meaning lively] night clubs. The whole place is very glamorous. Sunday evening we went to a fancy restaurant called "Tail O' The Cock." Speciality of the house is a rum cocktail, tall and cool like Planter's Punch, with a big red feather stuck in. Had French fried shrimp . . . yum.

Last night I had planned to stay in and write letters, but in the morning, Carrie's mother called up. She's down visiting Aunt Hattie, so we went out to dinner in Hollywood and had a real good old visit. Mrs. G. is still in a defense plant; she checks stuff. Carrie's dad is still out in the Admiralties [Admiralty Islands], likes his work. He's in charge of Jap prisoners. Mrs. G. had a lot of pictures in color that he sent. Many natives, and palm trees in the best tradition. Carrie is coming down the end of June and Grace said we could stay at her house. I will get a three-day pass, so we really ought to have a gay time.

News Flashes: We have our new work uniforms at last. They are extremely stylish and well made. Nice cotton material, heavier than Chambray, but looks like it; kind of a rosy-brown beige color, and fit like a sport dress from Lord and Taylor. We are very swish now. The weather has changed. We can see the mountains every day now and the sun shines and all is well. California is pretty after all. It's amazing how a sunny morning changes my outlook on life. Big fat rumor: we will get our T/5's by the end of the month. Ha! Last week fifty kids came in from Oglethorpe, just out of Basic, and quite rough customers—Hag Bags! Oh, well. All of Surgery is going on a Beach Party at Santa Monica this Friday. Should be fun—nurses and everybody. Thank you all heaps for the flood of mail this week. Very cheering it is to get letters almost every other day. Just had my "vibrations" read by an Englishwoman who is a Sergeant in our Detachment. She's on CQ tonight. She told me all sorts of amazingly true things about my personality, like my always wanting to rearrange people's rooms, and decorate. Also—hold your breaths—I'm to get a proposal very soon and will be married before the year is out. Pant, pant!

I'm very sorry for all you people's physical troubles. Hope you clear up soon. Me, I'm brimming with health now; those vitamins are marvelous. Write me all about the farm-hunt, all the details of what you find. I'm muchly interested. I *still* don't have my Class A summer uniforms yet, darn. I'm so sick of my ODs. List of clothes I'd like: When I'm at Grace's I'm gonna be a civilian, so there![63] Peach dress, green plaid suit, brown and white striped suit, spectators, white linen hat, white gloves, white purse, green pottery fish pin, pearls, green coat. Try to send this before Carrie comes. How 'bout this? But I'm tired of wearing khaki and everyone out here has such smooth clothes that I can't stand it another minute.

> Goodbye and much love and
> kisses,
> Annie

27 May 1945

Sunday

Dearest Family,

This has been a very quiet week; stayed in with the exception of Friday evening. No upsets in Surgery this week, either. I guess Snotsky is scared of us. Lots of ops and I scrubbed on about two a

---

[63] In California the strict rules about military dressing were beginning to be relaxed, even flouted, for off-duty hours, at least for women. The foolish aspect of my concerns about civilian clothes was that, once off the military post, service women were a rarity. The vast majority of women *were* civilians, and we in our civvies would look just like all other women. The army had me so indoctrinated that I really had to restrain myself from saluting an officer on the street while I was wearing normal clothing.

day. I was especially on the beam in a hernia case, snapping hemostats right and left, and ready with suture, scissors, and sponges like mad. After the op when they are sewing up, the tension is relaxed and they usually chat and joke over the prostrate patient. They discovered that everyone in on the case was from the South, with the exception of me. Truitt said, "She's a damyankee— from Minnesota." Whereupon Captain C. spoke up: "Oh, did you take your training with the Mayos in Rochester?" Heh! He thought I was a nurse! Went to a lot of movies on the Post this week. There's a moron patient who's been pursuing me for some time under the illusion that I'm the woman for him. As long as he stuck to kicking in fifteen cents for the pictures, that was OK, but when he started mangling my hand and whispering in my ear all during the show, "Honey, kin I kiss ya?" I decided that he must go. Why don't I ever attract interesting men and not droops? Maybe that's my fate in life. Friday evening, Brad and the Blonde Bomber and I went into the Brass Rail, the hottest spot in the Gay White Way of Van Nuys, to absorb a little beer. Numerous characters talked to us and bought beer, including some officers (Brad's patients) who are going to take us swimming tomorrow afternoon in the private pool of a friend of theirs. Also danced at the USO. This weekend I'm on call in Surgery and so have to stay on the Post, Cuss. And that, mes cheries, is all, absolutely all, the news of note. Haven't gotten any letters to speak of except from you and Grace. She says to send all that stuff I ordered direct to her house, and then I won't have to cart it around. Listened to the Symph this afternoon. Did you hear it? Artur Rubinstein was marvelous. Oh yes, heard from Ruth K., she's now a PFC. She really deserves more than that. I'd like to see her again; she's a good kid and writes rare letters. She has a subtle sense of humor that I like. Still haven't any summer uniforms yet. Patience is the highest virtue! I'm very happy and in good spirits. Hope you are the same. How's the wart, Dad?

> All my love, little family,
> Pvt. Bug

From Dad—May 27, 1945:
   Thursday we had a dull faculty meeting. On account of the vast

increase in "A" card gas, we are to have regular Saturday work next year. I hope The Old Man has trouble with the parents. He cut Saturday work when we went down to six gallons, but now that we go back up, on go the Saturdays. Some brain.

From Mom—June 1, 1945:

Would like to send you more cookies, and may, one of these days, except that fats and oils have gone way up in point value and I'm running a bit short on Crisco, but I may be able to squeeze out enough for a batch. Today I went to a luncheon at the Women's Club given by Mrs. Alder for Natalie Watson and her mother who are visiting here. You remember, Norm Watson was out at school as head of the Lower School a few years ago and was killed in the Pacific last summer. I'm sorry for Natalie; she seems very sad still. But she's fairly young—only 31—perhaps she'll find someone else.

29 May 1945

Tuesday

Dearest Carrie,

There is mine goot friend back in the groove! Just got your letter this evening and I'm making haste to answer same. Behold below a calendar which will show you to be somewhat screwed as regards dates; you said you had your last final on Friday the 23rd, which is actually Saturday. Methinks that the next weekend will be best—namely the 30th, etc. Come in Saturday evening and I will meet the train and we can go out and have a gay dinner. Of course you realize that by the end of the month I will probably be broke. I am now—completely. Yesterday I got extravagant—went to Hollywood and bought shoes, which caused a blister—damn—and a naked [two-piece] jersey bathing suit in a mad Roman stripe of chartreuse, purple, red, black, and white. It isn't really as bad as it sounds, honest. Then, with my and Carmen's last cent, we splurged on dinner. We wanted Creme de Menthe with our coffee, but even though we dredged in our purses and brought up hidden pennies, we didn't have enough. Then suddenly our waiter, Joe, spoke up: "Girls, let me pay the rest of your check. I was in the Army once, I know how it is. You want Creme de Menthe—you shall have it!" Imagine that happening in commercial Hollywood. Tomorrow I will have a heart to heart talk with Sgt. "Benito,"[64] our sergeant in Surgery, and see if I can work a little deal and get four days off instead of three. But at any rate, come in that Saturday night. Gotta rush now—going to the Ice Capades with some fellows.

Muchos love,

3 June 1945

Sunday

Dear Family,

It's Sunday evening again and I'm home early for a change in time to toss you off a note. This has been another of my social weeks. Monday was my afternoon off, but we didn't go swimming because it was too cold. Instead, Carmen and I went into Hollywood and shopped. I bought some new shoes, brown pumps. They're tres smooth, but I've discovered that they're too small. I'm going to have them stretched, if possible, and if not I'll just have to suffer. With my last money and five dollars borrowed from Carmen, I blew it on a wild bathing suit and I do mean wild. It's jersey two-piece, and the material is white with black, red, chartreuse and purple stripes. Sounds horrible, but it's not, really. But the style is what's wild. I'm almost afraid to appear in public in it. But I've been conservative too long. With our last money, absolutely, Carmen and I went to Mike Lyman's for dinner. I had to have enchiladas because they were the cheapest thing on the menu. We wanted Creme de Menthe with our coffee, but upon collaboration with Joe, our waiter, we feared it would be too much. We dredged our purses for all our pennies and dimes, and found, alas, not enough. Suddenly Joe said, "I'll pay the rest of your check, girls. You save enough for carfare. I was in the Army once, I know how it is. You want Creme de Menthe, you shall have it!" How about that? In Hollywood, things like that just don't happen. That little episode put us in a gay mood, so we toddled over to the Canteen to see what cooked. Mike must have gotten his "Joan Crawford" [autograph] by now. That ought to hold him! There were lots of fellows there and we were the

---

[64] The sergeant in charge of the enlisted surgery staff was named Tony Mariotti, and because he was so bossy I had started calling him "Benito" after the Italian dictator, Benito Mussolini.

only two servicewomen in the place and, amazingly enough, we got danced with! I got cut in on lots. Danny Kaye was there. He gives me a large pain. He's gone completely Hollywood, very blase and not at all funny. But a clever magician and a nice man singer compensated for the twerp. We had a lovely evening, even though I came home completely broke. For two days, all the money I had was three Minneapolis car tokens. Got paid Wednesday, though, so I'm solvent again.

Tuesday evening I went to the Ice Capades with PFC Chacon, and Cpl. Felix and his civilian girl friend. They are two guys from Surgery, and we went in Felix's car, big treat, four of us squeezed in the front seat—it's a coupe. The show was good, but not as funny as the Follies (loyal Minneapolitan, me).[65] The costumes were colossal, especially a South American number which, when special lights were turned on, turned out to be luminous. Also, I liked a gal juggler. In intermission, us soldiers went out and ate hot dogs and drank beer, which I spilled down the front of my utility coat because someone jiggled my elbow. I had fun identifying the tunes and themes that the orchestra amalgamated. Faust, Oklahoma, Nutcracker Suite, Dance of the Hours, Dancing in the Dark. . . . Wednesday I went in and drank tea and chatted with Grace. She's fixed my summer off-duty dress, which I finally got. We can have short sleeves! Thursday and Friday I stayed home and did necessary tasks. This weekend found me at Grace's again. We just laid around, same as before. Dick is attempting to teach me the principles of harmony. Don't worry about recompense for meals; I give 'em ciggies.

Notes and Comment: We have a new nurse in charge of Surgery!! Snotsky is out!!! The WACs accomplished this great deed!!! New nurse is Captain McM. Snotsky took her aside and filled her full of bull against us kids (we heard her), so the Captain is sort of leery, but we are eager-beavering to show her we are a good bunch. Sgt. Tony gave me Saturday afternoon off for some unfathomable reason. I nearly collapsed when he told me I could take off. I think it's because I took his side on a couple of arguments this week. We are definitely going to get T/5 within the next few

---

[65] There were two main ice skating and entertainment shows that toured nationally. One was the Ice Capades, and the other, the Ice Follies, had been founded in Minneapolis by Roy Shipstad and Oscar Johnson and was considered the original of the ice shows.

Sunbathing in my new nude bathing suit

At Ocean Park

Brad & Doug, my pals on jaunts into LA

Bessie, Coop, & I on a break from hospital duties

Los Angeles Times photo of V-J Day at Hollywood & Vine

months. It says here. In fine print. Carrie is coming down the
weekend of June 30 and July 2 and I have a three-day pass. We shall
have a whee of a time. I've millions of things planned, but there
isn't enough time to really branch out. William doesn't think he will
be out here after all. He has chances of going to OCS; I'm hoping
for him. EC wrote that she made Mortar Board, isn't that swell? She
really deserved it. Ruthie G. must be home by now. Gee, I wish I
were back. All the kids are going East for the summer. Now if I were
on the other coast I could see 'em all. Curses on the Ninth Service
Command. Hope you are all in good health now. Try vitamins—
they did wonders for me! Goodbye now; sack time.

All my love,

From Dad—June 3, 1945:

*And there's another week gone to glory, and what super-lousy weather
for the end of it—cold and windy yesterday—about 38 degrees. Thursday I
went to Scottish Rite for the Thirty-second Degree and they managed to feed
950—heaven only knows how as there just ain't no more meat to be had in
the markets. You are lucky to be in the Army and not starving here at home.
On Friday we had a cold fall rain all day and in the evening had supper
(some weird type of fish) and music and a nice visit with the Hodgkinsons.
Saturday Monroe and I took the gals to the Club for dinner—choice of fish
or chicken!*

From Dad—June 10, 1945:

*Well, here we are again with another cold, rainy Sunday. The weather
is getting me down; nothing grows but green mold and one's morale is worth
about a dime a pound. Exams are over and school has closed, which is a
comfort. Shube Owen was back for Commencement looking OK in spite of
his stop in a Jerry [German] prison camp. I hope he is discharged and comes
back next year, but I didn't have time to say more than "howdy" to him. We
went to a WAC movie on Thursday. I do not think you would have passed
the movie (*Keep Your Powder Dry*) even though some of the scenes were
taken at Fort Des Moines. The girls are made Grade V while still in training
and, of course, ended up as Second Louies! We did a big pot roast
yesterday—real meat—and will doubtless eat on that for some time to come.*

11 June 1945

Monday

Hello, everyone!

PVT Bug radio time. And now for our slogan: "It isn't LS/MFT, it's TS/BGH!"[66] And now for our theme song: "Send me a letter; Send it by mail; Send it in care of . . . Birmingham Jail." And now for our program. Ark! Monday again after a lovely but exhausting weekend. The week itself was quite quiet. . . . Ark! How did it get to be Wednesday all of a sudden? I'm a huge heel but you no doubt will have received my Father's Day offerings before this and you may be appeased, I hope. Well, about last week, it seems very far away by now. I mostly laid around and read and gabbed except for Wednesday evening when Brad and I went on a small beer bust. Friday evening I was on call so got Saturday afternoon off.

Carmen and I went into Hollywood and spent all our money again. I had twenty dollars when I left, and four when I returned. That girl has a terrible effect on me, but we had a lovely time. We shopped and ate and walked up on Hollywood Hill looking at all the gay Bohemian Bucky Bug houses[67] and went in all the second-hand bookstores and cologne bars[68] and smelled all the smells and bought some and played all the records in record shops and had some drinks and walked around looking at people. We did this all afternoon and evening until 12:00. I bought a pretty white slip with eyelet on top and a white hankie with a violet embroidered in the corner and some sweet smell. We went up to Grace's to sleep, and in the morning we made our own breakfast because they had all gone to church. That afternoon we went up to Huntington Park [in San Marino], which is a rich man's estate, avec a library of old books like Gutenberg Bibles and Benjamin Franklin's diary, and such. Also an art gallery with fruity old English painters of the Gainsborough period. Naturally the "Blue Boy" was the center of the collection. It was a typical foul California day—lots of fog and smog. It was getting late, so we went back to Hollywood for supper,

---

[66] LS/MFT was a slogan for Lucky Strike cigarettes: "Lucky Strike Means Fine Tobacco."

[67] Personal/family slang that could be translated as "small quaint cottages." These little houses perched on the hillsides above Sunset Boulevard in Hollywood.

[68] These were small boutique-type shops selling cologne, perfume, and makeup.

passing though LA. I *hate* LA; it's dirty and depressing, filled with bums and aimless people; has no atmosphere at all. Chicago and St. Louis are dirty but they're exhilarating and real people live there. Out here, nobody seems to be normal. People walk around looking like ghosts or dope addicts. The men look like women and the women look like men and they all look half-dead. The streets are empty of cars, but filled with dirty papers, and these dreary people walk up and down, and the watery sun filters through the mist on the whole mess. Back in Hollywood, which seemed almost human after the ghastliness of LA, we had waffles and sausages, and then went to two French movies: *Meyerling,* with Charles (pant, pant) Boyer who was in wonderful form with all his own hair. The other one was *Life and Loves of Beethoven,* tres dramatic, and spoken all in whispers. Of course I couldn't understand anything except oui, and merci, and quand and avec and little snatches like that. The last two nights I have laid around hating Birmingham and trying to shut out the noise of the barracks, but not succeeding.

Notes: LRs are rife about T/5s. We are—we aren't—we are—we aren't—next week—tomorrow—next month—and so on ad infinitum. Read a drooly novel by my pal Robert Penn Warren.[69] Our Surgery Chief Nurse, Capt. McM. is a swell gal. She invites us in for coffee in the mornings, knows how to handle people. Everything is OK. Mom (*poor* Mom) must know what I mean now about penicillin shots. You would be a good case to give them to. My subjects never had any meat on their bones, and so I was always hitting them, the bones, I mean. We are eating down in the Detachment mess, "Alvin's Barn"; Alvin is Col. Miller. We have PWs for KPs and everytime they knock down the tin trays, everyone shouts, "Hooray!" It is very noisy and the food isn't as good, but we haven't got as far to walk. Thanks for the *New Yorkers.* My clothes came. I gave Carmen a style show Sunday. Civvies feel marvelous— thanks muchos! I'm getting fat. Gray and I are having a hair race to

---

[69] Robert Penn Warren, poet and novelist, spent a couple of years teaching English at the University of Minnesota in the early 1940s, and my friend, EC, and I were allowed to take his advanced poetry class while we were still freshmen. We thought he was a great teacher and loved to hear him read poetry aloud, especially T. S. Eliot, in his melodious southern accent. He was kind to the students and always had time to talk with them during his office hours, even though he was considered a famous author. I do not recall which of his novels I was reading or why I thought it was "drooly."

see who can keep from cutting her hair the longest. Keep from, longest, not cut long—that would be impossible, huh? Hope summer comes to dear old Minneapolis, and that you all get well from your various troubles *soon.*

All my love, Peoples,

17 June 1945

Sunday

Well, how is my poor pin cushion Mom? The kids in the barracks just roared when I told 'em and I do, too, whenever I think of it. Naturally, it's unpleasant, I know, and I shouldn't laugh, but it is funny to think of my Mom getting what I used to give to the poor old guy with no stomach at La Garde. I hope you're back in circulation by now. This week has been ultra quiet. I laid around reading and fooling and not doing a durn thing all week. Went to a movie Friday: *Wonder Man,* with Danny Kaye. He's funny in the movies, I must admit. Last evening I battled for a tennis racquet and went over to the handball court and played tennis with myself. Today I slept late, did laundry, and went to the movies. Met a patient who's just back from the ETO (European Theater of Operations), and we went over to the Rec Hall. They were having a sort of program. There were two Negro tap dancers who were tres sharp. After coffee and cake, we adjourned.

Summer, such as it is, has arrived. Mornings: cold, with much fog. By noon it is hot, and by afternoon, completely breathless. Evenings cool down again and we sleep under blankets. Not very good for a summer, though. The sun is so pale and hot, and the mist obscures everything. Poo to California! And that is that, my dear family. No news whatsoever, but I chug along quite happily. Maybe things will be more gay this week.

All my love,

P.S.: Just about forgot the vital thing in my life right now, namely the need for money. I've gotta have some for when Carrie comes, two weeks from now. Send me my ten dollars, and any more you can scrape up, please, please!

From Dad—June 17, 1945:

The note which accompanied the Father's Day present has left me quite dizzy. If I have found such favor in the eyes of a critical offspring, I am indeed justified. That I occasionally enrage you to an extreme is as it should be as, otherwise, our relationship would be deadly dull. Beware, however, of looking for the virtues of middle age in a twerp suitable for matrimony. Remember that your Saintly Mother has had me in training for nigh onto a quarter century come next Ramadan and she has been able to do something even with unpromising material. In return, may I state that I consider you a most satisfactory daughter, at whom I can, and do, point with pride? There, that should hold us for some time!

21 June 1945

Thursday

Haloo, family,

Just a midweek note with answers to questions and comments: Mom, I'm glad you are out of the hospital and I pray for sun for Minneapolis every night so you can get tan and feel strong again. Thank you no end for the two dollars. Now I can pay back GeeGee who loaned me two dollars; I had twenty cents left. Again I reiterate, I need money cause Carrie's coming in a week and I'm what you might call low on funds, namely broke. Mom, don't you realize that EC was suffering from final jitters? No one is normal during or after final week. New York will be just the thing to cure her. Did you know that Ruthie G. is going to be a bed-pan commando [nurse's aide] this summer? That dope! Life is quiet again this week. I'm pooped every night because we're having a big rush in Surgery. My feet ache and I have an achin' GI back from running around so much. It's really rugged. OK, OK, so you didn't look closely at the envelope. Your little daughter is now a corporal, alias a Technician Fifth Grade, with sixteen dollars more buckos a month—not till next month. I'm stripe-happy. I'll send pictures of me all decorated up right soon. Isn't it wonderful? All of the old kids got them. We can't believe it's really true at last. Whee!

All my love, peoples,
T/5 Bug: T stands for tres chic.

24 June 1945

Sunday

Dearest Family,

I'm not in a writing mood this Sunday, but I know I should, so here goes. My midweek communique gave you the great news of my lack of "privacy"—happy day. I'm now a Non-Com, and my biggest problem now is how to worm my way into the men's NCO club.[70] I'll do it yet, by Gar!

Monday: Well, it looks as though I kinda sorta fell asleep Sunday afternoon. I was so floppy yesterday, just snoozed. We dragged ourselves up and went to the evening movie, *The Corn is Green*. Dad probably wouldn't like it but Mom would. Saturday evening I had a date! He's an awfully nice fellow I met last Saturday when I was playing tennis with myself. He came over from his ward to watch me and we got to talking and walking around. I saw him around during the week and we arranged to step out, because he had some money. Mac is an Infantry foot soldier Staff Sergeant, just back from the ETO, recovering from an abdominal wound. He's interesting because he is the most typical (if such a phrase is permissable) GI I have yet run into. Vital statistics: Twenty-two, six feet tall, blonde, blue eyes, regular features, silent type. In Army three years, overseas one and a half years; from St. Louis; after high school, worked in a machine shop until drafted; tres polite, excuses himself when he swears in front of women. He was with the First Army that ran into trouble in Belgium and the North, and was wounded during the German breakthrough. One night after the movie, we ran into a guy that was in his platoon and one of the few left from the original bunch. They had a huge old reunion, and sat around shooting the breeze about all the men they knew that had "got it." It was really grim to listen to them. These guys had passes in Paris, London, Bristol, Amsterdam, and lots of other places, but they can't tell you anything about what they were like. All they remember is what they had to drink and how much. But they'll sit

---

[70] The NCO Club was for noncoms. The post had never had Wacs previous to my group's arrival, let alone Wacs with ratings: *of course* it was the men's club! I think they finally allowed women to become members, but meanwhile we Wacs could get in as "dates," and most of our male fellow workers were willing to let us tag along in. The NCO Club had beer and what we thought was a really good snack bar.

for hours hashing over some little patrol: "Remember that hill with the barn on the left? And that Jerry hidin' in the bush? Jones got his watch and I took his Iron Cross. Geez it was cold that night, too." They go on like that. Mac's main activities are talking about the war with his buddies, and getting quietly soused when he has a pass. I bet he's a bit amazed about a person like me. Things we did Saturday that he had never done before: hitchhiked into town; rode in a convertible; saw Hollywood; went to Mike Lyman's for dinner—a very smooth dump—he was awed by all the fancy people; had numerous cocktails while waiting for dinner; went to a night club. Usually, he says, he goes to a little quiet bar and just drinks and drinks; came home sober—we ran out of money. Started with seventeen dollars, but living is high as you no doubt have noticed. We had saved out three dollars for taxi-fare, but in the last month they had upped it. We emptied our wallets of all small change, and still not enough . . . a la that evening with Carmen, so the dear cab driver said he would pay the rest and even gave us back fifty cents when we got out. Ain't life wonderful? Tuesday we are going out again because he gets paid tomorrow. What a time we will have.

Got my three-day pass from the Major. I was scared to death to ask him but he was in a good mood, and I gave him a big sob story, so I'm off from Thursday afternoon till Monday morning; good deal! Carrie is coming and all is fixed up. You probably won't hear from me again till next Monday and then I will have lots of news. EC wrote me she thinks that you think I'm off my nut because I bought you presents. I'm no psycho really, I just love to shop. Thanks for the check; it saved my life because we don't get paid till I get back from pass. The weather is still gray and stinky. This place doesn't have seasons or weather really. Oh, take me away from here; I hate it most passionately. Haven't heard from my friend William in ages. He's either half-way to Okinawa or in OCS. I sure would like to know what he's doing. Got an epistle from Alta and she "just loves" the WAVES and worships the officers. Oh, you kid! She'll get over that phase soon enough. We heard a lovely rumor from various sources, like the *Army-Navy Magazine,* that WACs can get a discharge after a year's service. I can hardly wait. I just ache to get back to school and lead a civilized life again. One year of stagnation is just about enough, methinks. Well this looks as though this were all the news. Gar, what a sentence—you can see how I have deteriorated—I can't hardly speak Englitch no more. Surge is very busy lately. We work like mad all day, seven cases per, and you should see the dirty laundry. Today we had 250 hand towels, 36 operating gowns, 56 sheets, and lots more stuff. I couldn't even see where I was going when I pushed the cart down. Adios now—got to put up my hair. New address: 78th WAC Medical Company, ZI, BGH, Van Nuys, Calif.

All my love,
CPL Bug

From Dad—July 1, 1945:

Dearest "Corpy," my gosh, that I should live to see the day where I should so address an NCO! I was much amused at your description of the S/Sergt. Have I ever soldiered with his father! He sounds about 100%. I have an idea that old Themistocles, S/Sergt. of the 9th Phalanx with Gen. Alexander, Macedonian Army, Persian Theatre of Operations talked just about the same way. Humans don't change much, which is one of the nice things about them. The only thing new in the picture which I can see is a female Corporal—and that's all to the good. . . . Meat just ain't, though we had roast beef and plenty of butter in Faribault and the markets had plenty, but that's a farm center for you.

2 July 1945

Monday

Halloo Family,

This will be just a short note to let you know I'm alive. I'm so pooped out that I couldn't write you a fat letter even for cash money. Surgery is surging with cases and I was plunged deeply into the grind the minute I got back this morning. Tonight I sewed the patches on my summer uniform, which I finally got, and that did me in completely. I had the most joyous pass, Carrie hasn't changed a bit, and we jabbered and giggled and had a gay time. Poor Grace—she's a martyr to put up with us kiddies. I forgot to say that to add to my poopedness I'm stiff as a Debark after his first pass. We went horseback riding Saturday and I still haven't recovered. It takes all my effort and concentration to just walk. I've been hobbling around like a Grammaw all day. Got your postcard from Faribault. I'm anxious to hear about your journey. I'll write a long epistle tomorrow, I promise. Mike, I'll write you a letter, too.

All my love,

3 July 1945

Tuesday

Dear Chumley,

Are you stiff? I still am. I could hardly walk yesterday, and today after I'd been sitting putting up gloves for two hours, I got up and immediately fell flat on my face. Yesterday I was thinking that by the time you got on the train, I had dusted and mopped an op room, brought in the sterile supplies, put up ten pairs of gloves, and had done a surgical scrub and was handing hemostats to Major L. on a bone graft case. Such is the Army. God, are we busy! Every afternoon I get back to the barracks all hot and sweating and panting and pooped out. You should see me heaving bundles of 75 sheets, 250 wet towels, and 40 gowns around. Maybe I'll sprain my back and get a discharge—hope, hope.

Yesterday afternoon who should call but my Staff Sgt. Mac. I went over to the bowling alley to meet him, and I've discovered that he's done a Jekyll-Hyde act on me. Last week he wanted to go out, and I told him I was going on pass and said, "Call me Monday and we'll see what we can do." So yesterday he says, "Well, you told me to call, so I called." Never a word about going out. Sounded as though I'd just twisted his arm and forced him to see me. We walked around for a while, and he's suddenly become very talkative and humorous. Before, I had to do most of the conversational honors. This time he chatted away no end, and I'm beginning to be interested. I suppose he's playing hard to get. Well, he can go right ahead and play; I'm not falling for that stuff. I had enough trouble with dear Joseph. Besides, I got a long belated letter from my darling William, with a picture, today. What a man! Starts out "My Dear One," and in between a dissertation on Socialism as propounded by Oscar Wilde, O'Neill's trend towards behaviorism, and Pvt. William's views on sex in the modern world. There's my man; just the right combination of intellectuality and earthiness. But to get back to Mackey-boy. He gave me a carton of cigs (which I sent off to you today) and as we parted, he said, casually, "Well, maybe I'll see you around at the PX." I had expected a repetition of last week's pleading for a date. Damn him. But here's the pay-off. Last Saturday when we went out, he ran out of money, so I volunteered $1.50—after all he had spent $17, so I figured I could do no more than chip in something. Now, one of the gals, Sgt. Denton, teaches class to the patients, and Mac knew that I know her. Sooo, in front of all the fellows after class, he hands her $1.50 in cool cash and says, quote, "Give this to Bosanko and tell her I hope to see her again sometime." How about that? I have become a laughing stock, no less. That is a dirty trick, methinks.

Well, my dear, I must rush off and do a bit of laundry much against my will. Give my love to your Mom and have a hugely fun trip—I know you will, I'm so jealous. I've been deluged with ecstatic letters from EC the last couple of days regarding her first few days in New York. Everyone I know is lazing around and enjoying life while I slave, and do you know what I did today? Signed a paper saying I was willing to go overseas. My God, what's my trouble? Write me jolly postcards on the way so I can get more jealous, will you?

> Love and kisses,
> Pansy

4 July 1945

78th WAC Medical Company, Zone of Interior, BGH, Van Nuys, California, Wednesday

Dearest Family,

Happy holiday—none for us in the Army, of course. Everyone in the barracks is out spending their yesterday's pay, but I decided to be an Eager Beaver and stay in. Suppose you're all having a picnic in the back yard or out celebrating with someone. Wish I could be home with you-all. I've been getting tres vague letters from Yorkside lately. The first I heard of your trip north was from Mike, and I still haven't had any news about the great Faribault farm hunt, except that SMH postcard. Better get together, folksies! I'm panting for information.

Of course I haven't been too sharp myself lately but then I have a good excuse. I got my pass signed by the Major all right, and

I worked a little deal with our dear sweet First Sgt. my pal. I was on call Wednesday night so got Thursday afternoon off, and my dear Sgt. let me go out on my Class-A pass till Monday morning; thus I got more than seventy-two hours. Grace met me at the car-line Thursday afternoon with the auto and soon we were at McCollum Place greeting Carrie who had just gotten out of the shower. She hasn't changed one bit—it's been two years since we'd seen each other and we had a lovely jabber session about everyone—who's married, and such. She hadn't heard any of my stale old Stagnantte news, so I passed it all on. For dinner we went to Mike Lyman's, me in my peach dress and green coat, looking about fifteen, and Carrie dressed to the nines, but not looking much older. We sat at the little bar, waiting for our table, directly under the juvenile-delinquent warning sign, drinking Manhattans and giggling profusely at my efforts to keep from talking about the Army, when suddenly a policeman came in. We got very scared, guilt written all over our faces, but nothing happened. I had lamb chops for dinner—meat! Think of it! Two girls in the next booth heard us talking about Minneapolis, and said they were from Minneapolis, too, and here we'd been thinking they looked like real native Californians. After dinner we went to an ancient Charles Boyer-Margaret Sullivan movie which was very good, and then back to bed.

Next morning we slept late—ah bliss. Grace had to go up to their cabin to do some cleaning, so we came too and made a day of it, with a picnic lunch. Down in the coast area it was a cold foggy day, but forty-five miles back in the mountains it was deserty, hot and sunny with BLUE SKY and wonderful. The country back there is very pretty—like Texas with sudden little green glades where the farmers have irrigated. Grace's cabin is in a canyon by a gurgling stream. Lots of sycamores, poplars, and evergreens surround the place. It felt so good to be back amongst nature. We all jumped into our bathing suits and lay on the stone dam crossing the stream, and went wading, and had water fights, and got sunburned. About five o'clock the sun disappeared over the mountain, so we headed back to town via the San Fernando Valley, stopping en route at a little wayside stand where we bought orange juice and sage honey which had a delicate and different flavor. Back in LA it was even danker and foggier, so we stayed in. Grace made biscuits, and we had a biscuit and honey and tea fest. We also had wine; this and all the fresh air made us very relaxed and we sat around and giggled. It was a good thing, we said, that Grace had the biscuits made before *she* got relaxed. Late sleep again.

This day we were to go horseback riding, me in blue jeans and Dick's motorcycle boots, and Carrie in Grace's horse stuff. Harriet and Grace had some errands to do so we got a ride over to Griffith Park. On the way, we stopped at a drive-in and had a hamburger and French fries lunch—it felt just like before the war. It was a fairly nice day for a change, and Griffith Park is very picturesque. It is wild, with small mountains interspersed with golf links, and parked areas. We cantered and trotted and climbed around on mountain trails and missed the trail somehow and got off onto the asphalt road in the park and scared little children and altogether had an enjoyable two hours. That is, enjoyable until we got off. Then we nearly fell flat on our faces and could hardly walk. I just got over being stiff yesterday. That night we went to dinner again in Hollywood. This time I was in uniform, and to another movie, an inane thing called *Valley of Decision*—don't see it. It's completely silly and senseless; anti-climax after anti-climax. We laughed during all the serious parts, and everyone got mad at us. After the theater, a chocolate soda, and then back.

Sunday, Grace and Dick were both out to church and if Grace hadn't called back to wake us up we'd have slept all day. But she did, and we staggered out of bed, got dressed, and hobbled to the bus. We went to visit the U.S.C. [University of Southern California] campus and Exposition Park. On the way we met up with a Socialist who thought we were students and, therefore, convertible. He was making all kinds of diagrams and bringing forth wild statements like "The world is made up of fools and thieves! The worker is robbed of 5/6 of his earnings!" etc. We argued and walked along, oblivious of everyone until we suddenly woke up to find ourselves in the quiet Sunday hum of the Art Gallery, screaming furiously and beating each other over the head.

He: No profits! Down with Capitalism!
Cay: Define your terms!
Me: Yes, but . . .
He: You are obviously a product of negative conditioning.
Cay: What authority have you got saying that the Marxian theory of surplus values is generally accepted?

Me: Yes, but . . .
He: I shouldn't have to tell a student anything like that.
       Down with money! Nothing that costs money is any
       good! No profits!
Me: Yes, but . . . Yes, but . . .

He finally left us because, he said, our little altercation would spoil our enjoyment of the gallery. The fact was that Carrie was getting so sarcastic that his ears were getting definitely chewed off. Immediately he left us, we went down to the biff and had a huge agreeing session, spouting off all the remarks we hadn't been able to get in edgewise while *he* was spouting off. Carrie having just gotten an A in a course on Social Philosophies and I having just finished Report on the Russians, we felt full of knowledge and rebuttals, none of which made any impression on our Socialist who wasn't there to appreciate it. We never did see any of the pictures, but saw some of the campus which is bare and dull compared to Cal and Minnesota. We had hamburgers at the local eatery and headed back.

We were to meet a friend of Carrie's for dinner, but we managed to get her and ourselves thoroughly lost, and we didn't get out to the restaurant till 7:30. We had a very nice dinner of fried shrimp—it was the same place I went on my weekend with those Kappas—we chatted and then back, very sleepy and stiff. Dear sweet Grace had enough gas to drive me back in the morning so I didn't have to trek back that night. We talked late, and then I had to get up at 5:30 and I was back on the treadmill by 7:00. Carrie leaves for Minneapolis this next Saturday. They are *driving* back through Yosemite, Tahoe, Yellowstone, Black Hills, et al. I'm so jealous. They get the gas because they are changing their residence.

I got a letter from William finally. He was home on furlough and loafing around Crowder waiting for assignment, and reading and such. I thought he was on Okinawa or someplace suffering untold privations. He included a picture, though, and letter was long, so I forgave him. I wish you-all could meet William. He's a darn good man, not like Mac, the "Typical GI" who did a Jekyll-Hyde on me and is now playing hard-to-get. Fooey on all men except William.

That seems to be all the news for now. We're still vastly busy in Surge and I nearly break my back every day heaving mammoth bundles of wet laundry around, and I get jumped on un-called-for-ly by the nurses but that is the usual rut. I scrubbed on a finger amputation yesterday by myself! Gore, Gore!

Goodbye and all my love,

8 July 1945

Sunday

Hmmm . . . all of a sudden it's really 9 July—how tempus fugit . . . and here I was planning to write a Happy Birthday letter to Mom. But somehow this week managed to get very full of doings and thus we see it is now Monday again. Anyhow, Happy Birthday, Mom dear. Monday last, and Tuesday I wrote letters madly because it seems that everybody in the world has been crashing through lately. Wednesday I collapsed in bed. Thursday, Baggie, Cooper and I went out and met two gals from the Detachment at Don the Beachcombers, a tres exclusif joint in Hollywood. These gals have been to college and are very smooth, but fun, and speak in words of more than one syllable. With them was a WAVE whom we called The Admiral. She was a good Joe and most witty. The evening was a gay trek from one night spot to another and we had a high old time. Friday night a gang of us from Surgery went swimming at Reseda Park pool and had a picnic and looked at the ducks in the duck pond and played tag. Whee! There were ten of us in Felix's coupe: three nurses, three WACs, three soldiers and one civilian. The guard at the gate roared when we rolled out. Saturday a gang of us went out to a western hillbilly joint and got quite jolly on beer. Your dear daughter distinguished herself by talking with a fake Cockney accent and convincing everyone that she was from London. I really created a riot—had crowds of people hanging around and buying me beer and stuff. That was quite a night. Yes indeed. Yesterday we took it easy and slept. In the evening, Gray and I went for a big hike and consequently I am pooped this evening. Last week was extremely active, but I'm too tired to recount any anecdotes. Have fun at the lake.

All love,

17 July 1945

Tuesday

Dearest Family,

By this time you are no doubt thoroughly sunburned and mosquito-bitten. I, too, am sunburned, but not bitten—no mosquitoes in California, remember? I had the loveliest weekend. The week was dull except for Thursday afternoon when I got a ride into Hollywood with a real wolf in a red convert, the first genuine one I've ever run into. I bought a nice tablecloth for Grace and some sun glasses—Hollywood Glamour, y'know—and went to a Van Johnson movie all by myself—swoon, swoon. Carmen and Baggie had a three-day pass over the weekend so Saturday I went to meet them. Got a ride into Hollywood with some UCLA fellows who were working in a machine shop during the summer. They also had a smooth convert, and we had fun playing tag with a friend of theirs all the way in on Ventura Boulevard. Going through the Cahuenga Canyon tunnel at fifty-per I thought sure something dire was going to happen, but nothing did. We got into town earlier than I had planned so we went to a joint called the Fog Cutter's and had a scotch and soda. Then I met Carmen and Baggie at the USO and we went to a spaghetti place for supper, after which we roamed around Hollywood looking at the odd people and ended up at a music shop. Since there were three of us, the clerk let us have a huge upstairs listening room all to ourselves.[71] We took off our shoes, loosened our skirts, lay on the floor and had a wonderful time. Played Lalo's Symphonie Espagnol with Nathan Milstein, and Tschaikovsky's Piano Concerto—the popular one. At that, poor Carmen got homesick and cried, so in a very bad mood we took off early.

We stayed at the Hollywood Guild Canteen, a real old house in Beverly Hills, converted into a place for gals to stay. It's sort of like the DG [Delta Gamma] House and absolutely overflowing with Marines, WAVEs, and SPARs. We were the only WACs there. Had

---

[71] In the late 1930s and 1940s record shops allowed potential customers to listen to records to see if they wanted to buy them. While still in high school my friends and I would squeeze into a listening booth at Dayton's with a stack of Glenn Miller and Artie Shaw records, spend all afternoon listening, and then buy maybe one Blue Bird record for the sum of thirty-five cents. The clerks gave us dirty looks but did not seriously object.

a swell sleep and when I woke up, the kids had gone to mass, so I took a shower and went to the men's Canteen about two blocks away for a free breakfast. Met a fellow from Surgery and we had a long conversation over our Rice Krispies. By the time I got back the kids were ready so we went to the USO and found out that we could go and swim at James Gleason's house (he is a movie star). We hitched a ride out to Beverly Hills, which by the way is most glamorous. The whole place looks like a movie set. We had an elegant swim. I was in the water for three hours, diving and having water fights with the fellows, and playing catch and getting sunburned. Then back to the Canteen for a small rest, lying out on the terrace and looking up at the mountains. For dinner we went to a little Chinese cafe in Hollywood which has much better food than John's. They serve family style, lots of different stuff and huge amounts. For seventy-five cents we had egg Foo Yong, pork fried rice, chow mein (but very Chinese-y and mostly bean sprouts) and then some stuff called Pow Yuk (beans and pork and celery). Tea and almond cakes for dessert. After nearly exploding with stuffedness we walked up to the Hollywood Bowl for "Symphony Under the Stars." Fog, really, and COLD. It was damp and clammy. The music was only fair. Stowkowski's brass section is too overpowering and the strings weren't very well integrated, but it was pleasant. It was entertaining to see all the cigarettes glowing in the dark. Listen to it on Sunday evenings—10:30 your time.

Surgery isn't very busy this week. We have a new man named Lido Ranelli. More Italians and Frenchmen in that place, but the doctors and nurses all have Anglo-Saxon names. How about that? Yesterday there was an Italian PW in for a hemorrhoidectomy, and Lido and Sgt. Tony had to talk to him in Italian and reassure him because he was afraid Col. Sheehan was going to kill him. A new gal just came into our barracks who used to be in a circus. She ate some fire for us—cotton soaked with lighter fluid! My gosh, lights out already.

All my love,

22 July 1945

Sunday

Dearest Family,

How! I am mucho hot. We are having a heat wave, and the Californians are groaning, but they don't know what's what till they have sweated out a Minnesota night. Here it drops to about 70 or 65, and you can sleep. It's really been quite nice this last week, I must admit. Moonlit evenings with stars, yet, and the mountains come out now and again. The week as regards social activities has been excessively quiet—evenings devoted to laundry, reading, and sleeping, with two movies to relieve the monotony: (1) *Call of the Wild*—an oldie with Clark Gable; has purty Oregon scenery. (2) *Blood on the Sun*—do see this. Cagney is really good—lots of fisticuffs, good dialogue and excitement, climaxes well handled. Friday saw us at another stupid Company meeting with our moron officers droning on and on about foot lockers and inspection and military courtesy and crap. After this little lecture a la Basic, we were all infuriated. Those damn meetings do more to disrupt our morale than anything else. Why can't they leave us alone???

This weekend I went in to see Grace. In the evening we went over to Harriet's (a friend of hers). Their house is on top of a hill with a view towards the mountains on one side, and towards the ocean on the other. Last night it was clear and we could see Hollywood, Beverly Hills, Santa Monica, El Segundo, and LA; pretty lights. We sat around and listened to the police calls. Of course, since Dick is a policeman, Grace and Harriet know all the codes. "Thirty-nine W down" means "drunken woman collapsed in gutter." And there was a "possible dead body" in an alley about ten blocks away. LA was really roaring last night—attacks, robberies, fights, and drunks in great profusion. Also we burned my name on the back of my new cigarette case I bought at the PX. And we ate chocolate cake and drank milk. Then we drove clear out to UCLA. Harriet felt reckless, I guess. It was very gay, buzzing along in a smooth car at night—felt positively pre-war. And such a night— moon, stars, bright lights. UCLA is very impressive and brand-new looking. It definitely doesn't have an academic atmosphere. Looks more like a big hospital or a sanatarium. Beautifully landscaped grounds—but I really prefer a messy jumbled-around campusylooking campus. Today I slept late, went horseback riding out at Griffith Park all by my lonesome, and nearly collapsed with the hot heat, then came back, took a bath, and returned to Birmingdamn Gaol.

Answers and Notes: (1) ZI means Zone of the Interior. (2) Cases we have in Surgery in order of frequency:

    a. Bone grafts
    b. Skin grafts
    c. Wound revisions
    d. Herniorrhaphies (hernia repairs) (I scrub alone on these!)
    e. Hemorrhoidectomies
    f. Miscellaneous orthopedic cases like:
       1. Finger amputations
       2. Fracture reductions
       3. Arthrodesis (shoulder repairs)
    g. Miscellaneous abdominal cases like:
       1. Appendectomies
       2. Nephrectomies (kidney removal)
       3. Cholecystectomies (gallbladder removal)
       4. Colostomy closures
       5. Intestinal explorations

(3) Dad: when I got your little map of the lake, my first thought as it fell out of the envelope was "Gosh—he's bought the farm!" I can't believe that you are actually going to buy it. Always it has seemed so vague and far in the future. (4) Mike: I'm very proud of your business career, and interested. How much do you rake in? Plutocrat! (5) Midge: Did you have fun at the kennel? Do write me all about it. (6) Mom: Hi, keed! Nothing special for you this time except Love from Grace. Oh yes, I was looking at her album and saw flocks of rare pictures of you and your little friends. Also ones of Dad and of me when small. Wonderfully funny. Old pictures of people you know always are! Lights are going out in a couple of minutes so I'd better hurry up. No more news now absolutely.

> All my love,
> Sunburned Bug

From Mom—July 25, 1945:

We came down from Cross Lake [in Crow Wing County] on Sunday which was the hottest day of the season so far—94, but it got to 96 both Monday and today. It was hard to leave the coolness and come back to town. Have settled back in to the routine of washing, ironing, and gardening. The garden was not in too bad shape except the cukes and squash which a blight had hit. We have had a lot of vegetables—radishes, onions, lettuce, kohlrabi, beans, beets, and chard—and we go through the old routine of gloating and counting our produce.

29 July 1945

Sunday

Dearest Family,

This is going to be a very groggy letter, cause I'm so tired I could pop. I was on call this weekend and so last night at 2 a.m. in the morning I was called out, and worked till 6:30, grabbed a couple of hours of sleep, and then worked again till 3:30. Woof! Some swabbie cracked up in his little car and they brought him here. Face kind of messed up, but nothing spectacular. Just enough to make a lot of work for this EW.

News of the Week: I got a permanent! Creme machineless. Now instead of looking like Mortimer Snerd's sister, I resemble a native on one of the lesser-known Pacific Islands. "Ittle grow" I keep telling myself. Friday was a big day on the Post—170th Anniversary of the Medical Corps, and of course Alvin C. Miller (Hubba, hubba) had to do things up in big style. Everybody that could be spared got off at noon. At 2:00 they had a baseball game between Birmingham and some guys from Slapsie Maxie Rosenblum's establishment.[72] Then crazy races and contests for the Post personnel and wives and dates and such. The Officers had a pie-eating contest, nurses had a sack race. The prizes—wow—you should have seen them. What I mean, they were sharp! A fifth of Hiram Walker, fancy leather make-up cases, Hudson's Bay blankets, perfume. Lucille Ball, a movie character dame with red hair (ouch) who is married to one Desi Arnaz, formerly of El Cinema,

---

[72] Slapsie Maxie Rosenblum was a former middleweight boxing champion who ran a nightclub in Hollywood.

now a Sgt. of BGH Special Service Department—well, she gave out the prizes and had her picture tooken with all the various winners. All during the afternoon and evening, free beer and cokes were dispensed. At five, feed was dished out. Picture 2,000 sirloin steaks ('ats right) grilled to a turn on an outdoor pit. The mess line was about a mile long. We had steak sandwiches, corn on the cob, carrot sticks, potato chips, pickles, celery, ice cream, and beer—YUM! Oh, yes, also French bread. Ah, those steaks—past all description. Then from 6 to 7:30 there was a Variety Show: Charlie Barnett and his band, the floor show from Slapsie Maxie's, the Delta Rhythm Boys, and "our own" Cully Richards—a jerk who thinks he's hot stuff (never heard of him before I got to BGH, but then I ain't been around). Lucille Ball and dear Desi. Mike—you should have heard the Delta Rhythm Boys—they were marvelous. We had next to the front row seats and the Boys nearly blasted us out. They sang "Take the A Train," "St. Louis Blues," and "Rum Coke," which was a slightly unexpurgated version. Barnett did "Cherokee," "Jersey Bounce," and all the moderner ones like "Laura," "There's No You," "Stranger in Town," etc. You would have liked it no end. At 7:30 the show cleaned itself up (Hayes Office-ly speaking) and went on the air, coast-to-coast and overseas. Col. Sheehan spoke and the whole thing was a large plug for the Medics. After that there was a dance on the tennis court for those who could still walk. But just think how much that must have cost. Big celebration, all right. Most of the patients got drunk on beer.

Notes: Got a new cigarette lighter. It's a flame-thrower, really. "Zippo" it's called and only 85 cents. Very good and holds lots of fluid. Captain Bates has one she bought overseas three years ago and it's still on the beam. Grace has gone up to Lake Arrowhead for a two-week vacation—lucky. I'm sure glad you had such a good time up at the lake. Wish I were home. Guess where William has finally been stationed? Beaumont, after all this fuzzy-muzzy about overseas and OCS, and they send him there. I wouldn't care to be there in the summer, thanks just the same. This next week ought to be quite social—we get paid Tuesday. Enclosed find some pictures. I'm awful sleepy now, so it's the sack for me.

All love,

From Dad—Aug. 5, 1945:

That certainly sounded like a real party the Medical Corps threw for you and how I drooled when you went on about the steaks! I have almost forgotten what one of those things looks like! When are you betting on the war being over? The smart boys here say 60 days, but I doubt it. And how do you plan to fit into civilian life? Still interested in the School of Nursing?

5 August 1945

Sunday

Dearest Family,

The last two weeks have been unutterably dull, enlivened by nothing more than an occasional Post movie. I'm so depressed about this dear Gaol and ache to get out of the Army, but no hope for another year no doubt. I live only for weekends, and I feel as though my youth were being wasted. Just think—next month I'll be twenty-one and there will be a whole year being spent with horrible people, doing horrible things. Groan and moan . . . Grace is coming back from Arrowhead this week and we are planning a trip to Chinatown soon. Wednesday was Carmen's birthday, so we two went out for dinner. Ate at a French restaurant, Maison Gaston, and had an excellent meal and not too expensive—$2.41 apiece. Here's what we had: one cocktail, huge tureen of pea soup (*good*), lettuce salad with real French dressing, little dab of spaghetti, two lamb chops, peas with celery and little onions chopped up in, potatoes, sherbet and coffee, French rolls, one bottle (small) of burgundy split between us. After stuffing ourselves we went to a record shop (our old standby) and listened to music, only this time we broke down and actually bought something. I got an album for your birthdays, Dad and Mom. I think you'll like it, I hope. Don't be downhearted Mike—your day will come. Also tomorrow I'm going to write you a letter all your own.

Yesterday I got mad at the Sergeant in Surgery. He's been riding me for weeks now, and I asked the Major for a transfer. Besides the Sgt. getting me down, I'm tired of those damned doctors swearing at me and treating me like a cockroach. I'm a human being but they don't know it. The Major was amazed to find someone who didn't like being picked on constantly, but I told *him*. He just couldn't understand why I wanted a transfer, the old so-and-so. Last night all the kids had to work late and they had to work today, too, so I've just been lying around sleeping and reading and doing laundry and am thoroughly fed up with this existence. I want a good game of bridge, and an argument about politics with my Stagnantte pals, and a walk around Lake Harriet in the rain, and Sunday evening supper with my family. Oh, yawn, I will end this sad missive before you all break down and weep. All my love, and sorry, no exciting news. How's your guitar playing coming, Dad? Why don't you and Mike play duets? I keep wondering if you've bought the farm yet. Sure wish I could help you look . . .

From Mom—Aug. 9, 1945:

Just a short note, as we are leaving about 4:00 for the Danielsons' island. We had intended to go by bus, but last night when we took Midge out to Cornish's kennels, dear sweet Mr. C. gave us two coupons!—so we are going to drive after all, which makes it so much nicer. I hope things are looking up for you. It looks very much to us as if the Japs would quit very soon, which would mean only another six months. Do keep your courage up. Saw Ruthie last night and she said she had sent you some cookies. Hope to do likewise soon when we are home. I've been awfully short on cooking fat. Canned seven pints of assorted beans, carrots and beets this a.m.—first I've done.

From Dad—Aug. 9, 1945:

We are off this p.m. for a visit to the Danielsons' island in Mille Lacs so you will miss a Sunday letter. This note is a substitute. We had planned to go by bus, but when we took Midge to Cornish's, he gave me tickets for 10 gallons of gas so we drive. No special news. The political news is cheerful and I feel the end is in sight, so keep up your courage and some day you will be only a civilian! I don't like these new bombs—we are worse than the Nazis, but some good may come of it in shortening this damned war. I must pop along and start packing or we shall never get off.

14 August 1945

Tuesday

U.S. Naval Photographic Services Depot
1357 North Vine Street
Hollywood, California
MEMORANDUM: DATE: V-J Day 2000
Tuesday nite, 14 August 1945
TO: the family of an inebriated WAC
        Hello family dear, I probrbly shoudn't be writing to you when
in this condition but I feel that you might like to know how the
Army reacts to the wonderful news of the end of this bloddy mess.
I'm at present slightly the worse for Schenley's at a naval offce as
you can see from the letterhead. I8ve been excited evre since Friday
when the nws started to come in. We were avsolutely glued to the
radio in Surge. Miss K. brought her radio in and in between ops we
rushed into the workroom ti hear thw latest. It was mad what I
mean aren't we living in thrilling times[Only six more months
before I8m a sweet little co-ed again. Mabe I8ll be home for Xmas.
Let us hope so. Hollywood is full of drunk wanton people even tho
all the bars closed at 4:00 when the news came. Noise—horns—
paper littering the streets—great surging mobs of fake people . . .
all being photographed like mad from every angle by the navy
army movies et al but still its fun and I'll never forget it. oh whee .
. especially the poor little swabbie here at the office who coundn't
hold his liquor and proceeded to regurgitate all over my nice clean
uniform . . how aboot thatz . . Perhaps you better not read this to
Mike . . he might think his sister was an old sot, But after all as I said
before its the end offnthe war and a little blowing off steam is
allowableand forgivable. You will, Won't you. Forgive me I mean.
All my love dear little family whom I miss so Much.

SIGNATURE ___*Bug*___

From Mom—Aug. 16, 1945:
        It still does not seem possible that the war is over! But after I keep
telling myself that it is, I realize how wonderful it is. I always had a
pessimistic feeling that it would last much longer, and I'm pleasantly
mistaken. Now we are beginning to look forward to your being home again.

It can't be too terribly long. I read in today's paper that WACs had to have 44 points for demobilization, but I haven't any idea how they are figured or how many you have by now. I hope and pray that maybe they will pass some legislation or what have you to let the women out sooner.

I was about to put supper on the table about 6:10 and sent Dad out for some parsley. He said "The sirens are going! It must be over!" We had listened to the radio so much for several days that it got tiring and I hadn't had it on since 4:00 in the afternoon. We tuned in and got Clement Atlee first. It was very noisy here. Good old Minneapolis finally broke down and celebrated—horns and firecrackers and guns and bells and the air-raid siren. About 7:00 the Seversons took Mike downtown with them to see the crowd and they said it was really a mob. Later we all went down to Petitclairs' taking along the quart of bourbon Dad had labeled "For the Defeat of Japan." We, too, celebrated—downed it all but a finger Dad is saving for you! We played some bridge, sang, argued, and felt very gay. Of course we are pleased too, that gas and fuel oil rationing is off. It's going to feel wicked to drive much or keep the house warm! Thank God this horrible thing is over—and now we'll hope for a real Peace! Tell us what your prospects are of getting out.

17 August 1945

Friday

Dearest Family,

Well, it's the morning after the morning after the ditto, and we're back in the same old groove. The past week seems like a dream or an hallucination, and yet it's all kind of dim and faraway. I've been so excited, and now—pooh—the Army looms up again and the gruesome life stretches ahead with no prospect of relief. As you can see, I'm depressed again. Lord, what I wouldn't give for a discharge and I'm sure I'll be in for another year at least. You know the medics will be the last ones out, especially the women, who don't have many points. Groan, also moan. Last week saw me over at the NCO Club to drink beer and gab with the kids Wednesday and Thursday.

Friday morning was the beginning of the big news. Sgt. Tony greeted us with "The Japs have surrendered!" I had to scrub on four ops that morning and so didn't get to hear the radio. I couldn't even leave the room; consequently I was frantic. The doctors would come in, saying "Well, it's all over!" Finally the schedule was over, and I tore into the workroom to listen. The commentators were stuttering and ad-libbing all over the place and that made it more exciting. I had the afternoon off and planned a big shopping tour and guess what? — we were restricted for retreat. But I was a wicked girl and snuck over to the film libe to see some kids and we watched cartoons all afternoon. On the way out that evening we passed an empty ward where moving pictures were being made. The scene was the happy reunion between patient and parents. It was hysterical to watch the "mother" standing in a corner crying away, whipping up a mood, and smiling and talking two minutes later. They asked us to be in it as background, but we declined. Went out to dinner and came back early.

Saturday the Major gave us all the afternoon off — amazing occurrence. Carmen and I took off for Hollywood to shop and I had my pictures taken. They came out pretty well and I'll send them next week when I get them if I have enough money. Which leads naturally into a plea for the *loan* of $15 till pay day. PDQ! Just a loan, mind you, but I need it cause I loaned money to Baggie, so I don't have any. Please, huh, please? Saturday evening, Grace, Harriet, Carmen, and I went to Chinatown for dinner, and shopping for junk, and then to Olvera Street, the Mexican Quarter. This is in contrast to Chinatown, fairly authentic and colorful. Night hid all the dirt and it was fun. I have prepared a largish box, mostly filled with junk, but with some presents.

1. Lots of little presents for Mike, but not the little dishes which were a present from Grace to me.
2. A long stiff present for Mom; it smells purty.
3. A long present for Dad to remind him of me.

BUT I can't send them till I have dough (bribe, bribe).

Sunday Carmen and I slept, then went to Mass, where I learned that the Catholics and the Virgin Mary have won the war:

1. War started day before Feast of Immaculate Conception.
2. War will probably end day before Feast of Assumption of Virgin.[73]

[73] The priest really did make these statements in his homily at the Mass on August 12, and he turned out to be right in his prediction about the war's official end. The surrender was on August 14; the Feast of the Assumption of the Virgin is on August 15.

Had USO dinners and breakfasts. Then drank beer to cool off. Then took a sunbath at Guild Canteen in the midst of which came the surrender rumor. We threw on our clothes and dashed into Hollywood only to find it all a fake. Went to the USO and had a palmist tell us all about our lives and characters. Father's life (I divulged all) is reflected in my left hand because I am ambidextrous—interesting, what? We next went to our favorite little bar to drink beer, because we missed our streetcar. This bar is very skinny and long—you can't get in the door frontways. The waiter's name is Jack, and he's always very nice to Carmen and me. Here we met two unusual Marines—different:

1. Handsome—swoon.
2. Intelligent.
3. Witty, on the cynical side.
4. Not in diapers.

The type that would be Staff-Sergeants in the Army Special Services, pulling all sorts of smooth office jobs, and here they were PFCs. Can't understand it. One of them and I discussed comparative Army and Marine Military tactics and psychology. Carmen and the other one discussed the place of women in the post-war world. We were loathe to leave, but Tom was leaning close and suggesting we go out and "make beautiful music together," and that always leads to nothing but trouble. So home.

Monday was another day of hovering around the radio. I was on CQ that night. When I got off at 11:00, I went in to see my Sergeant friends who have a Cadre room, and we heard the first news that the real surrender was on the way. Well, natch, we had to break out our bottle of Southern Comfort that we'd been hoarding. Upon which we got very gay, and found ourselves at 1:00 out in the middle of a bean patch, talking to the guard about the war. We had on our PJs, and I guess he thought we were trying to escape.

Tuesday the excitement was at a huge pitch. The commentators were so funny describing the Japs weeping on the palace lawn. At last, just before we went off work at 4:00, they announced that either Truman or Atlee was going to talk, they didn't know which. We had an idea that was the end, and we tore back to the barracks to get off the Post, because we'd heard we were going to be restricted. I was in the shower when the radio blared out: "World War II is now over!" At that rate, my friends and I were in

Hollywood one-half hour after the announcement was made, and what a mad-house it was. Impromptu parades, noise, horns, traffic jams. We went to a party at the Naval Photographic Depot (see letter of Tuesday—hmmmm—hope you weren't mad). We spent most of the evening tearing around in an open convertible with assorted people perched all over it. We kept collecting people: Army Lieutenant, two sailors, three WACs (us), one WAVE, and a soldier. It was crazy, but got in fairly early, too.

Wednesday and Thursday we got off, so I eager-beavered Wednesday—washed clothes, cleaned out lockers and slept. Went in to Grace's in the evening, and yesterday we drove all up and down the coast, sightseeing. It was a gorgeous day and the ocean was beautiful. Such fun driving on unrationed gas. Harriet let me drive some and I did right well, too. To bed tres early last night. All that fresh air laid me out. Grace drove me in this a.m., and here I am as I said before. Nothing has changed, and prospects for "OUT" are gloomy. So I shall continue in my little rut. Carmen and I are going to the Ballet tomorrow night. It will bring back happy memories of "ushing" at the Symph. All the papers are advertising fall campus clothes and it kills me. WOE, WOE. Now I'm interested to hear your reaction to all this hubba hubba. Did you break out Bottle #2? One reason I'm gloomy is because of the war news, and the Japs stalling, and the fabulous numbers of workers being laid off at the plants out here. There's going to be a mammoth amount of planning and working to be done before anything like peace really takes shape. On this serious note I will end.

> All my love, and don't forget
> about the money!

From Mom—Aug. 20, 1945:

Terribly amused by the letter written on V-J Day and so will you be when you look at it again someday! I was not too shocked—I'd have thought you less than human if you hadn't made a good deal of whoopee. After all, it was a big day. Now, brace yourself! We have bought The Farm! *And it's perfectly beautiful and gorgeous. Dad heard of it a little while ago and had a chance to go and see it on Saturday. It belonged to L.W., one of his old boys, who is a Lt. Commander, home on leave as his father just died. It's 320* acres—a dairy farm, in beautiful rolling wooded country. There is the most perfect site for our house on a knoll at the east end overlooking a long rolling sweep of the farm—wheat fields and the home farm in the distance and down below is a good sized clear lake! I never dreamed we would find any place so beautiful. I know you will be crazy about it. Now to hold a strong thought for you to be let out before too long—the time will go faster than you think. You may begin to draw plans for a low gray stone house with a south and western view!

From Dad—Aug. 21, 1945:

My dear and dizzy daughter. What a week! By now I feel about as dizzy as anything you could produce at your best. Your V-J letters came yesterday. The first one can only be described as a "Little Gem" and should be preserved to bring out at some future date if you ever tend to become too moral. I know how you felt on the occasion, for your Old Man was in Paris when the last war blew up. Now for a dull reaction and a trying time till you can get out. I have been through that, too, and urge patience and a realization of the fact that all things come to an end and that, rumors to the contrary, you will not spend the rest of your life in uniform, but will be returned to the bosom of your adoring family and the uncertainties of civilian life. I judge that by now you have checked to see what you can get for free from good old Uncle Sugar in the way of education, etc.

As though V-J were not enough to bowl me out, bang goes gas rationing, I "celebrate" my 50th birthday, and as your mother wrote, the Farm Deal broke with a bang too. We celebrated "Gas Day" by one of our pet drives on a hot evening over all the little side roads out by the Auto Club and Hopkins, and felt very wicked. Our V-J party has, I fancy, been covered by your Maw so I shall not repeat. I have saved a little from both the "E" and "J" bottles and have now have it marked "ALB" so you will have at least a sample.

The Farm has me down for the count and when I start on it I become rather incoherent. It is 320 acres and came to $100 an acre, a bit more than I had counted on paying, but I am getting so much for my money, its beauty and location only 28 miles from downtown aside, that it makes it an excellent buy at the price. The whole thing makes a young village. I am buying the land and buildings only, as the herd would run into too much money. L.W. will be off the place by Nov. 1st, when my manager finds me a tenant to move on and take over. I probably will not be able to get much back from the place *before next spring, so I shall have some highly complicated financing to work out, but that can be managed. And what a place it is and will be when we build our place and move on! — the Lord sparing us that long! This letter is rather full of US and not much of YOU, but I knew you wanted to hear as much as possible about the Farm and, of course, we can talk and think of but little else. It really is such a* marvelous *lay-out that it almost frightens me. How come that* I *can get a piece of property like that? It just doesn't seem possible and that's a fact.*

Part II
GETTING OUT

Birmingham

BIRMINGHAM GENERAL HOSPITAL
VAN NUYS, CALIFORNIA
22 August to 19 September 1945

22 August 1945

Wednesday

Dear Mom,

This is being addressed exclusively to you because Dad has been very remiss about letters lately. You have been carrying on through thick and thin and most nobly, too. I'm glad you weren't too mad about that exuberant, to say the least, letter. As I said, it was written in one of my few moments of alcoholic enthusiasm and you ought to be glad I thought of my family at a time like that. The thrill of V-J has definitely worn off, so much so that I can't believe it ever really happened. There is no change in our daily groove and we're having quite a groove. Ten and more cases a day. Death has really been stalking the halls of BGH lately. Sunday, even though I wasn't on call, I had to go over to Surge to help. A little Merchant seaman (only seventeen years old) had been injured in an auto wreck the night before. Internal trauma and hemorrhage, mesentary all torn, spleen ruptured. The blow just missed his aorta and stomach. It was an interesting case and Col. Sheehan did a marvelous job of surgery, but the poor kid died the next morning. He didn't have much of a chance anyway. It was a horrible sight to see the C-2 Wardmaster wheeling a guerney with a sheet-draped body on it down the hall. That same day, a patient was discovered to have hung himself in a grove just outside the Post. He was young, too—eighteen, and very depressed over his heart condition (rheumatic fever) and decided to do himself in. Yesterday we were in the midst of a busy schedule when "Daddy" (the Major) burst in with shouts of, "Hurry! Big emergency!" A truckload of German PWs en route to work on a nearby farm had overturned, and they were all banged up: what I mean, they were a mess—skull fractures, cracked ribs, huge lacerations, and such. We had two cases going in each room and the whole pavilion was a mess. One died at the time of the crash, one died today after the emergency op last night, another died this afternoon. This death business is a rare occurrence in an Army stateside General Hospital, luckily.

Carmen and I went to the ballet last Saturday. I don't think that they think too much of LA audiences because I felt they weren't putting out their best performance. In Minneapolis they were much better. Besides, the Hollywood Bowl is definitely not suited to stage presentations. Last night Jose Iturbi gave a concert here. I think he's the nicest guy; big friendly smile, informal and swell to the fellows. Though I don't know why. Every time he comes here, some boors walk out, talk during the program, and this time some even went so far as to clap in the middle of the "Moonlight Sonata" because I guess they didn't happen to like it. I was ready to personally choke them, but decided against it. These morons can't appreciate or even sit through anything that doesn't have an eight-beat. Jose should play his boogie-woogie number first so these ill-mannered so-and-sos can get out and let others enjoy the concert in peace.

Got your letter today and overjoyed at the news about the farm; it sounds made to order. At mess I was reading and suddenly screamed, "They did it!" and beat poor Baggie over the head. She couldn't imagine what was coming off. Since then I've been pestering everybody with descriptions of my family's farm "with TWO LAKES," and Holstein cows, and on and on. Oh to be home to see it in the summer. I think I have a pretty good chance to get a furlough the end of October or early November. Let's hope "Daddy" and Alvin (Commander of BGH) are in good moods then.

About my points: I have seven and that is all. These are months of service prior to May 8, 1945. Other points can be gotten for overseas, battle stars, and children, none of which I have. I don't even have a Good Conduct Medal; you have to be in at least a year for that. WAVES, SPARS, and Marines seem to be getting a quicker and better discharge deal than the forgotten members of the Women's Army Corps. Leave us hope fervently that we will be remembered eventually (Why not NOW?).[74] Keep up hope, the end is not in sight but everything has an end, it says here. Thought: Last year today I took my physical. Ark! Note: I think I will take a rain check on my twenty-first birthday present. Just send me my birth certificate so I can do my drinking legally. Also some Toll House cookies. And some new pants. Thanks: for the check. It rescued me from the Debtors Prison and will be repaid in part if not in full sometime after the thirty-first. Guess what: I've started a thrift campaign for myself; wonder how long it will last?

> Much love to you and Dad and
> Mike,

24 August 1945

Friday

Hi Dad,

Great humble apologies to you for slamming your writing endeavors. I fully realize the busy nature of your days. The most unprecedented thing happened tonight. Our C.O., who just got her promotion to First Lt. gave a beer bust after company meeting to celebrate the event. And we are very jolly in our barracks because one of our buddies, Cummings, who is generally super-circumspect, had two bottles and is now reeling around and being most amusing. Today was an exhausting day. A Major-General from the Surgeon-General's Office is coming to inspect. "Daddy" was in a great dither all day and had us beavering furiously. My feet are killing me. Sent on my picture today; hope you-all like it. Shows my insignia and everything.

Post-war Plans: Go to the University of Chicago. I don't want to go back to the U of M and get in the same rut I joined the Army to escape. Besides, if I stayed home I'd want to spend all my time working on the farm and I'd never get any studying done. I can do decorating long distance and on weekends. When I come home in November on furlough (hope, hope) I will discuss it at length. I think I can get two years' tuition free from Uncle Sugar with the

---

[74] I was adapting a slogan used by the General Mills Company to market Gold Medal flour: "Eventually—Why Not Now?"

help of the American Legion. The map of the FARM was swell. I'm eager for the photos. It all sounds, as Mom says, "Out of this world." Plans and schemes for our house whirl around in my head. Sure wish I were home to rejoice with you about it.

Love,

From Dad—Aug. 24, 1945:

On Wednesday we spent the evening with the Hodgkinsons and heard some music. His player is super, of course, and I told him that I was counting on one when we moved out. It seems that last summer in Rochester he was working on the famous atomic bomb project, knew all about it and had much confidential dope that is still rather hush, but which we will save for you. Hodgy is an odd and able man, who should be in a big job, but he doesn't quite dare to cut loose from the comfort and certainty of Blake.[75]

29 August 1945

Wednesday

Dearest Family,

Here comes another one of those typewritten letters but let us hope that this one is a little more decipherable. I'm on call tonight and figured I might as well combine biz with pleasure and snitch the Surge machine. News of the Week (not great news like yours, mostly trivia): (1) Annie was a naughty girl and got restricted for three days. Sgt. Johnson saw me going to the movies the other night and I had on white anklets. Oh wicked, oh sin!! Of course I and three-fourths of the rest of the detachment have been doing that for the past hot months, but I guess Johnnie thought she'd better justify her existence, so she called me into the orderly room and read me a small lecture on uniform regulations and then took my Class-A Pass away. Of course I'm simply crushed and filled with remorse at my wrong-doing. (2) Annie spent a respectable Saturday night last week. Accompanied by Brad, one of the better-known tanks of WAC Hospital Company 78, I hitched to Hollywood. There we had supper at a tea shoppe of sorts—chicken salad

---

[75] Hodgy was one of the science masters at Blake, and he and his wife, Ellen, were dear friends of my parents.

sandwiches and iced tea. Then on to the movies, *The Story of GI Joe.*
Quite good, I thought; did you see it? Then back to the barracks by
11:00. How about that????

(3) You (although you may not realize this startling fact) are
reading a letter written by the hand of one who touched the hand
of one who touched the hand of Van Johnson. Ask Mike who he is.
Van came to Birmingham yesterday and Gray saw him and touched
him and got his autograph. Pant, pant. She talked about him until
night paled into dawn. He is her dream man. I would have gone up
on the ward to see him but my feet hurt. Nobody interesting ever
comes to Surge except Colonels and Generals to inspect and see if
they can't find some dust or some EMs and EWs doing something
bad like smoking in the broom room. I told you, didn't I, that WACs
aren't allowed to scrub anymore? I'm mad in a way, but mostly I just
don't give a damn. I have become a shameless GB (gold-brick) and
an expert one, too. The Army is doing a lot for me—oh, yes. I used
to be an EB (eager beaver) but not anymore. (4) Routine prevalent
in Surge right now:

> Cpl. A. says, "I'm brown from the sun."
> Sgt. T. says, "I'm Smith from the Tribune."
> Both say in union, "Eh, eh!"

We must have our little jokes. (5) Dad—what is this you're
babbling about thus-and-so "when we move out?" Are you contem-
plating a removal to THE FARM in the near future? I thought we
were going to live Yorkside till Mike got ejected from Mr. Blake's
Academy for Manly Lads after his senior year. Please give more
detailed explanations. Say, what are we going to call our new
property? Are we going to be phunny, literary allusionical, clevah,
or merely naive? I think *THE FARM!* in large black letters on a
green background hung by the side of the road would be tres
original and would convey our state of mind very well. In Mom's
letter I told how I beat poor Baggie over the head when first I
heard the joyous news. She's still black and blue, a living testimony
to my reception of above-mentioned joyous news. (6) Next week,
just like PFCs (poor feeble civilians), we get Labor Day off. I think
I shall invite myself up to Grace's mountain cabin for the weekend.
That is, if she isn't doing something else. (7) Now you know darn
well that this would cover four or five good pages of handwritten
stuff so you'd better be satisfied. Besides my dogs are killing me (I

think I've got fallen arches or something) and my stomach is violently disagreeing with some pork we had for lunch which I am convinced was seething with Trichinella Spirillis. So, in other words, I think I shall head for my small fly-specked sack in 200 B.

Adios for the time being,

P.S.: I could do with a new wallet for my birthday. Make it smooth and leathery and with a place to put pictures in. P.P.S.: I watched a thyroidectomy today; very interesting. P.P.P.S.: Got the *New Yorkers;* thanks. P.P.P.P.S.: See the movie *Johnny Angel.* It's laid in New Orleans with some good scenes in the Vieux Carre. Only one thing was out of place; see if you can find it. We all made ourselves thoroughly obnoxious at the show by screaming, "Look! Look! N.O.!" whenever they showed Canal Street or some part of the Quarter. You'd think it was our home town instead of our station for only a month. Isn't that silly? FINIS and luv.

From Dad—Sept. 3, 1945:

Last week we heard MacArthur and the Jap surrender and got quite a thrill. MacA. certainly did a real job. And that's about the extent of the week. This morning Mike and I cleaned and sacked the onions—about 60 pounds—which inspired the following sonnet:

The tomato crop, it is a flop;
My onions, on the other hand,
Are unbelievably grand.

Then your maw and I policed the kitchen area and it can take white gloves, I can assure you. I like your idea of the U of Chicago. It is one of the best in the country and a degree from there (other than in science) has more prestige than one from here. We shall not like the idea of having you away from home again, but that is in the nature of things and we are getting used to it. That's why, with you brats getting ready to move out of the nest, the farm will be a life-saver to the old folks. As you say, you can get considerable government help and a Legion card will do you no harm. I'll sign you up in good old Peck Post when the next membership year comes on. There is a new all-female Post in town, but you will get more from one of the old established outfits. Wish I could offer you a membership in the Masons, too.

Next Monday school opens again. They are starting a drive for the new buildings which I fancy Alder wants to complete before he retires. I think his plans are poor, but I shall probably be out, too, by the time they are completed. I only hope real estate values hold up three more years so I can get a good price for this place.[76] My hunch is that they will.

I only hope that they do not keep you hanging around the Army too long, but that's anyone's guess. Once you are out, take a bit of time to get your feet under you. A too quick rushing into a civilian picture was a big mistake I made in the last war. And if you are going back to school, you will have to wait till a new term starts.

4 September 1945

Tuesday

Hello Family,

Back in the groove again after a lovely two-day vacation, I find it all rather disgusting. We have been having a heat wave; it was 100 degrees for about an hour yesterday and all LA is in a twit. They should come to the cold and frozen North to find real hots, no? Saturday I went in to Grace's, and after dinner we had to go and have me meet the family. I have already met Grace's mother—she seems like a nice old lady, but the others I find extremely dull and fuddy-duddy. What a boring evening, but as Grace said "It had to be done sometime." Grace tried to get me to go to church Sunday, but I craved sleep. So, quoth Grace, "A hell of a God-mother I turned out to be!" Around noon we departed for Long Beach with Harriet and Grace and Dot, a friend of theirs, and Harriet's mother, to visit Harriet's brother, a Lt. Col. in the Marines and his wife, and two cute little boys. Their apartment was a half-block from the ocean. A lovely bright day, cool breeze to alleviate the heat. We lay on the beach, which was semi-private and not crowded, and watched the surf and the beach, dotted with gay umbrellas. Had my first swim in the ocean and had a great surprise. I jumped in and bobbed right up, screaming, "It's SALTY!" Everyone stared at me doubtless thinking I was a poor little moron. But all along I had been regarding El Pacific as another Lake Michigan; that's just what it's like. Even Lake Superior has a more ocean atmosphere than this California brand—no sea smell, no sea gulls, no rocky

---

[76] Our house, a two-story, four-bedroom colonial with full attic and basement, cost around $10,000 for the house and lot when it was built in 1935. It sold for $20,000 in 1948.

coast. Had fun riding the surf and got a beautiful burn which has turned to tan.

Yesterday I lay around, panted, read, took many showers, and in the evening we had supper on the terrace at Harriet's with a gorgeous view of the mountains. Today I got transferred to Central Supply to work. At last no more Sgt. "Benito." We put up all the sterile supplies for the wards. My hours now are seven to three, with an hour off for lunch. Good deal, and the work is OK and not too arduous. Got in another sunbath this afternoon and went swimming in the newly opened pool at the Birmingham Country Club (alias GAOL) overlooking the miniature golf course. Bought a new Shaeffer pen at the PX for only $2.90. Got overpaid $10 on payday. Hope they don't discover it. I have eleven points now. The War Department made it as of V-J Day. Heard the broadcast from Tokyo Bay, did you? I laughed heartily at your news about Joseph carrying a torch. He must be bad off to do such an unprecedented thing. You know, he told me he never wanted to hear from me or see me again; this is rare. But I bet he doesn't write—he's too proud for that. Started a savings account with $20. How about letting me pay you back the $15 after my furlough? Can you let it ride that long? That is all the news, methinks.

Love you all,

From Mom—Sept. 7, 1945:

We have been having a heck of a heat wave this week and by the time evening comes I have been all washed out, or else we have gone out somewhere to cool off. It's still hot tonight—it's been about 93 today, but they promise us a thunder shower later, so we are hoping. Your picture finally came and we were so glad to get it. At first I didn't think I liked it, but the more I look at it, the more I do. You certainly look very smooth and sophisticated. No doubt your close proximity to the glamour capital has done it! Your summer uniform is very becoming, I'll bet. I always thought you looked so pretty in that tan, or pongee shade, even as a little girl. I was glad too that your stripes and insignia all showed up so well. Thank you very much—you are now sitting in the middle of the mantle. As Dad said, you looked very well nourished, too!

I have started the fall season being very gay and social—everything

*starting up again. Tuesday Dad and I went with the Danielsons to a place
in St. Paul for dinner and there we had the most beautiful piece of roast beef
I have seen since the war started. Last night Dad and I went for a ride to
cool off—drove down to Shakopee. It still seems devilish to go riding! If you
aren't allowed to scrub anymore, what sort of work do you do? Why did they
take the WACs off that work?*

7 September 1945

Friday

Yesterday was my day off so today feels like Monday, and my
regular writing day. This day-off-in-the-middle-of-the-week business screws me all up and I can't decide where in the week I am.
Such a creature of habit and sot in my ways. Wednesday evening
Carmen and I took off for the Beach-side, planning to stay at an
Army Rec Center that we'd heard about from the kids, not knowing
exactly where it was. Result was that we hitched all over Southern
California. Each person we rode with gave us different directions
and it got darker and darker and we got more and more lost. No
map with us, of course. Finally a nice man in a station wagon who
was going down to the ocean picked us up and we toured up and
down from Santa Monica to Venice looking for this camp. In
desperation we appealed to the men at a fire house, and they put
us right. Seems we'd been talking about Ocean Boulevard, and
what we really wanted was Ocean *Park* Boulevard, which makes a
world of difference in these parts. That nice man dropped us off
right at the door of the camp, too. We drew our bedding at the
supply-room and made up our bunks. The women have a little
dorm in the Headquarters Building. After which we strolled out
into the night. Went down to the Pier and rode on the Merry-
go-Round and the Ferris Wheel. The ones in California are double
and all lighted up with neon lights. When you're up high, you can
look back and see all the lights on the shore. Also we went
"twenty-five feet below the surface of the water, right down to the
ocean's floor and then up—speeding skyward at a speed of sixty
miles per hour" in a diving bell. It was fun; we saw funny fish and
it was all green and very bubbly. We went in the Penny Arcade and

strolled around and ate stuff and then went back. Harry James was at the Casino, but we couldn't go because no dates, natch.[77]

The next morning we slept late, then went up to Santa Monica for breakfast. We had "pancake sandwiches" which were two pancakes, then in between an egg fried, and then between or in amongst the egg, a sausage cake. Carmen had to buy some slacks so we went shopping. It killed me to look at all the cute fall clothes and accessories. Then we went back to Ocean Park, changed, and got a ride down to "The Bitch" with one of the GIs that work at the camp. (The above is a common GI term for the ocean-side.) We cooked in the sun for a long time and swam. The breakers were mammoth and very good for diving over. For lunch we had fried shrimp. We bought some stickers for our luggage. I got a gorgeous one of Minneapolis with little pictures of the Nicollet Hotel, the Gateway, Foshay Tower, Minnehaha Falls, and the Capitol. Also have Hollywood, LA, Texas, and Louisiana, and US Army. My suitcase now looks very gaudy.

Later: Just got back from a Company meeting where we learned the worst, which is, namely, NO FURLOUGHS for the next few months. I'm so mad I could spit. The civilians are working only forty hours a week, and there's a shortage of civilian workers here anyhow. Also Lt. C. said she doesn't think there will be any separate demobilization for the WAC. And as I'm only almost twenty-one and unmarried and have only twelve points, it could conceivably be two more years, unless something unprecedented happens. I have every strike against me and the outlook is gloomy in the extreme. If I could only get home this fall, even for fifteen days. Damn Col. Miller and damn everything. We had been hearing all kinds of good rumors the last couple of days, too, that seemed to have some foundation. But, like all LRs they have definitely petered out. The only way I can be discharged, it seems, is to wait for the "duration plus six." And remember in the last war, the duration wasn't over for two years after the Armistice. In 1947 I'll be twenty-three, a hell of a time to go back and finish college and try to get started on a profession. Well, Dad, you did, so I guess I can, too, only I'm afraid my mind will rot away in the interim. Oh God, I'm so depressed and mad. All I can see is barren years stretching ahead, being bitched at

---

[77] Carmen and I could not go into the Casino Ballroom on Santa Monica pier without male escorts.

by snotty nurses, wearing thicker callouses on my palms, and getting sore knees from scrubbing. All the PWs left today, too, so we'll be doing heavier work. Probably will be mowing lawns when we get off our day's work, pooped out. I'd better stop this before I have myself crying. It's rugged, believe me. Better take a long look at my pictures, family dear, because that's all you'll be seeing of me for the next year or two.

All my love,

From Dad—Sept. 9, 1945:
    Fall faculty meeting yesterday. My own schedule is super-simple: French I, every day, 2 boys; French II, every day, 5 boys; French III, every day, 3 boys; French IV, two days, 1 boy; Spanish II, every day, 10 boys; Spanish III, every day, 2 boys; for a total of 23 boys. The war and practical subjects certainly have knocked languages in the eye. If I were ten years younger, I should be worried and re-study my Russian. As it is, the Farm is the answer and when Michael is done with Blake, we shall move out and probably make more than I do now.

10 September 1945

Monday

Dearest Family,
    Let's see . . . I haven't done very much since my gloomy letter of Friday. That evening I GI'ed. Saturday evening I read three murder mysteries; everyone else had gone out so the barracks were nice and quiet. Sunday I had to work and it was very boring, but I got through at three, so Carmen and I went swimming at the Birmingham Pool—it's really quite a lay-out. In the evening, Brad got me a date, my first in months. There was me, Brad, Doug, and Jean, Brad's cousin, and accompanying us were four Air Corps Lieutenants—no, three, and a Captain.[78] We had some drinks at the Hitching Post, and then went on and had some marvelous steaks at another place. The pianist there was very obliging and played all kinds of college songs, which we rendered with great

[78] With the war over, the rules about nonfraternization of officers and enlisted people went by the boards. These rules were bent frequently anyway.

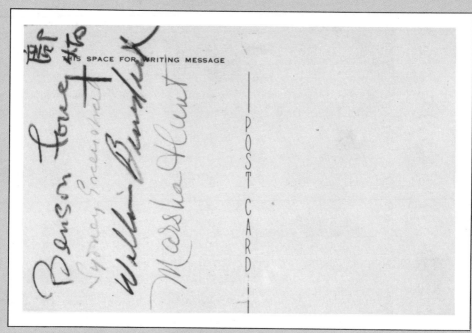

POST CARD

Benson Fong #6
Sydney Greenstreet
Willie Beavers(?)
Marsha Hunt

Autographs I got at the Hollywood canteen

Grace Symons in front of the NBC Building
at Vine & Sunset

Hollywood Boulevard

effect (we thought). Then on to another place for more drinks and rug cutting. My Lt. was a good Joe, good sense of humor, not a wolf, and a swell dancer. After we got kicked out of the night club at twelve (curfew still, out here) we started to drive one of the guys down to Long Beach where he's stationed. It's forty miles from downtown LA and more from out here in Hollywood, but at Santa Monica we decided it was too far, so we let him hitchhike, and we went wading in the surf. There was so much palavering and deciding which way to go that we didn't get back to camp till 4:30 a.m. The net result was that I had exactly one-half hour's sleep.

Tomorrow I start on the three to eleven shift in Central Service. I don't like it because it messes up the day so; you can't go anywhere or do anything except read and write and lie in the sun and sleep. It won't last long, though, because . . . because, dear family, brace yourself for a shock. No, I'm not getting out, but I *am* going to New York for a month!!! I found out for sure only today. Here's the deal: it's been cooking since July and I thought the Army had given up the idea. I'm going to a four-week Occupational Therapy School at Halloran General Hospital on Long Island, no Staten Island (just found out). In July they took applications for it and I put down my name when I heard the school would be in New York. Let me say first off, I don't think this will have much effect on a sooner discharge. I'm sure I'll be out by next summer, at least. This hospital is getting deader every day and things are really falling off in spite of what the Ma'am says. One thing, though, I won't sign any waivers saying I'll stay in three more years or anything like that. If I'm in a few more months than the other kids, I think that month in New York will be worth it. The school starts on Saturday, Sept. 29 so I'll probably leave here in a couple of weeks. Also I'm working on getting a Delay en Route on the way back, so I may be able to see the farm, after all. Just think, I'll be able to see Cousin Frank, and Ruthie up at Holyoke, and plays, and museums and all kinds of stuff. If this is too incoherent, just ask me some questions in your next letter and I'll try to answer them. Ahh . . . October in New York. I just can't believe that it's really come through at last. I gave up the idea long ago; that's why you didn't hear anything about it before. This will frost EC; she leaves the fifteenth, and I arrive the twenty-ninth. I so hoped to get in the first class, which started September first, but Ninth Service

Command is very slow in these matters. Now to toss off a couple more notes and fall into the sack. Write me your reactions to this news, quick-like.

P.S.: The pictures of the Farm are swell. Everyone in the barracks is going to come and visit me apres l'armee. They like the white barn with the green roof, especially.

From Dad—Sept. 14, 1945:

A brief mid-week line to say that I think your New York deal is a good one. This post-war waiting is very trying, as I can well remember and the morale is none too high. Anything that will get you around and keep you interested is all to the good. I very much doubt if it will hinder your discharge, particularly if you politely refuse to sign anything. Armies are the same old deal and just when you figure you are in for life, they throw you out without warning. In Paris we figured we never would be out and I went with about four hours notice! School is getting organized and should be fairly good this year. But are languages taking a beating! Harvard is planning to drop them from its entrance requirements. With the farm I should worry! Last night your maw and I canned ten and a half quarts of corn off our patch.

14 September 1945

Friday

Hello,

This is just a short note written before going off duty in Central Service at 10:30. Mom, please send your large suitcase. I abhor the idea of toting my dirty duffle bag across the country and I'm sure I can get a month's supply of stuff in two suitcases. My left upper wisdom tooth is coming in. I can't see it, but I can feel it. Gray and I are going to Santa Monica tomorrow to get sunburned again. I'm very excited about New York. I hope fervently that nothing happens to cross things up.

Goodnight,

18 September 1945

Tuesday

Dearest Family,

Things are moving swiftly. Today I signed my request for a Delay en Route and I get *ten* days! So I should be home around the first of November. We are pretty definitely leaving this Monday, the 24th. *And,* dig this, Sgt. Malone told us to take *all* of our stuff with us because something will probably break while we're gone and we may be transferred or something. Things are really cooking here at the GAOL. Patients are being discharged at a rapid rate. Col. Miller said all the nurses have to be out of here by December 15; they are being discharged thick and fast also. The Doctors were told that the sooner they got the patients out, the sooner they can get out. Lt. K (WAC) said that it was fairly definite that there won't be any peacetime WAC and that the WAC will probably be demobilized all at once. Most of these aren't too rumor-ish. Who knows, I may be out by Christmas. The only thing that throws me is: why are they having this school and spending so much money on transportation when things are closing down so fast? It just doesn't seem logical, but natch, the Army is seldom logical. It may be an oversight. At any rate, it's wonderful and New York here I come.

When I think of all the junk I'll have to pack, I get a violent headache. I've acquired so much more stuff since I've been out here. I think I'll leave my radio and civilian clothes at Grace's in case I don't come back out to the Coast; then she can send them on to me. Oh, happy day, caloo, callay!!! I haven't been doing too much lately; I'm still on the swing shift at Central Service. In the mornings I sleep and read. I'll have to start washing and ironing and getting stuff together this week. Hope your suitcase gets here in time; I still can use it. Goodbye for now, dear family, I may write again before I leave and maybe not. Anyhow I'll keep you posted while en route.

From Dad—Sept. 16, 1945:

As this letter will reach you about the mystic 20th, I really should have some Message for you on the occasion of your Coming of Age. As it is, what I would say I think you already know; my Paternal Blessing and a Memorial suitable to the Occasion will have to wait till you are once more with us. With proper changes to fit nationality and sex, the old Four Rules for the Soldier are still sound ones for a Father to hand on to his son or daughter on a Serious Occasion and as such I give them to you as I received them: "Fear God; Honor the Queen; Shoot straight; Keep clean." To which I add, "God bless you, my daughter." This denotes time out to listen to Cedric Adams and find out what is going on. Cold tomorrow and probably rain, but I do not mind as oil is off rations! Now to hit the hay for Monday is always Monday, no matter how you spell it.

From Mom—Sept. 17, 1945:

This is to wish you a very happy birthday and to wish you could have spent it at home. No doubt you remember what we did last year! I well remember how fussy they were at the Covered Wagon about your having a drink, and how Dad assured them you were celebrating your 21st birthday.

19 September 1945

Wednesday

Dearest Family,

Thank you all so very much for the birthday box. Natch, I couldn't wait till tomorrow to open it. The lipstick is swell, Mike— the shade is just right. And my smooth wallet is the envy of the barracks. I have transferred all my pictures and my money (what there is of it) and it proudly rests in the back compartment of my satchel. Mom, *how* did you know I needed new pants (heh, heh)? As soon as I saw them I quickly bestowed four raggedy pair on Carmen to use as dust rags. Muchos gracias also for the fancy PJs and my favorite cookies. My best present, though, was my birth certificate. My wish now is that I could stay at this age forever. I don't want to be any older but I guess it can't be helped. It's so funny; lately I've been feeling terribly ancient and as though I were getting old very fast without having much time to be young in. Always before I never thought much about getting old, and if I did, it seemed like such a long time off that it wasn't very important. I suppose everybody feels like this on his or her twenty-first birthday, but even so I don't like it. Well, enough of this morbid chit-chat.

Tomorrow I shall endeavor to sleep late through the early morning madhouse of Barracks 200 B. I shall iron clothes and sew on patches. Then lunch. Then sleep for a couple of hours. What a gala birthday I'm not having. Last year's celebration will have to do for two, I guess. I pulled a good deal on Sgt. Stark, though. Friday I have off, and Gray and I are really going to Santa Monica this time. I'll work Saturday, then have Sunday off, because I gave him to understand we're leaving Monday and I needed time to pack. But in reality we're not leaving till Tuesday evening at 6:35 p.m., so I'll have Monday off, too. There are five of us going; one girl I know slightly, and three other aging WACs who are nice but dull. They were Girl Scout leaders in civilian life or something like that. Ah well, such is life in the Army. How nice to be out some day and be able to talk to interesting people and friends again instead of babbling small talk with a lot of duds. What a waste of time it all is, says I, the intellectual snob. But my attitude is not at all unusual. All of the kids I've ever talked to who had anything on the ball, have experienced the same feeling. So sad about us.

Further notes on the New York set-up. School starts the 29th. Johnson is convinced that we'll have ten o'clock bed-check because they did when she went to Ad School, with maybe one late night during the week and a late Saturday night. And no weekend passes. I am prepared for the worst, but maybe I can get a special dispensation to go up to Hartford to see relatives. It's only about three hours by train, isn't it? And don't think I won't be out every night till the stroke of ten as long as my money holds out. I've got to do as much as possible in that month. Unit personnel is having our clothing records sent with us, which means, as I said, that we'll have to take everything we own (gas mask, too—ouch) which seems to indicate that there is a possibility of a transfer. If it has to be on the West Coast I'd just as soon be here, though. I have a good deal with Grace, and I know my way around by now and I'd loathe to be stuck out in the desert somewhere. Uncle Sugar Able will probably cook up some fiendish scheme to make me miserable, of that I have no doubt. It's just about time to close up the joint and hit the sack, so I'll finish this off with much kisses and love and hugs and I'll see you in November for sure.

From Mom—Sept. 21, 1945:
   This is to wish you bon voyage. If you by chance go through any of the places where we have relatives or friends and you have any time off the train,

why don't you telephone them? Aunt Kate in Omaha, or the B's in Chicago. They would love to hear from you. I thought of something else. Rachel Katz is in New York City, and you might like to get in touch with her sometime. Here is her address. You might write her a note and perhaps get to see her. She has a medical discharge from the Army Nurse Corps, you remember.

Halloran

HALLORAN GENERAL HOSPITAL
STATEN ISLAND, NEW YORK
26 September to 28 October 1945

In Transit

26 September 1945

Wednesday

Hello Family,

Bumpity, bumpity, this train is really giving my writing a bad case of the twitches; hope you can read it. We're whizzing through Utah now, having passed through California and the southern tip of Nevada. The country is gorgeous, of course, with lovely pastel hills, rugged mountains, sagebrush, brilliant blue sky with little drifty white clouds; cool, too. We left last night at 6:30, had mess on the train, sat in the lounge car till our berths were made up, and then hit the sack. I'm sharing a lower with a nice kid who's been around at BGH since before me. Very uneventful trip so far, except for some drunken Marines who tried to give us a snow job. Naturally, we gave 'em the frost. It sure is fun to be on a train again.

My last week in California we had perfect weather: cool, clear, and sunny. Friday, I had off, and Carmen and I went over to Santa Monica where her brother is taking a course at Douglas Aircraft. We stayed at his hotel. First off, we got into our jeans and hiked up along the coast for about three miles, playing in the surf and exploring for shells. Exhilarating day, with the wind and sand in our hair. We had dinner with her brother and a friend of his; then we all went to Ocean Park and danced to the music of Harry James. Good, good, good. He broadcast from the hospital last week and the great man actually ate in our mess-hall beforehand. In a

T-shirt, he was. Saturday was a sparkling day, and curses, I had to go back to the hospital and work. Sunday I lay around and packed a little. Monday also. Carmen and I went out for a farewell dinner at Mike Lyman's, which was up to previous standards, and went to a double feature French movie; *King of Virtue* and *Confessions of a Newlywed*. Both farces, both lewd, and wonderfully funny. Even though I didn't get all the cracks, they were broad enough, 1920's style, for me to catch most. Just remembered, Sunday I went in to Hollywood with some stuff to leave with Grace and spent most all afternoon trudging the ten blocks between the USO where I left it, and the Information Center where Grace works. For my birthday she gave me some beautiful old gold filigree earrings that belonged to her mother, I think. She's going to have them polished and have regular clips put on; they're made for pierced ears. Took some pictures of dear old Hollywood. Nobody thinks we're coming back, so it was fond farewell. I hope I do come back, in a way; if I have to be in the Ninth Service Command it may as well be BGH.

As for this trip: we get into Chicago at 9:00 Friday morning, and don't leave till 6:00 that night. I can use a nine hour layover in good old Chicago. I'll call Mary B. and maybe she'll meet me somewhere for lunch. In William's last letter, he included a pamphlet from the University of Chicago and a blank, which I sent in for more information, and I'm sending it on to you. Sounds like a good deal to me. This clear (relatively) penmanship is due to a small stop in the wilds of Utah. Then we get into New York at 3:15 Saturday afternoon. When I return, I have to go coach and take a layover in Chicago and round-trip it up to Minneapolis, or else swing up from Chicago and down to catch the train again in Omaha, whichever takes the least time and money. I get four days travel time from New York to the Coast, and ten extra days. Any traveling I need to do up to Minneapolis must be out of these ten, which isn't too bad. Gosh, I wish you all were along. We could have fun on the train and I know you'd appreciate the overwhelming scenery. We've been winding up through deep canyons all morning. We'll be going through Salt Lake City, Denver, Omaha, and Chicago, and after that, I don't know—probably Cleveland. Yes, Mom, I'll call up all my relatives.

Goodbye for now,

27 September 1945

Thursday

Last night I was very sick. Felt better today though. It's very cold; snow in Cheyenne and Laramie, sleet and rain in Nebraska. We're huddled around the radiator, feeling slightly numb. This trip is rather dull, I'll be glad when we hit Chi.

All love,

New York, New York

29 September 1945

Halloran General Hospital, Staten Island, New York, 8th WAC Co., ZI, Saturday

Dearest Family,

Here I am perched in my upper bunk in the barracks; the wind is howling and spasmodic rain beats down on the flimsy roof. Sounds cozy; in fact I think I'll hit the well-known sack. I'm kind of tired and I think the lights are supposed to be out . . . My gosh, Monday already. I'm waiting around for a little meeting we're supposed to go to, so I'll try to add some on here. I posted you from around Cheyenne, I think. The scenery was dreary and we read all day. The next noon we got to Chicago, the train being four hours late. We got out to pouring rain, and me with no Utility Coat, but no matter. I called Mary and went up to her office. We went out to lunch and then over to Time, Inc. to see Marge, after which we went to the Wrigley Building and met Billy. I heard all the family gossip which I'll relate to you when I get home. They saw me onto my train OK and we sailed away. Chicago looked swell even though it was cold and rainy. I got to ride on my favorite double-deck bus and saw Michigan Boulevard.

On the New York Central we had a first-class Pullman. I nearly collapsed when I saw it. We're so used to those gruesome green plush tourist-class deals. The dining service was wonderful, and I had a lower berth all to myself, so naturally I didn't wake up till Schenectady. It's a beautiful ride through New York State and down the Hudson. Saw West Point and Sing Sing and lots of blue mountains. Coming into New York we came through a lot of real slums with wash hanging out, and second-hand outdoor shops, and kids in gutters, and people leaning out of windows, and garbage. Just like Sociology I, Fall Quarter. We pulled into Grand Central about three and dashed right out to look at the place. Walked up 42nd Street to Fifth Avenue; saw the Library, Rockefeller Center, all the big stores, all the swarms of people. Then we went to a place recommended by Lil and had an elegant seafood dinner. I had six cherrystone clams—raw, Dad!—and fried scallops, and kibitzed on another girl's boiled live lobster. After this we thought we'd really better go out to the hospital, so we got a subway over to South Ferry and took the boat over to the Island. It was wonderful; the harbor all full of ships; saw the Statue of Liberty; spray got all over our clothes; marvelous sunset. People ran full tilt off the ferry to catch a bus. Never saw the like of the way everyone tears around here. A cop with a great Irish brogue directed us; heard all kinds of weird accents.

The hospital is way to hell and gone out on Staten Island. A mammoth place; big brick buildings with colonial-like trim; eight stories, some of them. Natch, we live in dear little white barracks with wood stoves. It's not too bad, just good old Army style. There's a big PX, fancy Service Club, telephone center—all on a larger scale than BGH. The next day, Sunday, we couldn't get passes till ten in the morning, but then we took off. A bus going from the Hospital to Times Square took us through Bayonne, Jersey City, under the Holland Tunnel, and thence to Manhattan. It's wonderfully easy to get around New York; I feel as if I'd been here for weeks. I had a little trouble, though, in getting to the apartment where EC stayed this summer; there's a lot of Minneapolis girls still there. What I did was walk all over the West Side from 34th to 44th, when I should have been on the East Side, which I remembered after I had walked all over the joint. Saw Times Square, the theater district, and more mobs of people, and finally found the apartment. We visited and then some more kids came over. There's a whole nest of Minneapolis kids on the East Side there. We made supper and had a good bridge session. Ruthie's coming down in a week or so, and Alta's coming up from Washington on the tenth, so it should be fun.

Here's the pass deal: 11:00 week nights; one late pass a week—2:30; weekends free from 5:00 Saturday to 6:00 Monday morning. It's a swell deal and I'll be able to get up to Hartford. I

have all kinds of mad plans to meet people for dinner and stuff. I
don't know when I'll get any studying done. Who cares. I'm here
frankly for a good time. I'm wiring you for some money cause we
missed the September payroll and I'm desperate. Got to go to class
now—more later.

From Dad—Oct. 2, 1945:

*Your telegram arrived this morning and I hasten to answer. New York
is a poor town to be busted in, as I know from experience. May I call your
attention to a basic rule of finance which you have evidently overlooked?
Never go barging around without a small reserve for emergencies (which
always come). Make the reserve your first goal and* get it, *for, without it, you
are at the mercy of a harsh world—*I know. *Learn this early and you will
save yourself some bad beatings in the future. This week we went down to the
Athletic Club to dinner and had excellent steak. Meat is getting easier here
now.*

7 October 1945

Sunday

Dearest Family,

First let me express my great gratitude for the money order. It
saved my life—of course, it's practically all gone by now but we
should be paid pretty soon now; I signed the payroll yesterday.
We're going to be gypped next month, too. It ain't right, but that's
the Army. I'm having a lovely time and also working like a slave.
They really pour the work on and we have to do things every night
to get our projects done. We have a WAC Captain who is an
Occupational Therapist to teach us. We have lectures on OT
methods, and how to do things like weaving, finishing wood,
carving, etc. Last week I wove a belt, carved out a shuttle for netting
and finished it off, wove a length of netting, chip-carved a linoleum
block, made four leather patterns, carved a wooden box and
finished it, cut out pictures for my scrapbook, and read in our
textbook. I don't quite know whether I like this yet.

I alternate between periods of depression and sloughs of
despond, and times of self-confidence and interest, which is

wearing on the nerves. I don't have much time to relax. I did take one night off, though, and came into town to have dinner with Barbie O. (she works nights at Associated Press) and Betty P. who is studying ballet. Barbie had to go back to work, so Betty and I went up on top of the Empire State Building. It was dreadfully cold but such a view—millions of lights. It was like looking at a map, it was so high up. After which we went over to the apartment where I reveled in a bath. We met Barbie for a drink at 12:00, and I bounced back to camp on the Journal Square bus. This weekend I came in and stayed with the kids again and we went to a most wonderful Swedish restaurant, the Three Crowns, which has a smorgasbord on a revolving table, and you pop back for more every time your plate gets empty. I hogged madly, I couldn't resist anything. After we ate, we couldn't think of anything to do but go to a movie. Reason: no men, no money, no tickets. Without those in this town, civilians don't have such a hot time. If I'd been with fellow WACs, we'd have bummed around to Service Centers and stuff. Today we slept late, went to the Drury Lane for dinner where I had excellent shrimp curry, and then I bid the kids farewell and took off to go museuming.

First I went up to the Museum of Non-Objective Painting. The pictures would probably give Dad a huge ache, but I thought they were rather interesting; mainly Kandinsky things. I even went so far as to buy a particularly colorful print for the large sum of twenty-five cents. Next on my program was the Metropolitan, so I walked and walked up through Central Park, which is quite wild and woodsy to my surprise. By the time I got up there, my feet were pooped and the thought of the museum appalled me, so I sat on a bench, watched the squirrels and little kids, and then took a bus back downtown, finding myself in the midst of a parade for Pulaski Day and horray for Poland. No sooner did the parade start than did the rain—great drenching sheets. But it was a swell parade, and everyone stayed in the rain to watch it. Many bands, and colorful costumes and people carrying banners. After I was thoroughly soaked (even through my Utility Coat), and the parade ended, I went over to the Museum of Modern Art and gazed. Saw lots of stuff that I'd studied about. I felt so brilliant when I recognized them before reading the signs. Had to fight with myself to keep from buying prints, but my better self, allied with my emaciated wallet, won out. For dinner I went to the French Cafe at Rockefeller

Center and had cherrystone clams, French fries, and chocolate cake. I'll probably have nightmares tonight but it was good.

Even though it was night, I wanted to glance at Columbia. In the subway I had a horrible time trying to find out which one to take. The ticket man had an unintelligible accent which I couldn't hear through the roaring of the subway. Luckily a nice sailor who was going up to Columbia took me under his wing, and I got up there OK. He didn't have to be in till 8:30 so he very kindly showed me around the campus. It reminds me a lot of Minnesota. We strolled around and then had a hamburger and coke. He's a nice kid from Tennessee in the NROTC [Naval Reserve Officers Training Corps] at Columbia. He wanted me to go to the football game next Saturday but I can't get off till five, darn it. But if he isn't on watch, we're going out that night. He's the first sailor I've met who isn't a wolf, and it will be nice to have a date to see the night life with. Life is getting very complicated: Ruthie can't get down till weekend after next, which is the twentieth, and my last one, because school ends the twenty-seventh. Also, Cousin Frank won't be back in Hartford for another week, so you can see things are getting jammed up.

I told you about my ten days Delay en Route with the four days of travel time. I have to be back at BGH on the eleventh, and the swing up from Chi to Minneapolis is on my own time. It takes two nights and a day to get to Minneapolis from New York, in other words, thirty-six hours, getting in on Monday night. I had a brainstorm: why not fly from here to Minneapolis? Then I wouldn't have to grind myself down on the coach. I could get in on Sunday night if I left on the 1:00 afternoon flight—it takes eight hours, and costs $52, meals included. Do you think it's worth it? I'd have to have an advance of more money to pay for this journey, but I promise to pay it all back. IOU already: Mom: $15; Dad: $25; this will be paid back, too. I am absolutely going to be frugal when I return to California. Please give me your opinion and decision— since the money angle is in your hands. Remember I'd have to pay anyway from Chi to Minneapolis . . . of course, this is beside the point, but I'm dying to fly—never have, you know. I hope you can understand all this. Got your letter of the second. At last I hear—gosh, that was two weeks without any mail. I kept wondering what you all were doing; you sound very social. I must stop now and catch the bus back to the Island. I'm at Barbie's now as you can see by the paper . . . Beekman Tower.

From Mom—Oct. 19, 1945:

Yesterday evening we had Mu and her husband Bill to dinner. Our farm manager had gone hunting with Karl Danielson over the weekend and he gave us two pheasants, so I got some wild rice and we had a real Minnesota dinner. They brought the baby; he's a cute little thing only he yelled most of the evening! It's a hard life for a baby, living in a hotel and getting dragged around. Bill has had offers of a couple of good jobs here, but they still can't find a place to live. Housing is an awful problem here, as well as all over the country.

15 October 1945

Monday

Dearest Family,

As you can see from the stationery I was up in Hartford last weekend; a spur-of-the-moment excursion brought on by a feeling of to-heck-with-everything. My sailor deal didn't work out, and all my fellow students go home over weekends, and the Minneapolis kids didn't have any money, so I just suddenly decided to go up. I knew Cousin Frank wasn't back yet, but I thought Lena would let me stay. It turned out to be rather a mess, and really funny, but it's all too involved to tell here. As it was, I stayed at the Bond, slept well, went to 11:00 service at Christ Church where there was a swell sermon by a young Navy Chaplain. Then I had dinner and went over to Kenyon Street. We sat by the fire and chatted and listened to the Symph. We had to make supper because the maid was out, so we slummed in the kitchen, as Lena put it. That Lena sure is a character; she's strictly two generations behind the times, and more class-conscious and imperialistic and white man's burden and all that rot than any Kipling character ever thought of being. The biggest event in her life, that she's still talking about, is the sinking of the *Titanic*.

This last week has been another grind: ceramics, lumber construction, cord-knotted belts, weaving, paper decoration, block printing, plastics, and Lord knows what else. Next week it's leather work. I can't see what there is left to do but no doubt the Captain will dig up something. I'm so tired all I want to do is sleep for days. Also to add to the gaiety I have a lovely cold. I knew I couldn't go through the fall without one. Last year I sniffled all through Staging at Fort Des Moines. Thursday night I went into town and braved the mobs at Macy's to get some stuff to block print on. Got a square yard of imported Irish linen but have decided it's too nice to ruin with my feeble attempts at "Arts and Craps," as we call it. Right now I'm in the throes of a huge lumber project which will eventually turn out to be a record cabinet, we hope. I can't get the joints to match. How would you like to saw nine-ply wood with a completely dull saw? My shoulder ached for days. Oh, to be out of the Army and rest; maybe back at lenient BGH I can relax. You'd better decide for sure about flying soon so I can get reservations. They are supposed to be two weeks in advance. I'm awaiting your word breathlessly. Ruthie is coming down this week, but most of my other plans have messed up. No more now, too busy. This is being written during break.

All love,

20 October 1945

Saturday A.M.

Dearest Family,

It's all set. I've got tickets on the 11:00 p.m. plane Sunday the 28th. I'll get into Minneapolis at 5:45 Monday morning, Wold-Chamberlain Field. It was too late for the afternoon plane; it's too bad because at night I won't get to see so much but it will be fun anyway. I had to borrow $30 from Lil to buy my ticket, so would appreciate $50 money order or wire quick-like so I can pay her back.

This week has been another mad rush. Met Jeanne D. Wednesday for dinner at an Indian place and the Ballet. Tuesday I spent rushing around trying to get theater tickets; finally got some to *Dark of the Moon*. That crazy Ruthie wrote too late to get anything else. She's coming in and I'm meeting her tonight. I think Cousin Frank tried to call me, but the orderly never bothers to find people when they have calls. They just tell you casually a couple of days later. If

I live through this week it will be a miracle. I have to: finish a mammoth box; make linoleum block prints; make plastic coasters; make a leather case; pack everything (horrors!); make a scrapbook; copy notes. Give me strength, oh Lord.

Goodbye and all love,

BIRMINGHAM GENERAL HOSPITAL
VAN NUYS, CALIFORNIA
18 November 1945 to 7 February 1946

18 November 1945

78th WAC Hospital Co., ZI, BGH, Van Nuys, California, Sunday

Dearest Family,

I have put off writing till now because of the messed up condition of my situation and my possessions. But today I moved into my old barracks, unpacked everything, washed mountains of dirty clothes, mended stockings, spread myself around, and definitely feel as though I am back in my same old rut. Few things have changed. Cooper left the week after I did; her husband was discharged and she likewise. Cummings was made a Sergeant. The hospital is booming; three thousand patients as against 1300 when I was last here. Far from closing as we all thought it would, it is being made into a paraplegia center (men paralyzed from the waist down). More personnel are being shipped in, and our Detachment mess is going to be opened again. All personnel will have to work seven days a week, says Col. Miller. I don't think this will affect OT though. We have a super deal, at least up to now. I worked Thursday, Friday and Saturday, so I got some idea of the set-up. Civilians run the whole thing. They are very nice and pleasant. We work eight to five weekdays and Saturday mornings for four hours. The civilians are gone then and we putter around getting stuff ready for the next week. Our work consists of cutting out plastic and leather, finishing up projects for the patients who are in bed, tracing patterns, and just being useful. The men come in from nine to twelve and one to three, and we circulate around giving advice and helping them with their little problems. When they leave, we sweep out the place and then we all whip out our own projects. I

216

made three large plastic buttons, and four little ones; and am working on a salad fork and spoon. The facilities are wonderful, with all power saws, drill presses, and electric buffing machines. Next week I think I will be assigned to the newly opened Functional Shop where they do more weaving and knotting, which I like. You can see that we aren't worked to death as yet and it's all kind of fun.

The trip back was quite horrible. I got some sleep the first night although I was sharing my seat with a Sergeant who seemed to expand mysteriously during the night. Morning came and I found myself squished up against the wall and the Sergeant comfortably swarming over five-eighths of the seat. We had some time in Omaha and I called Aunt Kate. Then at 10:00 a.m. I got on the Challenger and my troubles began. It was a twenty-five coach train, with not more than fifty civilians on it. All the rest were GIs; swabbies on their way to the Coast to ship out, Marines and soldiers on their way to be discharged, and numbers of the already discharged, and all with the consuming desire to tank up. Which they did, with a vim. I have never witnessed such a mass absorption of alcoholic spirits and such a resultant mass drunk in all my young life. It was frightening really and I was badgered and slobbered over by so many high GIs that I never wanted to see a man again. Great bunches of them ranged up and down the car all night, greeting long-lost buddies and imploring people to have a little drink. Little sleep did I get. During the day it wasn't so bad; I knit and looked out the window. The scenery was, as usual, overwhelming. We saw the Rockies covered by a fresh fall of snow up around Ogden, Utah, which is a cute little town set in a nest of mountains. Got off for awhile in Las Vegas, Nevada—a wild town that was still going strong at 1:00 at night. It was very hot in California—just like summer in LA. The rains haven't started, luckily. I took a taxi to Grace's and washed off the accumulated filth, and I *do* mean dirt, and had lunch and a nap. After supper she and Harriet took me out to the hospital.

Well, my sweet family, that seems to be all of the news. One more thing—bad news: we can't be paid till January on account of they have paid so many liberated prisoners they don't have enough money or clerical help to take care of us.[79] Christmas will have to be a few weeks late for you, therefore, and I can't send any money till

[79] United States troops liberated from Japanese prison camps had piled up a lot of back pay from time spent in captivity.

later either. I'll try to get along on what I have and they might give us a partial pay in a couple of weeks. I hope so. Goodbye for now and I'll write again in the middle of the week.

Love,

From Mom—Nov. 16, 1945:

I'm sitting under the dryer at DuVal's, improving the shining moment. Dad had his examination Tuesday a.m. and had to go back again in the afternoon. The doctor gave him barium and looked at his innards with the fluoroscope. He said there seemed to be nothing at all wrong with his stomach, but that there was a certain amount of spasticity in the duodenum. He gave Dad some medicine and told him if he wasn't a lot better in ten days, to come in again and they would really go after it. I think he got a stomach flu bug and then got worried and nervous and built it up into the same trouble as before. If he will only relax and forget his insides, I think he will be all right. He really is feeling better; can eat more now. We haven't done a thing all week—Monday it rained hard and was very dismal and I missed you a great deal. I do hope you didn't have too bad a trip . . .

From Dad—Nov. 16, 1945:

This has been a long week since we popped you on the train and it seems as though you had been gone for ages and not just seven days! At present, having just laid the fire, I am writing this on the corner of the couch, waiting for your Maw to bring on the toasted-cheese sandwiches. My visit on Tuesday to Old Doc Johnson was as unpleasant as those barium exams usually are, but I was much relieved to get a relatively clean bill of health. I have doubtless produced the whole thing, what with getting into a tizzy about the Farm and whatnot, but I shall try to be a better man in the future, s'welp me. My new guitar is a real treat and I want to keep at it all the time. My insides still fuss at me, but now that I know there is nothing serious there, I can take it for a while, and I fancy that a week or so will clear it up.

From Mom—Nov. 23, 1945:

We were so glad to get your Sunday letter today (Friday). I was beginning to get worried because we had not heard from you—I thought you might be sick after that long and tiring trip. What an experience, to be mixed up with such a wild bunch of drunks. *Dad is feeling much better. He is able to eat and enjoy his food again, and ate quite a man-sized meal yesterday (Thanksgiving Day). I'm sure it was all nerves and tension. That's most of the trouble with both of us. Take heed—learn to always be relaxed and don't stew over things! I'm feeling pretty good myself, at the moment, anyhow.*

25 November 1945

Sunday

Hello Family,

I meant to write in the middle of the week but somehow I got sidetracked. It has been a full and pleasant week. Monday evening we had a spot check of all our GI clothing. We had to get everything out and the barracks was a mess, and it took a long time, and an evening was wasted in feeble red tape. Tuesday afternoon I went into Van Nuys with practically all my clothes for the cleaners. Also I did some shopping for our little group: Postum, tea-balls, crackers, and cheese. Then went to the Post movie. Wednesday I took off for Grace's. We cleaned house madly for the next day. My fingers had been itching for a long time to dust her living room and at last I had my way. I dusted and vacced and swept the whole place. We made pies and stuffed the turkey and made gingerbread and drank beer and gabbed and had fun. Thursday I actually went to church with everybody. Usually Grace goes to early service and I want to sleep so I don't go. But this time it was at ten with a good choir under the able direction of Dick. His three brothers and their wives and his mother and father are all in the choir—it's like a club. After church we had breakfast and then lay around in the afternoon waiting for the turkey to cook. Dick and I went over to get the relatives and then we ate and ate and it was all most good. Friday night a bunch of us went into Hollywood to the boxing matches. It was just like in a movie—blue smoke hanging thick and the ring glaring out in the middle. We yelled and threw peanut shells around. Saw a few movie stars, like Dane Clark—big thrill.

Saturday afternoon Baggie and I went shopping. I bought only linoleum blocks and paper for Christmas cards, but Baggie went to a make-up bar and had the woman give her the works. What a line! Baggie bought specially blended powder and rouge and lipstick and lipstick brush and eyelash wax, and they stunk us with all different kinds of perfume trying to get us to buy some. We had an early dinner and then went to a movie, *Confidential Agent*. After which we went to my favorite skinny bar. Here we met two nice Marines who were just back from overseas and had never talked to any WACs before. They wanted to have some fun so we went to Mike Riley's Madhouse, a crazy place with continuous crackpot stuff sort of like Spike Jones. We had a fine time laughing and making cracks back at the MC—we were at a front table. These Marines were extremely nice. They bought us flowers, and didn't get drunk, and didn't try to pull any rough stuff, and they hitched clear back out to BGH with us. One said, "I never take out a girl that I don't escort home," which is rather unusual with GIs. Today I accomplished nothing. We saw a funny movie, *Pardon My Past*, a double people mix-up with Fred MacMurray. Then we went scrounging around all the wards getting milk and coffee and teacups and bread and crackers and lemons and sugar and knives and spoons. We have gone into housekeeping. Dick got us a hot plate from the Police Station and Grace gave us a saucepan, and we're all set. It's great sport. Of course the plate blew out a fuse tonight but we'll fix that.

My job seems to be shaping up rather well. Through sheer bluff and a good memory I have gotten myself put in charge of the weaving department. I said I knew how to set up a loom. Fact is, I had watched El Capitan back at Halloran start to do it, and I had the general theory, but that was all. At that I seemed to know more about it than most of the Janes around there. They say, "My, you must have had a lot of experience," and I say, "Oh yes, I'm never so happy as when I'm puttering around a loom." (Cough, cough.) I work by myself in another room; no noise and nobody butts in and no one hounds me or watches. As a consequence I do twice as much work. Did you see in the paper married WACs can get out December first? Soon there will be no one left but hags like me, because about 75% of the WACs are married. Baggie, Brad, GeeGee and Doug will all be gone, 200 B will be almost empty, and we'll rattle around back here. I have thought of a wonderful Christmas present for me. *Time* is offering a special subscription rate for GIs: two years for $6. Usually it's $5 for one year, so if you could send me the money now, we could take advantage of the rate and I would consider it an excellent present. How about it, huh? My area is in chaos so I must go clean it up. I miss you all so much, I do wish

I were home. Though I'm happy and busy, I think constantly about the day when I can get out. All I can do is think though, unless I quick get married—to whom I have no idea. Such is life.

All my love,

From Mom—Nov. 30, 1945:

Let's see—what have we done this week. Monday I went downtown and did a few errands and then to the Study Club where I heard a rather gloomy lecture by Professor Luyten of the University called "The War of 1965." He said that unless the atom bomb secrets are shared by all the big powers and then outlawed, there is little chance of escaping another war. I trust the politicians will take this point of view.

Wednesday night we all went to hear Fritz Kreisler. The concert was good and some of the numbers very lovely but I do feel he is losing his touch somewhat—he is past seventy. There is a rather severe flu epidemic here, but to date the family has escaped it. There are an awful lot of boys and masters out at Blake. Write often and keep cheerful. Why not try to be philosophical about your present job and make the best of it that you can? I don't mean to be preachy but just want you to be as contented as possible.

From Dad—Dec. 2, 1945:

It is grand to know that you like your new work and that you are able to really get going with the weaving. You should be a real expert by the time you come home. Maybe I should build a weaving-house for you and we can organize the St. Keverne Klever Krafts Korp. Ink. and make some real money. Your Maw ain't too old to learn a trade, and Mike and I could peddle the products of the loom and loam. Think it over!

3 December 1945

Monday

Dearest Family,

Well, guess what? Our hot plate blew a fuse again last night, and do the Post engineers hate us! Dick had put in a new element and I guess it's just too powerful. But all is not lost; Dick's getting another one, and Margaret, Grace's friend who is at the Information Center with her, is giving us one also. We are deluged. Much excitement is going on in the rear of 200 B. Brad's husband came back Monday after one and a half years overseas and she went out on a three-day pass. Saturday Baggie's husband came in after two and a half years and *she's* out on a three-day pass. Doug is pregnant, and all four of 'em, Brad, Baggie, Doug, and GeeGee are getting out of the Army next week. I'm so happy for them, specially Baggie. She was with Tony only five days before he was shipped overseas. The barracks will sure be empty when they go. I wouldn't mind the Army so much but it's so damned cold here. We have no heat whatsoever and the cement floor is clammy and freezing. If we don't get Pneumonia, I will be surprised.

Everyone is being terrifically artsy-craftsy. Lena is creating dolls at a rapid rate; I painted a face on her latest one, a clown. Cummings is crocheting, and embroidering guest towels. Carmen is knitting scarves and hats. Doug is crocheting baby bonnets, and I carry on as best I can. I cut out two linoleum blocks last week for Xmas cards; I'll send you samples when I start printing them. And Saturday morning I wove a rug for beside my bed. It's red chenille with yellow and gray stripes. I was doing it at top speed, so the department wouldn't discover I was using their chenille. I was hurrying so fast that when I cut it off the loom, the strings all slipped through the heddles. So I had to come in early Sunday afternoon and restring the whole blasted thing. The wages of sin!

Let's see—social life: Monday: Company meeting. Rough. Tuesday: rushed into Van Nuys to the cleaners, and had supper at the USO with a former Surgery buddy. We had some beer at the Brass Rail and home early. Wednesday: knit and read. Thursday: saw a *very* funny movie, *Stork Club;* Barry Fitzgerald at his best, Betty Hutton was also funny. Friday: met Carmen and GeeGee in Hollywood. We grabbed a hot-dog and then went to see *Spellbound* which was very good, at Grauman's Chinese Theater, a very amazing place. It's huge and every inch is thick with lush imitation Chinese decor. Saturday afternoon, Lena and I went to the USC-UCLA game, which was a big rivalry to see who would play in the Rose Bowl. It was a fun game with lots of running around and fumbling and passing and enthusiastic tackling, not like the fairly sluggish powerhouse technique of most Northern teams (except Indiana). But sad to say, UCLA lost 26 to 16. At the half there were special stunts. At the fifty yard line on both sides were special rooting sections all in white with colored pom-poms which they waved in unison when they cheered. At the half, they had flash cards, all colors, and they spelled words and made pictures of Bears and Trojan horses, and the coaches, and the Queens of homecoming and stuff. After the game I met Grace, and Harriet and Dot, and a friend of theirs who's a Lt. in the WAVES. We all went to Harriet's for supper and a cribbage tournament. Sunday I slept late and had a hot surging bath. Then went into Hollywood with Grace, had dinner with her and Margaret, then hitched out to the Post where I worked from 4:30 to 7:30 on that accursed loom. I was so pooped I went right to bed; that's why no letter till tonight.

I'm rich now. I got my partial back pay check and we are being paid this Wednesday, too, so I'll send you a check soonly. Give me some Christmas ideas, now. For me: sweet smells, powder, stockings (if you can get them), and maybe some pretty PJs (not a nightie—too cold), and a pretty slip and some new fuzzy slippers—just things like that, and $6 for *Time*. About my work. I teach the patients how to weave, and I get them out of jams. I had to laugh; there were three OTs gathered around this one guy, talking about his weaving, but he yelled to *me* to come and tell him what to do next. Also I string looms, sort yarn, and do odd jobs. Fun and easy. Got to do some laundry and wash my hair now. No rain here yet; it's real warm in the middle of the day still.

Love,

6 December 1945

Thursday

Midweek communique: I'm on barracks detail and thus I have an extra hour in which to do it, but it doesn't take an hour to do, and so I have time to pen you a note. You have been so nice to write so many little letters all week—nearly every day I get one and I don't feel neglected at mail call. Tuesday night I printed my Christmas cards of which I enclose two samples. Last night Carmen and I had our favorite dinner at Mike Lyman's. Then we went to Olvera Street and shopped for presents, for you people, EC, and Ruthie. Carmen bought me a wonderful ring—a jade knuckle-duster with a Mayan face. I bought a ring for her, too, so we are even. I am enclosing a check for $30, leaving $70 yet to pay, in small installments, natch. I have opened my savings account again and it makes me feel most virtuous. Must go to work now, so goodbye till Sunday.

All love,

9 December 1945

Sunday

Dear Family,

Things have changed. They have changed me to a new barracks. After eight months, I have to leave my little buddies. It is warmer here, but I don't like these kids' choice of radio programs. Tomorrow I am sending you a box of presents, mostly for my friends. If you could send or take them to the kids, I would appreciate it. I shopped madly Saturday, covering about forty miles by the time I was through, from Van Nuys to Wilshire to LA to Hollywood to Van Nuys! Wilshire has such beautiful stores, one is afraid to buy anything. Bullock's Wilshire is just like a dream or a fancy movie set. I was actually awe-struck and walked around drooling dazedly. You just can't imagine what they are like. This weekend I have done nothing but laundry and moving and knitting. Life is just very calm and somewhat dull, so no more to say except goodnight and I love you.

13 December 1945

Thursday

Hello Family,

Hope the flu hasn't taken hold with you. It's going around here and all my patients have colds, but as yet no signs with me. I have a small wish: could you address the enclosed cards for the relatives and shove 'em in a post box for me? Thanks. Would you be satisfied with not so many presents till after Xmas? I sort of ran out of money last week. Another package is going to be en route as soon as I can find a large enough box. I'll write news on Sunday.

P.S.: If somebody wanted to give me some purty stationery, I wouldn't cry . . .

13 December 1945

Hello Again,

I'm kind of thick this evening. I forgot to tell you about Grace's Christmas present. They have a gruesome wooden lamp in their living room, and Dick is always grousing about how awful it looks. So I thought I would get them a lamp and I did, last week at Bullock's Downtown. It is a lovely yellow pottery one. I had it sent to Grace and was planning to call and tell her not to open it till Xmas, but I forgot, and they opened it, mystified as to where it had come from. When I did call, Dick said, "So *that's* who sent it! I had been complaining so much about that other lamp to everybody, I couldn't figure out who had taken the hint." So they have it on the table—the non-Christmas present. We had a fire in the supply room Saturday morning. Just before Col. Miller was about to come on inspection of our non-burning stoves, the supply room one blew up. Hope he really does something about the situation now. We are freezing to death.

Love again . . .

From Mom—Dec. 9, 1945:

Heard from Mu. They bought a house in St. Louis Park. It's a pre-fabricated and quite tricky, Mu said—all one piece kitchen unit, a living room, two bedrooms, kitchen and dining room together, and a full basement. But they had to pay a fantastic *price—$8,350—which is almost what we paid for our house.*

From Mom—Dec. 16, 1945:

Tuesday I went downtown early to shop and got practically everything done. By being an early bird I also got one *pair of nylons! Was I ever thrilled. They look so nice and feel so good. I hope after New Year's they will get in plenty of them.*

16 December 1945

Sunday

Dear Family,

Sunday again, and this week I listened to Charlie McCarthy, too, because I got home early from Grace's to finish wrapping the last of my presents. Let's see—what did I do this week? Seems to me I spent most of the time huddling in bed trying to keep warm. We, too, are having a cold wave of sorts, and the smoke from the smudge pots [protecting the orange and nut groves] covers the Valley till noon. One night I went to Hollywood with Georgia, and met The Admiral for a show. Afterwards we were in the Knicker-bocker [Hotel] having a peaceful Scotch and soda when up popped a weird character in a black shirt, blue tie, and brown suit. He was a cameraman at MGM and knew The Admiral, who is a civvie now and works at Universal. He had the queerest line; I thought he was kidding. He was telling all about how he was a poor little Jew-boy, brought up in the slums of lower East Side New York, selling newspapers for a living, and laying it on very thick. So I popped up brightly with, "Just like Georgie Gershwin!" at which he was very insulted; he meant it. We went to the Brown Derby and saw all sorts of famous people and listened to the cameraman go on about the movie game in the familiar cliches. I didn't think people really talked that way . . . fascinating.

Saw *The Bells of St. Mary's* Friday evening. It was a very good rambling sort of movie, funny in a quiet way and not as tear-jerky as *Going My Way*. Baggie left for Camp Beale today, and so all the kids that I know have left. How frustrating. Maybe I could find some guy, marry him, get out, and have the marriage annulled afterwards. I must work on this. I will spend next weekend at Grace's helping them trim the tree. I sure wish I could be home. It isn't the least Christmas-spirity here at all. Phooey on California.

Farewell till next week,

21 December 1945

Friday

Hello Family,

It's Friday and is it ever raining out and has been all day; sheets and sheets of it, beating all around our poor little wallboard barracks. I guess winter, as such, has come at last. The area in front of the Detachment is a sea of mud and the ditch is a great river. I'd rather have snow than rain, any day. This week has been extremely lazy as I spent most of it in bed. Monday morning I went on sick-call and had an influenza shot, because I'd been exposed to Grace over the weekend. By that afternoon the reaction really hit me, so I stayed in, and all day Tuesday. It was almost worse than having the flu itself. Fever, chills, headache, etc. Wednesday I worked and in the evening saw a very good British movie called *Vacation from Marriage*, with Robert Donat. It was about a fuddy-duddy clerk and his sniffly wife. He got called up for the Navy and she went into the WRENS. It changed them both for the better—put hair on their chests; then they have a reunion after three years apart. It was very well-done and funny, but Robert Donat sure is getting old looking. Thursday afternoon I spent in bed again. I had a terrific headache. Today I went on sick-call again and got sent back to quarters for the day. My bed is really getting quite a groove worn in it. I have also a headache around my eyes like last spring, and great pains in my back and thighs like arthritis or something; maybe it's the damp. I don't feel so bad when I'm in bed, though . . .

Things are popping in the Company. On one hand, we are getting more kids in from all the hospitals that are closing. They are cramming more beds into each barracks till we bulge at the seams. On the other hand, Captain C. gets an order from the Ninth Service Command to inactivate the 79th Company, and authorizing our strength at 100, which means putting about 140 people on the surplus list. They will either be transferred or discharged. I hope and pray I get on the list, but I don't know what basis they are using. Kids from all over the country have heard that we are getting out in March; it's a very persistent rumor. I told you, didn't I, that BGH will become a Vet's Hospital then? One kid I was with at Halloran wrote me from Washington that she heard BGH was closing up. Rumors are very funny. Got a Christmas card from Ruth K. and she's a civilian. She was my friend in Basic and went to Denver as a Lab Tech. The so-and-so didn't tell me how or when; she said, "For further details, you will have to write me." Needless to say I dispatched a letter at once.

I opened all my presents tonight. I guessed what they were, and had to open them to prove I was right. Score: Slip; right. It's awfully pretty, Mom, and I will wear it Christmas Day. Slippers; right. I guessed the color, too, but I didn't guess how gay and original they were. PJs; right. Thanks very much. They will be a nice change from GIs. Package from Mike; wrong. I thought it was stationery but here it was wonderful sweet smells. Thank you, Mike; you are the cagey one—you win. Mom, your cookies are the marvel of the barracks and were eaten all too fast. I kept the marzipan to myself though. Ain't I selfish? But some people don't like it and there's no sense wasting it on them. The fruit cake and jam we are saving for later. I have a three-day pass for Christmas—goodie. Carmen got off for Saturday afternoon and Sunday, and so to pay for that, has to work twelve hours on Monday, Tuesday, and Wednesday. You should see the barracks. We have it all decorated up; cellophane red bells over all the lights, streamers from the rafters, poinsettias in pots, Christmas cards tacked up on the walls, and a cute little tree in the back part. We have put all our presents around the bottom and it looks almost homey. I like my new home. I'm sorry to be away from Carmen and Lena but the sum total of people on this side are more congenial and not so irritating as most of the people on the other side. It's warmer, too, as I said.

Other notes: I have only one sleeve and the neck left to do on my sweater. I'm reading *Wuthering Heights*. I glazed my pottery Wednesday; it ought to be pretty. When it is fired, I will send it back. I love you all. Merry Christmas. Happy New Year.

29 December 1945

Saturday

Dear Family,

This will probably be a very interrupted letter because I'm on CQ and the phone keeps ringing. They finally nabbed me for duty, and here I've managed to escape it for a year. Remember I was on CQ last Christmas morning? The holidays were very nice although not very "spirit-ish." There just has to be family and snow to make Christmas. Carmen and I took off in a driving rain storm Saturday afternoon, and had a terrible time getting rides into Grace's, but we eventually arrived while Dick was out getting the boys, who turned out to be two sailors, Harry and Jake. We all trimmed the tree that afternoon, and sat around drinking beer. The fellows were most surprised; on the card Grace gave to the USO, it said, "No Drinkers," and the first thing they get in the door, they hear, "Have a beer?" Dinner was fried rabbit (good) and after dinner we sat around drinking more beer and gabbing. Dick's brother Joe and his wife came over, and there was much chaff and persiflage. We made some funny records, too. Sunday we all slept late. Carmen and I went for a walk, but we spent most of the day dozing in front of the fire. In the evening we decided to go to the movies, but after a few drinks we thought better of it and went to the Palladium and danced. Carmen had to go back to camp that night, poor child, so Dick drove us back. It gave me a good feeling not to have to get out of the car.

Monday afternoon Joe drove us kids around in Beverly Hills to see the movie stars' houses. They aren't nearly as pretty as around Lake of the Isles [Minneapolis upper-class neighborhood] or out in Rolling Green. The guys got a kick out of it though, and took lots of pictures. They're from St. Louis, Mo., by the way. We had supper and lay around by the fire some more. In fact, that seems to be the way we spent most of the time, but it was nice. Soon we got dressed and went to Midnight Service. The choir under Dick did itself proud. When we got back we opened our presents; Grace gave us kids spinning tops and little humming horns, and the fellows got toy aircraft carriers to play with in the bathtub. Their ship is a baby flattop so it was very appropriate. I got notepaper from both Grace and Harriet. The boys gave Grace and Dick a large good-looking painting for over the mantelpiece, a sort of Mexican scene, and me they gave a bottle of Rock-and-Rye. It was sort of a standing joke about me using it for cough medicine. Along about four we finally went to bed. Christmas morning we all went over to Glendale and played tennis. Joe played with his friends who are all a bunch of fiends; Joe is a tennis teacher, so he was too good to play with us. Jake and Harry played, and they let me play some with them. I wasn't in too bad form, and Jake graciously said, "You're not bad, for a girl," but I hastened to assure him I wasn't an example of what the fair sex could do on the courts. This unprecedented exercise had whipped up a terrific appetite, and we did full justice to Grace's turkey. Our appetites had been further whetted by a bottle of Canadian Club that Dick broke out. More sleep followed this repast, and about eight, I roused myself and declared I wasn't going to spend the last night of my pass in a stupor. So Jake, Harry, and I all went out. We went to downtown LA, and Harry dragged us around to a lot of horrible beer dives. He was in search of local color because he aspires to paint. He favors the sort of Steinbeck-Dos Passos-type of realism to be found in joints—butts on the floor, air blue with smoke, crummy characters staggering around being friends with everyone—he goes for that. Poor boy—he has yet to see Chicago and New York. I regaled him with tales of what I'd seen in the great metropolis and he was enthralled. We rode on the one cable car in LA. That was fun; we were just walking along when we discovered it. It's call "Angel's Flight" and we felt just like San Francisco because it was real foggy. Well to make a long story short, I gathered my possessions, and Dick drove me back to camp and my pass was over.

The rest of the week I've just been existing. My cold waited till after Christmas to be over with, cuss it. I feel swell now. Assorted notes: Got a ride to Hollywood with a man who had a pet monkey in the front seat. I have a date with Jake tomorrow night. I hope we go dancing because he's right good in the rug-cutting department. The wind blew the back door off our barracks tonight. I hate being CQ. I have another three-day pass this weekend. I shall spend it sleeping and cleaning out my wall locker which is so full I get a concussion every time I open the door. I got a letter from Pal Joey in which he spends a page talking about how it is so cold in the mornings that he hates to get up, then says there is nothing doing on campus and then signs off. What is that guy's trouble? . . . Did you know that the "Ford Sunday Evening Hour" is back again? I made a fuzzy dog yesterday. His name is Gizmo. I will send him home with some more stuff soon. I miss you all. I love you all. XXXXXXXX

From Dad—Dec. 30, 1945:

To start things right: HAPPY NEW YEAR! Well, having lived through Christmas I think I shall survive the Season and see 1946. It is always a question, but I am full of hope. It was grand sitting around the fire on Christmas Day, not having to go anywhere and watching people get stuck in the snow. We missed you heaps, as you may imagine. Two Christmases away from home is quite enough. May the rumors that you will be out by March prove sound—no fury.

From Dad—Jan. 6, 1946:

By cracky, but it has been a long time since we had a letter from you—Dec. 31st to be exact. I trust that the delay merely means that you have been having a good time over the holidays and not that you have been laid up sick or something unpleasant of that kind. Your poor Maw is in a bit of a tizzy over the lack of news. I hope that tomorrow will bring a letter and put her mind at rest. Nothing special at this end. I have been doing a mess of minor chores and managed to get some money and get all my bills paid—a job that took me most of yesterday to clean up. If the Farm does not pay off we are certainly going broke in a grand way—but I am not worried since I saw that fleet of cattle.

Last night we had C.W. in for dinner and she showed us how to put glass mounts on our color prints, so that should keep us busy for several evenings this winter. I hope that film is easier to get, for the Farm offers many good subjects. Any further LRs as to discharge? I trust that it breaks soon. From all reports the schools are so full of GIs that many of the boys are quitting for lack of room in the classes, let alone the trouble of finding any place to live, so you may be just as well off having to wait a bit till things calm down and they can find out what it is all about. What with all the strikes and general upset that we are having, I am glad that the family has a good farm to fall back on. I only wish that I could quit and go out there this summer for good. But that time will come soon enough.

7 January 1946

Monday

Dear Carrie,

To you goes the honor of being the first to receive a letter written on this most elegant and much-needed stationery. What a coincidence; I was just about to go to Van Nuys and buy myself some when your package came. All the thanks I can possibly drum up in my present incoherent and somewhat hungover state are for you. Your description of White Christmas made me absolutely green. Here it rained and was foggy and I was suffering from the aftermath of a flu shot. After which I had a cold on my Christmas pass. I spent it with Grace and Dick and two sailors. Imagine having all of us people in that minute house. Every time anyone went to the biff it sounded like thunder, and we had to hibernate in the kitchen till the boys got up in the morning. It was fun, though.

Carmen was in for a day and night, and we all went to the Palladium and danced, played tennis, hung around and read *Forever Amber* [by Kathleen Windsor] aloud, and ate. The last night of my pass, Jake, Harry and I went to downtown LA, which was interesting because I had never been down there at night. Harry dragged us around to a lot of horrible beer dives.

I was very lucky and got another three-day pass over New Year's and thence ensued a most horrible week from which I'm only now recovering. Here is the schedule: Saturday: twenty-four hours CQ duty. Sunday Evening: date with Jake. Much dancing, much drinking, and much battling. Why in hell can't men be buddy-buddies and leave my poor battered virginity alone? Rhetorical question. Nature is nature, I guess. Monday, New Year's Eve: I went to a wild party at the Non-Com's Club. What I mean, it was really a brawl, and of course this weak-willed one distinguished herself by being thoroughly inhibited and disgusting. However, I did wind up with a date to the Rose Bowl Game with Terry, the Sergeant-at-Arms. After four hour's sleep, I dragged myself out and we hitched out to the Bowl. This was Tuesday. It was a good game; I saw it through an alcoholic haze and it all looked fine. Then out for supper and much deep conversation at Jule's over creme de menthe. Wednesday: dinner again with Terry and a dance on the Post. Thursday: went to a show with the kids. Friday: had a date with another Harry, a patient who has a draining colostomy. Right after dinner it started to act up, so we jumped in a cab and asked for the nearest hospital—you should have see that cabbie's face. He looked as though he thought I were going to have a baby in his back seat. We got to a hospital finally and I helped the doctor change his dressings. I guess he thought we were married. Ark! Poor Harry is really beat up. No movement in his right arm, a kidney gone, and the incision from that isn't healed yet. But despite these drawbacks, we danced at El Palladium till all hours. Saturday: in the afternoon we went shopping for cars with no success, then hitched out to Santa Monica to the house of a friend of his who has a fun wife and a cute baby. Here Schenley's flowed like water. People streamed over, and we danced and sang dirty songs and had a big party. The hell of it was that Harry started proposing and getting serious instead of being funny which is why I went out with him in the first place. To hell with men except William. His friend drove us back to camp about 3:30 a.m. very much the worse for wear. Sunday night:

Terry and I went out to dinner and *he* proposed. The problem here was that I had had four beers and two Manhattans, and was thus feeling silly, so I said "Yes," but he meant it. Now I am in a jam. He's getting discharged today, but he'll be back. He has the names of all his children planned. Oh God, give me strength. I'm really worried about this because I don't want to hurt him. Luckily I got a letter from William today and he cleared the air for me.

We are having a terrible situation here. All the water on the Post has been unfit to drink for the past week—fecal contamination—and we are slowly dying of thirst. One guy said, "I always thought that the water tasted like crap, and now I *know* it!" The WACs get three pairs of nylons issued on 1 February. Hooray! I'm down to wearing lisles again, and you can't buy a stocking in the whole of Southern California. Gotta stop this babbling; I have about twenty more letters to write. Carry on . . . I wish I were in your shoes—with my family, going to school, and no lecherous men hanging around.

> All love, Carrie dear,
> Panzy

7 January 1946

Monday

Dearest Family,

It's Monday morning and at last I have time to draw a deep breath and write to you. This last week has been completely a mad rush and I haven't done anything but run around in a social whirl. This week I absolutely am not going anywhere. It all started last Sunday when I went out with Jake, one of the sailors who was at Grace's. We went to Hollywood and ate and drank and danced and had a good time. I stayed all night with Grace and came back Monday afternoon—I had another three-day pass. Monday being New Year's Eve there was a big party at the Non-Com's Club and I had a date with Sgt. Terry, one of the Detachment men who is a PT instructor in Reconditioning. It was quite a wild affair by the time 1946 came in; sort of reminiscent of the Nu Sig brawl because everybody knew everybody else. New Year's morning I crawled from my downy couch, and Terry and I hitchhiked to Pasadena to the Rose Bowl Game. It wasn't much of a game compared to Midwest football standards, but it was a thrill to see all the crowds and realize that practically everyone in California had battled for tickets to the game and couldn't get them, and here was little me. That night Terry and I tried to get steaks at the Pump Room but couldn't so had hamburgers and conversation. Wednesday Terry took me out and this time we did get steaks. After dinner we came back to the Post and went to a dance at the Rec Hall. Thursday I was going to write letters, but the kids dragged me off to the show after which we went to the Club. Friday (this goes on and on) I had a date with one of the patients who has been in for a couple of weeks doing leather stuff. This guy is really remarkable; he has lost one kidney, the incision of which isn't completely healed, has an open colostomy, and has lost almost the entire use of his right arm, but still he's up running around, and is always cheerful and kidding. We went to Hollywood and after supper were about to go to the Palladium to dance, when Harry's colostomy started draining. So we jumped in a cab, and asked the driver where was the nearest hospital. That poor cabbie was most startled. After going to about three stupid hospitals, none of which had night surgeons, we finally found a doctor who would fix him up. Then after this interlude, we did go back to Hollywood and danced. It's amazing what the human body can stand. Saturday afternoon I went with Harry to look for a car, but the prices for old junk are just outrageous so he didn't buy one. Thusly we had to hitchhike out to Santa Monica where his best friend lives. We had supper, and then a slew of people came over to the house and we danced and sang and had a big old party, and I didn't get back till 3:30 in the morning. TIME OUT FOR WORK

7 January 1946

Monday

Dear Family,

I started a letter this morning containing the multitudinous facts of my past full and hectic week, but I left it over in OT, and it's all so involved that the thought of retelling it appalls me, so this will be notes, and I'll finish the other one tomorrow. Gosh, I'm sorry I haven't written oftener. You sound as though you've been as hectic as I was. Mom, I'm amazed at your stamina; how you can hold up under the social whirl and flu too is truly great. I was all over my colds and stuff right after Christmas. We are having quite a time with the water supply here on the Post. It's been contaminated for about a week now and we're all dying of thirst. People stream down the halls chanting "How dry I am," with their tongues hanging out. I am very unhappy. I'm having men troubles. This Terry, of whom you will hear in tomorrow's installment of The Trials of Anne, thinks he's in love with me and wants to get married right away. Unfortunately, I, in the heat of a couple of Manhattans and the spirit of a gala dinner party with a newly engaged couple, accepted him, and now he refuses to believe I was just kidding. What a horrible thing to kid about. I feel so awful and I don't know whether to be tactful or truthful. I don't want to hurt his feelings cause he's such a nice guy, but not as nice as William. William and I have been having a fight again, but all is well now. I got a letter from him today. He's somebody I want you to meet; I just know you'd like him as much as I do. It's been almost a year since I saw him; he's a corporal now and should be getting out of the Army in a few months on Length of Service.

No more news here about discharges except a formal announcement by the Colonel that "Sometime after March" this hospital will be turned over to the Veterans Administration. Hope for me. The rains are still holding off here, although they're having floods in San Fran. It was over 80 degrees New Year's Day and it's pretty warm every day. Nippy in the mornings, though. Did you get the money order OK? Now we stand: $30 plus $30 equals $60 paid; and this from $100 equals $40 IOU. We have a new supervisor in OT and she is tres efficient and is reorganizing the whole department. Which is a good thing because things were beginning to get snafu-ed and I was getting disgusted. Now she is having me write pamphlets of instructions for Ward Crafts. Ark! She doesn't know what she's getting into. My eyelids are drooping and I think I shall turn in.

Goodbye and all love,

Portrait taken for Mom + Dad

Boggie with me + our dates at a Hollywood nightclub

Minneapolis Tribune photo of women lining up
to buy nylons at Dayton's

8 January 1946

Tuesday

Tuesday Afternoon: (continued from yesterday): Sunday night I went to dinner with Terry and that's when the unfortunate occurrence of the proposal took place. That really finished me off. I had a good sleep last night though, and plan to lead a life of retirement from now on. Jake called last night to say he was shipping out today. Harry went to surgery this morning, and Terry is getting discharged Thursday. My life will then go back to its accustomed calm.

Last week I applied for entrance to the University of Chicago. I had had a letter at last from Bergie who was home for Christmas vacation. She's teaching in Texas for a while. She said that her brother Fred had had a hard time getting back into Chicago and to get my application in early. She also said I could stay with them and ride with Fred to school because he's going to commute too. In view of the housing shortage I don't see how I could possibly find an apartment that wasn't too expensive, and I don't want to live in a dorm if I can help it. Of course I would pay room and board, but it still might not be as expensive as living all alone. It sounds like a pretty good deal, what do you think? William wrote that he isn't going to Chicago because their journalism department just doesn't have what he wants. He mentioned Columbia and Northwestern but he hasn't made up his mind yet. Hope it's Northwestern because then I could see him now and again.

I got my American Legion pin and card. Thank you for paying this year's dues, Dad. Who'd have thought, three years ago, that I would be a Legionnaire? I can't belong to the 40 & 8 Club, though, can I? I must get back to work, now.

All love,
Annie

From Mom—Jan. 3, 1946:

Did I ever write you that I was asked to be the chairman for the Thirteenth Ward Red Cross fund drive? I'm just a "Big Deal on Campus." I accepted and now find it's going to be more work than I thought. It's so hard to get people to do anything now that the war is over, but I've been doing lots of telephoning and hope that I'll get my district chairmen lined up before long.

From Mom—Jan. 11, 1946:

Yesterday we got your letter of Jan. 7. Now I await avidly your previous one. I hope and trust that by this time you have gotten yourself unengaged! I mean—after all—that's a heck of a situation to be in, and you should not string along a poor fellow like that. Things must have been pretty gay over New Year's!

13 January 1946

Sunday

Dearest Family,

I hope by this time you have gotten all of my various and sundry missives: namely, 29 Dec., 7 Jan., and 8 Jan. I think the mails must have been sort of screwed up because Dad said that you hadn't heard from me since 21 Dec. I will be a better girl now, so help me. My man troubles are slowly straightening themselves out, praise be. Terry came in from Fort McArthur Tuesday evening and we had a heart-to-heart talk in which we agreed "It could never be." He has gone by now and I'll never see him again, I hope. It's all pretty funny now when I think of it; I'll tell you all the rare details sometime. Wednesday evening Carmen and I went into Hollywood and had our traditional dinner at Mike Lyman's amid much talk. I had seen so little of her since Christmas that we had much news to impart. After dinner we shopped around in bookstores. One of them is very tiny but has many nooks and crannies and is sort of like stacks. We were crunched in a corner in the back for about an hour reading and thumbing through stuff and nobody bothered us or anything. We went home early, getting a ride from a thirty-year man just back from overseas. He was going to Long Beach but had nothing to do, so took us clear out to the hospital. We picked up a couple of fellows from the hospital and took them along too. When we arrived we decided to go to the mess hall and scrounge some food, but it was closed. To kill time, we all traipsed up to the clinic where one of the guys works in Electrocardiograph and Basal Metabolism. The one who runs the clinic is a graduate of Columbia, and did work at Yale in biochemistry. In the Army, he is a PFC. Irony of the Army. He ran EKGs on Carmen and me, and we fooled around so long that suddenly it was 12:30 and the mess hall had closed up again. One o'clock found us on C-2 where Joe knew the nurse, making fried egg sandwiches and drinking buttermilk. Result of EKG: Me; extremely normal. Carmen has a right axis deviation but it isn't serious.

Thursday we all went to the show—*Harvey Girls,* a gay, light musical in color, and adjourned to the NCO Club for sandwiches and coffee and dancing. Friday I went up on the Ward to see Harry. He feels pretty good, the Wangensteen is out and he's on a Sippy diet.[80] He still proposed every other word and I try to convince him that we're just buddies—what a hopeless task. Yesterday I spent the afternoon on the Ward, too, playing cribbage and gabbing. Harry has had the most fantastic life. He's only twenty-one but he claims he's been in the Army five years besides having finished high school and two years of college. He's lived all over the United States, gone to school in Burma and the Hawaiian Islands—that's where his family is now. He was with Patton's Third Army in France and Germany and was in that mad race across France. He was in charge of a half-track. Sometimes I wish I were a man and could have gotten in on some of those shows, but when I think of how messed up Harry is, and has only a slim chance of pulling through his next operation (he's had ten so far) I am thankful for the safe life I've had.

Things are really popping now around here. See clipping—it's definite that the Veterans Adminstration will take over from the Army on March 31. They've started shipping kids out. I'm on the surplus list—what that means I'm sure I don't know, but within the next six or eight weeks we should all be gone—somewhere in the US. I hope I get out of the Ninth Service Command; I've had enough of California to last me for quite awhile. It doesn't look much like discharges are in the near future, darn it. No more news for now . . .

[80] A "Wangensteen" is a postsurgery drainage tube named for its inventor, Dr. Owen Wangensteen, who was associated with the University of Minnesota Hospitals. A "sippy" diet is a light liquid diet prescribed for postsurgical or seriously ill patients.

From Dad—Jan. 13, 1946:
Your life seems to be an even madder whirl than ours, but I am glad that you seem to be having a bit of fun out of it all. Let us hope that some of the rumors are founded and that spring will see you free again. The Farm and the Family are both waiting for you. I am sorry that you have been playing fast and loose with an innocent boy's affections. Look out or you will end up being haled before justice for breach of promise; and do not expect me to pay costs. Your Maw was quite a one along those lines in her day, so you doubtless come by it naturally. Personally, I was always able to keep my women happy and divided. I saw in the paper as how you had a bad wind storm. I trust that it did not hit BGH though it might have been an ill wind and blew you in some potable water. What do you drink; vodka?

From Mom—Jan. 17, 1946:
You certainly had a hectic time the week after Christmas, but it must have been fun, at that. This other poor boy you told us of—what a sad deal for him to be so cut up and knocked around. I hope he gets better. As a family, I think we were very fortunate that you were the older and Mike did not have to see service. With you we did not have to worry that you would be wounded or killed.

21 January 1946

Monday

Dearest Family,

I'll try to get this off this afternoon, time and the OT Department permitting. Got Mom's newsy letter this noon. You sure are an Eager Beaver! What you need is a year in the Army to teach you how to be a G.B. (Gold Brick) like me. It's too bad the weather is stinky, but then it usually is. Here it continues to be lovely. We haven't had any rain since Christmas and very little fog. The mornings are quite nippy but we seldom have to wear coats. The mountains are out nearly every day, too.

Last Sunday afternoon Flo and I and some other kids went for a walk, ending up at Metro Air Field. All the GIs but sixty have left and they only use the field for jet plane testing. The guys let us go up in the control tower and we had a glorious view out over the whole valley. We could see almost to Hollywood through the binoculars. When we came down we went over to the mess hall for some water, and they were just finishing noon chow, to which we were invited. We compromised with turkey sandwiches and super coffee. Then the guys drove us around the runway in a jeep and thence back to camp. You should have seen that poor little car—two guys, five WACs, and two dogs! Sunday night Bill called me from Beaumont. His voice sounded so funny and neither of us recognized the other. He thinks he can get over here sometime after the first of the month and then we can have a reunion. Monday, Tuesday, Wednesday, and Thursday were completely uneventful. I think I went to two movies, and I knitted and read and wrote letters and sweat the week out. Friday I went up on the Ward to see Harry. He'd been sending guys down to OT who were saying, "You'd better get up there and see Harry—he's mad!" This got a bit tiring by Thursday so I went up, *and* I discovered he had a present for me—a pretty bottle of perfume from the Islands in a carved wooden bottle. It's called "Ginger." His family got it on the black market, which is all there is in Hawaii. Saturday afternoon I lay around and luxuriated in slumber and literature. Terry came back from Frisco, all dolled up in civilian clothes and looking most sharp. He'd been calling all Friday night, but I wasn't there. We drank beer and danced over at the club. He still says he loves me with a passion, and keeps asking me to marry him. He thinks he will beat me into submission by constant reiteration. Well, he has another think coming. Mrs. Anthony . . . what shall I do?[81]

Sunday Flo and I were invited over to Miss Ohlssen's for breakfast and all day. She works in OT but isn't an OT—sort of like us, only a civilian. She has a cute little house and chickens and largish garden and orange grove in the mountains up the Valley a way. We picked our breakfast oranges right off the tree and had fresh-laid eggs and buckwheat waffles and swell coffee until we nearly burst. We lounged around most of the day, knitting and drinking beer. Her mother is a little old lady with a thick accent who does beautiful crocheting in bright colored wool. We are all inspired to make purses now. I finished my sweater and Miss Ohlssen is going to have it blocked for me. I can just barely get my big head through the neck but I think it will be OK. For supper we had steak (T-Bone) and baked potatoes, and carrots browned in

[81] There was a radio show featuring Mister Anthony, who gave advice on etiquette and love problems. "What shall I do, Mister Anthony?" was a catch phrase of the day.

honey and salad with a swish dressing for which I got the recipe. What celestial food. She is a good Joe and let us mess around and do anything we wanted to . . . and asked us to come again anytime we liked. The water is cleared up now, or did I tell you? About half the Company leaves tomorrow for East Coast hospitals but it doesn't look as though I will be leaving very soon. However— everything is so confused one never knows what will happen. Just so I get out to go to school next fall . . . that's all I ask. Gotta rush away now.

All my love,

28 January 1946

Monday (Just before Company Meeting . . . urp)

Hello Family,

Life is extremely quiet lately so I will devote myself to news and notes and odd thoughts in paragraphs. (1) "Information Please" just came on and so I'll finish this later.[82] Off to a fine start! (2) Hey, how is Mom? Did she go to the hospital? How sad that you should have so darn much sick trouble this winter. I sure wish I were home to help around the house and stuff, but here I am being not too useful at BGH. (3) Those orders sounded very confusing but it had to do with making out a surplus list and disbanding the 79th Company. All the extra people have shipped out by now and Flo and I are back in the 78th. Purely paper work. I'm still doing odd jobs around OT and keeping fairly busy. (4) After much hubba by the War Department and General Omar Bradley, BGH has finally been designated as a Vets Hospital. Col. Alvin C. Miller, the Great, announced it over the PA system today. Which alters nothing as I have said before. It will probably be at least two months before we ship anywhere. I'm just in a rut and have ceased getting excited over rumors. (5) Had a letter from Alta the other day and guess what the Navy is doing? All the WAVES get a promotion in rank *plus* a fifteen-day leave if they enlist till September. Natch, the WACs

[82] "Information, Please" was a radio quiz show. The radio audience sent in questions on a wide range of topics to stump a panel of experts who were well-known wits and know-it-alls. They were editor John Kiernan; Franklin P. Adams, columnist for a New York newspaper and member of the Algonquin Round Table; Oscar Levant, pianist and bon vivant; and a weekly guest panelist.

are just stuck; we've never gotten any good deals like that out of the Army. She also put me a deal: she's considering a special journalism course at the U of Chicago and wants me to live with her but where, we don't know. Maybe Bergie can take two boarders, even if they are rugged Vets. (6) I am decorated now. Last Monday evening at Company meeting those of us who had been in a year got American Theater of Operations ribbons. Hot stuff—chest lettuce! We have a new CO who is a prize stinker. Much GI and stiff inspections and rotgut about "Carry on," and "Service," and "Remember, you enlisted". . . why can't they leave us alone? (7) Bill wrote that he will be discharged the first of April and has been offered the Civil Service position of editor of the paper at Beaumont. He's going to take it because he can make some money and get good experience while he's waiting to go to school next fall. Nothing much else of note. Grace wrote me a little note. I haven't had a chance to go over since Christmas. She has just lately gotten over her cold that she's had since before Christmas. Asked after you-all. Yawnnn . . . sack time.

P.S.: Another wisdom tooth is coming in and it hurts. P.P.S.: I told Harry off Saturday night, and so goodbye to him, thank heaven. Jake, the sailor I thought to be safely at sea, called last week too but I staved him off also. I'm tired of men. Take me back to good old bridge-playing Stagnantte days. I've almost forgotten how to play, it's been so long.

3 February 1946

Sunday

Dear Family,

Life has been somewhat gruesome the last few days and it leaves me in rather a hurry and mess of which I'll write later in the week. My evenings this week were spent reading, drinking beer at the NCO Club, and seeing a very funny movie called *Tars and Spars*. There's a guy in it, Sid Caesar, that's every bit as good as Danny Kaye. Last night, Carmen and I went to Hollywood for dinner and had superb sirloin at Maison Gaston. How is the meat shortage in Minneapolis? There doesn't seem to be any out here, not in restaurants, at least. This morning we woke up to a terrific rain. I guess it's started at last, cuss it. But we have had such wonderful weather since I got back that it really couldn't last forever. Family, I'm very desolate tonight and not at all in the mood for writing. I'll pen some later on.

All my love,

From Dad — Feb. 3, 1946:

Last evening the gang had dinner at the club, but it was late and I ate too much too fast and had a tummy ache in consequence. I should know enough not to get mixed up in that sort of foolishness. Not again. At the Farm today spent time going over finances with the tenant. His are not too hot, so I think that the smart trick would be to step in and take over myself. It will not run to any very large sum, and the security is fine. I do wish I could be out there more often this winter and less of an absentee landlord, but it sure is hard to get away from dear old Blake ("We care for your damn brat all day"). The place looked fine and the barns are full of cattle. Continue to have what fun you can. I trust that William is able to get out and that you do not stay off men for too long a time. Now for a bit of reading and beaucoup sack — I need it.

From Mom — Feb. 8, 1946:

Today I went downtown again for a few errands — bought some new black pumps. Dayton's have been staging the "Battle of the Nylons" these last three days. They announced in the paper that they had 60,000 pairs of nylons to be sold at 20,000 pairs a day for three days. They had a special section on the second floor roped off, with iron gates and special sections for each size, extra guards and policemen, etc. I did not go near the place but from what I hear it was a real shindig. I went past today about noon and there were throngs of people waiting in line to get in, and out in front a firetruck and a mob — I think they were using a pulmotor on someone![83] People are so crazy and so greedy *— it is really disgusting!*

[83] A pulmotor was a 1940s artificial respiration machine.

7 February 1946

Thursday

Dearest Family,

It has happened again—I'm shipping out. This time to Fort
Lewis, Washington, near Tacoma. Address as follows, as far as I
know: WAC Detachment, Madigan Convalescent Hospital, Fort
Lewis, Wa. It all happened many weeks ago when some civilians
from Ninth Service Command OT Headquarters came down and
said they need two kids up at Madigan. Lil said she'd go. Flo and I
said definitely NO, and Schuts was off on pass. When she got back
she said she'd go, too, and Miss Poland wrote Headquarters the
deal. In the meantime this dame got hold of Flo's and my names,
and last Friday comes in a request for Flo, me *and* Lil. Well, we
disrupted the whole OT department with our loud wails, mine the
loudest because Bill was coming this week, and dear old Sgt.
Johnson won't give me a Delay en Route. Flo got fifteen days and
she doesn't want it because she can't get back to Philly on that time.
I rushed around frantically all day Saturday trying to see what I
could do about a delay—saw the chaplain and cried around, but it
didn't do any good. Sent Bill a telegram Friday to call me Friday
evening, and waited . . . but this Tuesday when he did call, he said
he didn't get the wire till Monday night . . . efficient Orderly
Room—ha.

Carmen and I went out Saturday night as I said. Flo and I went
out Sunday night to supper and a horrible show—*The Dolly
Sisters*—DON'T see it. Monday night we all went to the show on the
Post. Likewise on Tuesday and drank much beer in NCO Club with
our little buddies, one of whom is from Owatonna and is sweet on
Flo. From Monday afternoon on, we were relieved from duty and
have been doing laundry, sleeping, and running around on last-
minute errands. Tuesday we went shopping. Haul: one girdle, one
pair slacks, one cute brown jersey blouse to wear with them. I
needed something for my morale, sadly sagging by this time. I leave
this afternoon in a couple of hours—all alone because both Flo and
Lil have delays here in California. Fort Lewis is the second largest
Army Post in the states and I'm kind of scared to arrive by myself
not knowing anyone at all. It's the first time, because every other
time I've been with someone I know. I'm very desolate but maybe

it will be interesting. We will hope for the best. Gotta rush now and shove off.

All my love,

MADIGAN GENERAL HOSPITAL
FORT LEWIS, TACOMA, WASHINGTON
8 February to 12 July 1946

In Transit

8 February 1946

Sacramento, California, Friday, 9:30 a.m.

Hello Family,

Here I am, en route again. This time I'm lucky. A Chief [Petty Officer] traded me his lower berth so I sleep in luxury. Pretty day. I saw a horse roll over in a field all by himself—clever—and I saw a little Chinese girl peeking out of a window in a station as we whizzed by. I see many wine fields. The vines are all cut back now. Many Italians up around here. I should get in tomorrow afternoon about 5:00.

I love you muchly,

Tacoma, Washington

11 February 1946

88th WAC Hospital Company, MGH, Fort Lewis, Washington,

Monday

Dearest Family,

Well, here I am rotting away at dear old Fort Lewis. Never have felt more useless, never has life seemed more futile than now. Got

248

in Saturday night—always a bad time to arrive. Nobody knew who I was or anything about me. The Company is divided into two sections about seven miles apart, and I got into the section that has no administrative people around. Some gal gave me some sheets and indicated a bed, and I stowed my gear away after I had gone over to the Service Club and had something to eat and got two books out of the library. Sunday I found I was sleeping next to one of the kids that was with us in New York. She took me over to mess—steak and French fries, no less. I read and did laundry all afternoon, and in the evening we sweated out a huge line to see *Road to Utopia* with Hope and Crosby. This morning I popped up at seven, all alert to go to work, and waited four hours for the CO to come over from the other section so I could report to her. Sometime after lunch I was informed that she was too busy to see me for a couple of days, and for me just to lie around. None of my records have come, nobody knows what section I'm supposed to be in. The girl that works in the Convalescent OT Section which urgently requested all three of us, says that there is no work to do and they're falling over each other in the department as it is. Good old Army game . . . only in this case it was a bunch of fool civilians trying to be efficient. I *knew* it would be like this but it's no joy to have my worst expectations confirmed. So here I am, plopped down in the middle of nowhere—barracks are freezing cold, too—the furnace is broken. The Post is mammoth, all spread out and confusing. Hundreds of soldiers walking aimlessly around. There's a big Basic Training camp here and the place is crawling with eighteen-year-old rookies trying to act tough and military. I feel like a Civil War Vet in comparison.

The trip up was quiet. Played cribbage all day Friday with a submarine sailor from whom I learned a lot about the game, especially the psychology of getting pegs during the play. The second game he double-skunked me, but before the day was out I had him skunked once. He was amazed that I learned so fast. Saturday in Portland we had a three-hour lay-over. Who should I see in the station working for the USO but Char McK. from my class at St. Mary's. We didn't have time for much of a reunion but I gathered that her husband was out of the Army and they're living there. Jimmy-the-sailor and I had breakfast, then took a walk and came back for lunch. Northern California has beautiful scenery and likewise up here. Many evergreen trees and very, very damp but beautiful in a hazy blue sort of way. Of course, some conversation intervened and I can't remember what I was going to say . . . but I am slowly going mad.

> Goodbye, dear Family, much love,

15 February 1946

Friday

Dear Family,

Here it is Friday and I'm still sitting around waiting for that moron of a CO to do something about me. If I weren't laid out with a nasty drooly cold I'd do something myself, but I'm just as content to stay in bed some more. The only thing is, I feel so cut off from the world. I haven't had any mail for two weeks and I know only two kids here, so that leaves me feeling lonesome. Tuesday they had me in my full uniform perched on the edge of my sack waiting to be taken over to Section 5 to see the CO. All day I waited—couldn't sleep, couldn't go to the PX, couldn't go to mess—because the driver "was coming *right* over." Finally at 5:30 I was taken over to see the Holy Captain. After talking to me for a half hour she finally came to the bright conclusion that I should work in OT. But to make it all legal and by the numbers, I should see the Classification Officer the next morning. While waiting for the driver to take me back to the main Fort, I had a couple of beers with Challford, one of the kids that was with us in New York. I will be working with her over in Section 5 where they do need another person, instead of in the Convalescent Hospital which requested us in the first place, but which doesn't really need any more people. The old Stupid Army at work again. What a snafu it is, to be sure. If they'd left us back at BGH we would have been shipped East for sure. But no. Anyway, Wednesday morning I trotted over to see the Classification Officer. He pondered over my Form 20 for a lengthy time, then asked me if I'd ever worked in OT before. I gently informed him that I'd taken special training for OT, that my M.O.S. [Military Occupational Specialty] number was for that, and that I'd been transferred up here for the express purpose of working in OT. He then decided that since I made 37 words a minute in my typing test taken in

Receiving at Fort Des Moines, that I'm an experienced secretary and should work for some Lt. in Reconditioning and maybe help out in the shop on the side. By this time I'd given up trying to tell anybody anything and said OK. So Wednesday, Thursday, and Friday have passed, waiting for the CO to inform the right people of where I'm to work and waiting for orders to move over to Section 5. God knows how many more days it will be. In the meantime, I have no baggage, no radio, I've used up all my knitting yarn, and I can't go out because I have no pass. You see why I'm somewhat depressed? Wednesday night I did get off; went skating at an arena with some kids here. It was fun because I haven't been on skates for two years. A sailor and a Lt. skated with me. Big thrill.

Last night we had an earthquake. I was scared into fits. All of a sudden there was a big noise, like an explosion, nearby, and the windowpanes rattled. Then the whole building rocked back and forth, and the wall lockers almost tipped over. What a horrible sensation; we live in a big three-story brick building with steel girders and cement floors, and to feel a structure like that bouncing around beneath one is something I never want to feel again. Yesterday was Valentine's Day but I didn't get any—nobody loves me anymore. The scenery up here is really quite pretty, just like the North Shore [of Lake Superior]. Nothing but huge pine trees all over, which isn't unusual because we're about on a line with Duluth. The sun has been shining all day for a change. Mostly the skies are gray with a light mist all over everything. Since this is a Regular Army Post, they play tattoo and taps over a loudspeaker at night, and in the morning they play reveille followed by gay rousing band music. It is rather ghastly and all I do is moan and turn over for more sleep. I wish I were back home in my own little bed with Mom to bring me chicken soup and cold drinks and put cold cloths on my head. I had a two-degree fever yesterday and I ached all over but that has gone away, thank heavens. Instead, I'm living in the equivalent of a classroom on second-floor Folwell Hall at the U[niversity of Minnesota]. It is just the same—dun-colored wall, black radiators and the equivalent of University Avenue traffic just under my window. Not conducive to rest. I'll be glad when I get over to Section 5 which is small, quiet and peaceful like Birmingham. No sound of Basics hutting back and forth, or of cars and trucks splashing through puddles. I'm very sad; last night in the dark, I knocked over and broke my little ash tray that I've had with me ever since my first week at Fort Des Moines. Let us hope that is a symbol of the termination of my Army career. My only hope now is that the Month's Service number will be reduced to twenty sometime this summer. In May I will have twenty. Otherwise I'll have to wait till September when I will have twenty-four; that's the figure now. I'm tired of sweating the months out. It seems like a waste of precious time, but that's all I can do. I guess I'd better stop before I break into another gripe session.

Love from Homesick Bug

P.S.: Guess what? Pal Joey wrote me a sonnet. Poetry, yet. I think that poor little medic is degenerating. It was a good poem, however.

From Dad—Feb. 17, 1946:

I have been much involved with farm finances and income tax returns. I am discovering that a 320 acre dairy farm with a herd of better than fifty cattle makes me a "Big Time Operator" and takes time, judgment, and above all, moolah. Fortunately I have a reasonable amount of the latter and some of the other two, so that I fancy that we shall come out the right end in the long run. To date it takes all our income to buy feed, but once the critters are able to chew grass we should have some real milk checks to make up for a slim winter. We continue to jog on as usual and life is a bit dull and complicated to suit me.

Poor little Cpl. Annie. Your last letter just came and we all feel very sorry for our Bug. Your trials have more and more a familiar ring. How many times, having given particulars as to my special skills (which ran to languages) have I been set to learn typing, work on a fire guard, or even spend long happy days policing the area for ciggy butts. Only in my case, when I wrote home a good gripe, the censor picked it off, sent it back to the CO and I just missed getting a General Court Martial for being a damned Yankee. All armies are alike and they all smell.

20 February 1946

Wednesday

Hello Family,

I am now having a prolongation of my last week's rest—this week in the hospital. Saturday and Sunday I really felt like h---, so bright and early Monday morning I went on sick call and landed here with acute sinusitis, about which they have done nothing except surfeit me with aspirins and put me on a soft diet. I'm slowly starving to death and my sinuses haven't started to drain yet. The doctor keeps ordering cocaine packs but the nurses never do anything about it. Everyone on the ward is getting sulpha for the common cold and aching feet, but me, I don't get nothin'; I just sit here and pant through my cracked, dried-up lips. I should be on the EENT Ward getting diathermy and such, but you can't tell these dopes at Madigan anything.

Speaking of dopes, I finally found out the reason for the big snafu about my assignment. Saturday afternoon I was finally allowed to move to Section 5, and I was to go to work on Monday. It seems that there was no record on my Service Records about having gone to Halloran or ever having worked on OT. That must be Johnson's fault, the doddering old yes-woman. Only after the Captain called in Challford and made her swear on innumerable Bibles that I was in New York with her and that I did attend the school, and so on, did she really believe what I was reiterating about OT. She's going to write Birmingham and raise hell about my records not being up to date, which is some small consolation. Last week I got my one letter in two weeks. It was from Mom, written about the 14th, and most welcome. Since then all has been silence. My letters are probably floating all over Fort Lewis and will reach me several months from now. Dad's Valentine package is over at the Convalescent Hospital and the ward girl said she'd get it for me. But since she is somewhat understocked with gray-matter I fear she will forget about it. Oh well, nothing matters much any more. I live in a sort of gray void, sleeping between my hearty meals of toast, gruel and milk, and have no ambition to do anything whatsoever but get the hell out of the Army. Rumors are thick again (they seem to come in waves) that the WACs will disband in March. This in spite of the fact that the Army has specifically outlined the discharge procedure past April. Foolish girls! Most of the kids up here have been in less than a year and they have no hope at all of getting out on Length of Service. Me, I will be released no later than September, unless the Army pulls a fast one and renigs, which it hasn't done yet, but that doesn't prove anything. There really is no news at all. I can't even tell you what other people told me, because I haven't heard.

A few weeks ago EC wrote that she's graduating in March, and medical school doesn't start till fall, so she has dreams of hopping down to Mexico with one of her Theta sisters. That ought to be fun. I myself would give up all the travel in the world during the next year for three month's stagnation on the farm. But I probably won't be granted even that. My life has struck a new low with nothing working out right. One thing, though—they give furloughs up here and I'm due one in May. Between now and then I'll save much money and then fly from Seattle round-trip. No more filthy Northern Pacific trains for me. Oh, by the way, I doubtless will not get paid this month and I may have to nick you for $10 to help along. It's nearly sack time so I will finish this and pull the sheets high over my head.

All my love,

27 February 1946

Wednesday

Dearest Mom and Dad,

My sinuses have cleared up (as much as they ever do) at last, and they let me out of stir today. It wasn't too bad being in the hospital. The nurses were good Joes, oddly enough, and the first part of the week I got lots of rest. Towards the last, a bunch of crude characters came in and at night they would have loud and lewd bull sessions which made me mad and kept me awake, so I was glad to get out. Flo and Lil got up here Sunday and came to see me, bringing my Valentine candy which got eaten up at a rapid rate. Thank you so much, Dad. I am using the pretty box for hankies. Yesterday afternoon I got a pass, and Flo and I went to the show and ate at the Service Club. It felt very festive after lying around for so long. Poor Flo has been put to work in the Orderly Room, since she was a clerk before going into OT, and she hates it. But she put up a stink to various people and ought to get back to OT, especially since Lil decided to take a discharge. A new order came out that everyone who was eligible under marriage, age, or points, should get out, or sign a waiver to stay in for the duration plus six. I sure wish I had a choice; guess what I'd do???? (Two words . . .)

Rain is raining all around still. Big puddles lap up against the barracks. Luckily the one I'm in is on relatively high ground so it doesn't leak the way the other ones do. I'm supposed to go to work tomorrow, but I'm going to try and get the day off and sleep because I still feel rather shaky. Then Friday to work. That will make a clean record of absolutely no work during February. Flo and I relieved ourselves of Duty on 1 February when the dire news came. Ha Ha on the Army; serves them right for not giving me a Delay en Route. I'm most sorry to hear of your sore throat, Dad. February is really the worst month of the year; it should be dropped from the calendar. Everyone roars around doing too much work and then gets sick. No social news whatever to report. I will write again as soon as anything of interest occurs. I have some little Army books of phonetic Russian, Spanish and Italian which I have been looking at. Now I can say "Where is the toilet?" in three languages. Hot spit!

Love,

Bug

P.S.: I'm stuffing vitamins faithfully. Thank you, Mom. P.P.S.: But those pills taste terrible; they make me burp.

7 March 1946

Thursday

Dear Mom,

OK, I can take a hint. I'm all well now and taking my vitamin pills like a good girl. I've been very busy and fairly happy. Aside from having a fight with the old Bag in charge of our department, my work (ha) is going smoothly. I'm just piddling around doing the same old stuff, helping string looms and doing odd jobs. Not very exciting. One thing has brightened my life though. I've met an amusing little guy who works in Educational Reconditioning, and who has promised to help me learn Spanish.[84] He spent about four years in Brazil going to school and doing some sociological research for the Rockefeller Foundation. His name is Jerry; that can go in my gallery along with Harry and Terry. Now all I need is someone

---

[84] Educational Reconditioning and Orientation were programs for wounded servicemen on long-term recovery in the hospital. Enrichment courses, basic high-school courses, and discussion groups on current events were offered, partly as occupational therapy and also to help with the transition to civilian life.

named Larry! I have a date with him tonight. We are going to eat
steak and argue politics. Will write a huge letter Sunday.

All love,

10 March 1946

Sunday

Chere Maman et Papa et Michael,

I can hardly hold a pen today due to the great exercise in which
I participated. You are related to a great skier. But of that, more
later. BIG NEWS!!!! At last comes the news the world has been
waiting for! Annie gets out of the Army in June! Hooray! Caloo,
callay! Frabjous Day!!!! Saturday afternoon orders came out that all
those with twenty to twenty-four months service will get out by June
30, and I will have twenty months in June. Flo and I are overjoyed.
Everything is rosey. I can endure the most horrible things now that
the end is really in sight. Ah, bliss!!

Social News: Flo and I visited Seattle the 2nd and 3rd of
March. We went up Saturday afternoon in a pouring rain, standing
up in the bus all the way, planning to just have dinner and then
come back. While looking for a USO in which to relax and look up
a good restaurant, we ran into the Servicewomen's Club and
decided to stay the night. It is a cute little three-story building
tucked in between some huge structures on a steep side street.
(Seattle is very hilly.) Most picturesque, with wild decorations
inside. Elizabeth Arden make-up bar and all such. We went out and
had crab meat au gratin at a place called Don's, and then saw a
movie at a theater much like the World [in Minneapolis]. The bill
was *Adventure in Music* and *A Star Is Born,* the former a concert in
film avec Jose Iturbi, Vronsky and Babin, and a good string quartet,
the latter a revival with Janet Gaynor and Fredric March, and very
good it all was. Sunday we slept late, and after a yummy breakfast
in the food bar at the Club, we went for a walk down on the
waterfront. This section is quaint and quite colorful. Fishy smells,
lots of ships tied up at dock, many Alaska expedition stores, gulls,
and the harbor filled with tugs and ships. Had lunch at a swell
seafood place, then took a ferry over to Bremerton. Then came
back and saw a movie until our bus left. We got back to Tacoma at

10:30, but due to horrible connections we didn't get to our Section till 1:30. Groan.

Tuesday night at chow I got talking to a guy who had been to the University of Illinois and was going to the University of Chicago when he got out. (See postcard of 7 March.) Very amusing guy. We had a hot political argument about the State Department's actions in the Argentine elections, and also discovered that we both were planning to be teachers of history. Naturally such a great friendship should be nurtured so we went out to his lakeside cottage with his roommate and girlfriend and we spent the evening pinning maps on the wall and drinking rather horrible homemade Manhattans. Wednesday Flo and I went to Mass and got ashes on our foreheads, thence to the moving pictures; *The Seventh Veil* . . . not bad. Thursday: dinner and more arguments with Jerry, much fun. Friday: GI Night. I'll reserve this weekend news for tomorrow's letter. I'm so pooped, I must get some sleep.

P.S.: Bergie wrote that all is set for next fall. The only drawback is that her father wants everybody up at 8:00 for Sunday morning breakfast. Ark! How will I stand that? To be continued.

17 March 1946

Sunday Eve.

Dearest Family,

This night finds me, as usual, exhausted from the weekend's junketings, and the week's labors. (1) News of last week; party given by the Engineers Battalion—beer bust. Met a nice guy who had lived in N.O. and L.A. He's been trying to date me all week but we just can't seem to get together. Sunday skiing: twenty-foot snow drifts high up on Mount Rainier. Gorgeous scenery. Was scared to ski at first, but, egged on by one of the Detachment men, I went, or rather fell, down the ski run and found it to be a wonderful sensation. (2) Thanks loads for the cookies. Flo and I are scraping up the remains right now. (3) I read and like very much Dad's paper on clandestine Masonry. I have saved it in my file of Good Things. (4) I'm awful sorry to hear of Mike's chicken pox. I'm just lucky I have had it before; it's going around the Post like mad. (5) In OT I arranged a display case—tres artistic. Also, I am painting a barrel a la Pennsylvania Dutch to be used for yarn. I have decided to suck up to the old harridan in charge and maybe I can get a T/4 rating out of it. (6) Thanks for my Blueprints [transcripts of courses taken at the university]. I filled out the papers and sent the $5 application fee—what a rook that is. I am now broke. Maybe Dad could go over to the U sometime during vacation and needle the Admissions Department into sending my transcript to Chicago real quick-like. (7) My Spanish is coming along slow, but—well, slow. I study every noon and my accent isn't too bad, according to Jerry. (8) All last week we've been leading a rugged life. No heat, no wood to start fires, no hot water, no lockers, no nothin' except mess. Now we have moved into squad rooms in the Hospital proper; fifty women in a room the size of our ground floor at home. Cramped is an understatement. Two hundred people to three ironing boards. (9) I will write about this weekend in a letter to Mike. (10) Sending home a package of stuff including a hide from which I plan to make a purse. Please roll same up in a roll of paper and put in cedar closet. (11) Have heard no further news about discharge. Things are still subject to change; you know the Army, but I feel sure it will be this summer sometime. (12) William was discharged last week. He's staying on at Beaumont as Editor of the *News* till July to make some money. We had another fight but made up again. We might get married when we finish school. Pleasantly vague, n'est-ce pas? I'll have him out to the farm in August. You must meet him. I'd kind of like to see him again myself. You can see by the brevity of this that I'm tired but happy. Life is full.

All love,

From Mom—Mar. 20, 1946:

I haven't had a real *letter from you for some time now—perhaps there will be a letter in tomorrow's mail. Busy as usual this week. Monday I was invited out to lunch at Jeanne's; we had a very good lunch and later a woman came and gave us all beauty treatments. Jeanne is thinking of going into the cosmetic business and the woman was demonstrating for J's benefit. We got all sorts of goo put on our faces, and a complete paint job. We all looked elegant, we thought, only Marian G.'s husband told her she looked like a woman of the streets, and someone else's husband said the eye shadow made her look as if she had kidney trouble. What's the use? Yesterday Thelma entertained the Doll Club en masse and we had a super lunch of fresh shrimp salad and all sorts of lush food. We sewed and gossiped. Today went over to church to help clean the kitchen cupboards. Tonight we celebrate a real event—one of our silver anniversaries: twenty-five years ago today, Dad and I met. I have a large amount of money to deposit in the Red Cross office again. Do write soon—I look every day for a letter.*

From Dad—Mar. 25, 1946:

Last Tuesday my damned old stomach started to go spastic on me. Johnson assures me that it is nothing but nervous fatigue. I cannot say that I like it under any name, but I have about pulled out by this time. If teaching brats, even under reduced efficiency, gives me these attacks, I might be a smart boy to call it a day and move out to the farm for good this summer. I want to in a couple of years anyway, so the change in plans would not be too radical. I am going to see Johnson this week and see what he thinks about the idea before I get my mind made up one way or another. I am planning a day at the farm with McN. and the Soil Conservation man from Stillwater to get summer plans set up and see what the East House may need. Your last letters were welcome. You seem to be having a tough time, what with skiing parties and such. Do you ever do any work, or is that just incidental now that peace has come? Sure hope that the Army lets you go on schedule. I'll hold back on my taxes if they do not, so there!

27 March 1946

Wednesday

Dear Family,

Life is wonderful. Spring has sprung, although it snowed last night and it was lovely this morning with feathery white on the fir trees. I'm filled with a euphoria which is senseless but fun. I go around singing merrily and despite the fact that I've had no letters except from family for about two weeks, I hate no one. Maybe it's the vitamin pills. I saw my first robin in two years last Sunday. It was a fat, healthy one. I also saw daffodils, hyacinths, forsythia and violets. Rain hasn't been in evidence as much as before. Gee, ain't it wonderful? OK, I'm crazy.

I have a three-day pass starting tomorrow. No travel is planned because no dough. Just before Lil left for Beale, the dear woman loaned Flo and me five smackers which has saved us from starvation and stagnation. I shall sleep during the day and be social in the evening. The calendar looks quite promising. To the boxing matches at North Fort tomorrow evening with Scott, a new guy in our department. He's an artist, a real one, and is going to teach watercolor, charcoal, oils, and ceramics to the patients. Handsome character he is, too. Very blond and tan and deep blue eyes. Last night we went over to the gym and played basketball and badminton, and then watched a game between Madigan and Main Fort. We won, of course. Friday night a jaunt into the jolly metropolis of Tacoma with Rose, this gal who was at BGH with us and is now up here as a clinical psychologist. We are going to investigate the possibilities of a skiing three-day pass next month. We have mid-morning breaks for coffee and chat; handy because I'm up on the NP Ramp every morning.[85] In the afternoons I now dispense tools in the main shop. This is hard work but a good deal because I don't get "clock-eyed." I'm far too busy and also it's fun to chat with all the patients instead of sitting back in a corner creating. Miss Miller has been extra-sweet to me the last couple of weeks. I can't understand it. What foul move is she planning??? Saturday Jerry is taking me to the play he's in. The civilians up here are great community do-ers. The area bristles with WPA Rec Houses, Little Theater groups, etc., all of which flourish. The plays always play to packed houses, and the performers and technical personnel have a swell time in the doing. The people that Jerry, Bob, and I visited last Saturday were also in the group and a large part of the conversation revolved around the approaching performance.

My God, someone just turned on the radio full blast just behind my left ear. I can see where we shall have no peace in the joint from now on. The kids from Section One just moved over and there are now over two hundred in the Company. It's like living in a subway station; the five o'clock rush would be hard put to it to beat the ten o'clock rush for our two showers for forty-two kids. In the midst of my jollity and cheer came the most disturbing news from Carmen. She and Lena and Cummings were recently transferred up to Bushnell Hospital in Brigham City, Utah, a desolate hole, seething with aggressive Mormons. According to Carmen, some officious so-and-so felt called upon to tell her she should not smoke

---

[85] This was the neuro-psychiatric ward. My occupational therapy technician job took me to different wards with a cart filled with craft supplies for the patients.

while in their fair city. Anyhow, the news is that Lena tried to commit suicide, failed, and is now locked up on the NP Ramp in an acute state of depression. That poor kid was somewhat off the beam, as I was, when we first got to BGH, but she never pulled out of it. She used to cry for hours on end and we were terribly worried, but never did anything definite about it. I guess those last five months of hard physical labor with no days off and getting bitched at by those fool nurses just broke her down. So she took a huge slug of Seconal so she could "just sleep her life away," as Carmen said. They found out in time to apply the stomach pump, and when she came to, she was hysterical and cried till her mattress was soaked through. Then she would have periods of excessive hilarity—typical symptoms of manic-depression. Latest news from Carmen says she is much better and will be moved onto the open ward soon and will get a thirty-day furlough. Carmen is working twelve hours one day and nine hours the next, but she will never crack up, I feel sure, because she has a full life in her mind. Lena doesn't have as much recourse to anything in herself.

I feel like a heel because I'm having so much fun up here. Such a good deal working, so much time off, meeting so many interesting and fun people. Ever since I got out of the hospital I've been tearing around. I hope it keeps up till September, but that's too much to ask. I shall probably be depressed in a couple of months but till then, whee! Everything is rosy. Got to go bone up on the Russian situation with Jerry's PM's[86] and *New York Times* (that should provide good balance) for our next week's orientation. We're having an open discussion and all the kids in Recon and Psych, the intelligentsia of the hospital, are planning to make it a free-for-all. Rose and I want to put in our twenty-five cents worth. Till Sunday or Monday, then.

All love,

From Mom — Mar. 30, 1946:

I certainly have not been doing right by you in the matter of letters. Dad's vacation plus my Red Cross job have interfered terrifically with my letters. Monday I had to preside at the Study Club—one of our joint

---

[86] *PM* was an evening newspaper in New York City whose editorial policies were considered left of center.

meetings at the Y—and we had a most interesting speaker, a young chap from Iran who is visiting professor of history at Macalester College. He gave us the background of the present trouble in Iran and had no good word for the British—most countries hate their guts, he said. Tuesday I was busy all day raking in Red Cross money and by nightfall had over ten thousand dollars to take down to headquarters. That night we went to the Builders' and Auto Show—saw some interesting things. The new cars are not very good looking—Packard is best. Yesterday Dad and I went to Monkey-Wards to look for certain things we might want on the farm—could find none of them. It's still awfully hard to buy anything.

For the last two weeks we have been talking almost constantly about our future plans. Dad has been having trouble with his stomach again, although it is better now. Dr. Johnson says there are no ulcers, it is only a nervous condition due to tension and strain and fatigue. Dad has about made up his mind to retire from Blake and I think it is very sensible. He is always a new man when school is out. McN. says he knows we can count on a good income from the farm by August and we think we could get along with some economizing. The main consideration is Dad's health, and I know that all he needs is to get out of school-teaching. We so wished you were here to plan with us, but the final decision is Dad's.

Now for your news. I'm so glad you are having fun. There must be more interesting people there than you have run across yet. All those fascinating men you meet! Are there any good prospects among them? I have been acquiring a few nylons—three pairs now—I've had one pair since before Christmas. Nearly four months of hard wear and they are as good as ever. The other two pair I haven't opened.

From Dad—Mar. 31, 1946:

We went to the Builders' Show one evening to see all the Post War gadgets that are not yet for sale. They are, however, making deep freezers and I think I shall get one for fall use when food is really coming off the farm. Our real garden will be at the farm where we should be able to raise proper crops. I think I shall resign from dear old Blake this June, go out on the farm and do my best to get things in shape. If we can put the East Farm in condition, I can sell this place and move out there, with Mike in the dormitory. To run that place properly is going to take most of my time from now on and, after twenty-five years, I have had about all the teaching that I want. I will take something of a cut in income during the first year, but I do not think that I shall have very much less than I have been making before we got the farm and that was enough for all of us. So that is how things stand at the present moment.

So sorry to hear about your friend Lena. Life seems to give some poor souls a frightful beating. I have seen men go completely off the beam in the last war and it was hard to tell just why they should smash under what just made the rest of us bitch with enthusiasm. You are one person about whom I have never had much worry. You may be in the dumps at times, but you never stay there and you come of fighting stock when things go wrong.

1 April 1946
Monday

Dear Family,

Pride goeth before a fall as the old saying has it and I am now suffering from an incipient cold. Damn and blast. I feel lousy; partly cold and partly too much roaring around over the weekend. Things didn't work out quite according to schedule but it was still fun. Thursday Scotty and I did go to the fights and drank beer at the NCO Club afterwards. When they closed we went over to the Sergeant's Club and got halfway into the bar when great shouts of "No Ladies Allowed!" greeted us. It was Stag Night and I should have guessed it from the blue haze and coarse roar of voices. So we slunk out. Friday night we went to the play. It was *A Good Fellow* by Kaufman and Hart, all about Lodge Brothers, Eagles and Elks and such. Rather amusing, followed by a party at some people's house. We played "Ziggy Za," a crazy Brazilian drinking song that Jerry taught us. Hilarious time had by all.

Next day went to the Daffodil Festival and parade in Puyallup (that's right). Many bands and pretty floats with forty million daffodils used. Had a street dance after the parade. Everyone stared at my nylons. That evening I sat backstage during the play and attended the cast party which migrated to Bob's and Jerry's house for more drinking and singing. Sunday I tried to catch up on my sleep, and that evening Scotty and I went to the show amidst great difficulties. Missed the early show at Number One, walked miles down to Number Three, saw terrific line and decided not to sweat it out, and thus walked clear back to Number One for late show. Healthy evening. Scotty is a very nice Joe—opens doors, lights my cigarette, helps me up and down curbs, pulls out chairs, etc. I feel like a clinging vine insead of the dray horse that the Army considers a WAC. Heard from Grace with all the latest which isn't much. She at last is over her cold and is resting as much as possible. I'm sorry to hear that Dad's stomach is on the hop again. I could get a furlough in June if you could help me pay for it—watcha think?

Goodbye from germ-ridden
Annie Bug

From Mom—Apr. 7, 1946:

Thursday night we went to the Parish House for a Lenten supper. I had a talk with Helen A. The WAC certainly dragged her down; she smokes publicly and said "damn" once! She has let her hair grow again and looks very pretty.

From Dad—Apr. 7, 1946:

Spent most of Saturday at the farm getting some records in shape and taking a chattel mortgage on everything in sight. My insides are coming on, but they are not yet all they should be. The Doc assures me they will be OK before too long; I trust that he is right. Well I crossed the Rubicon and burned all my bridges this week by going in to the Old Man and resigning my job! Twenty-one years at Blake and twenty-five of teaching are enough for any man. From present looks, we will be right in this house this coming winter and in the mean time I shall have plenty of work with the place to keep me busy; I am going into the butter and egg business in a big way. I think that I will be able to turn quite a nice penny selling what we raise to City Slickers and have a whale of a lot of fun doing it. "Maw, the egg man's here again." Shortly you will be the daughter of a full-time Minnesota farmer.

9 April 1946

Tuesday evening in a great rush

Dearest Family,

I guess you know by now that when you don't hear from me I'm having a good time. Frankly, I can't even remember what I did last mid-week, read probably. We had a very sharp orientation

Tuesday. Jerry, me and Bob against some Hearstian reactionary on the Russia-Iran-UNO question.[87] One evening Dorian, Harkins, and I had a bull session about Liberal politics. Life seems to be one big bull session lately which is a wonderful change from vapid gossip fests. Friday night Scotty and I went down to Tacoma for a drunk. It's so funny here, you feel as though you were going to a "speak" [speakeasy]. We got our liquor cards and queued up for our fifth apiece, then went over and joined the Racy Roberts Club where one is provided with mix and ice.[88] Danced to the juke box and had a fairly good time but the fair Scott is getting out of hand. I took off Bill's ring[89] because I was mad (he hadn't written for three weeks—all OK now) and El Artist thought that gave him license to move in, which it doesn't. We made a date for Saturday evening which I broke because I had a lousy hangover, and since then he's gone around in a blue mood, thinking he's in love with me and I'm a cruel woman. Men are so sappy sometimes. You'd think that he'd have some sense, being twenty-five and married once before, but some people never grow up. Luckily, Jerry suffers under no such delusions and is quite normal acting.

Saturday, Rose, Harkins and I went down to Olympia, a charming little town and the Capital. We bummed around shopping and viewing the sights which included an Army Day parade. I bought a gray sweater and a silver Peruvian belt buckle which is very swish and which left me practically flat broke. Sunday we three went skiing again. I'm getting really good, falling down hardly at all, and doing snow plows, Christies and schusses with a confident air. I'm getting to be a ski afficionado, reading ski mags and instruction books assiduously. Ski Heil! I'm really looking forward to our three-day pass up at Mount Baker. It should be fun. Last night Bob and I dropped into the Catholic Forum and crossed up

[87] In the spring of 1946, the great powers—the United States, Great Britain, and the Soviet Union—were jockeying for spheres of influence in Iran because of its oil and because of its strategic geographical position.

[88] Washington had strict liquor control laws, and alcohol was sold through state-run stores. Rationing cards were issued to residents and visitors. Alcoholic beverages were not sold by the drink, but private clubs (with nominal admission fees) let customers bring in their own bottles and have beverages mixed at the table. Texas had much the same system. I recall being in El Paso's nicest hotel and seeing people in the elegant dining room having crumpled brown bags with liquor bottles in them on the table.

[89] Bill had sent me his fraternity ring sometime previously as a "going steady" gesture, similar to pinning, as the custom was then in college. This was not the same as an engagement to be married.

the Padre with some sharp arguments. Little did the Father know that I was a heretic and that Bob, although brought up a Catholic, is half Jewish. Then out to the Chateau to listen to Norman Cousins' "On a Note of Triumph," have a highball and back early to bed. Tonight Dorian, Jerry, Bob and I are going over to some Lieutenant's house for a chat. I met them at the Puyallup Festival and they are fun people.

I wasn't too startled at your decision about quitting Blake, Dad. First because you've been threatening to, all spring, and secondly I've grown so used to sweeping changes and upheavals that it doesn't seem soul-searching, only sensible. Hooray for the farm. I have gotten over my cold only to have a nasty sinus again. This climate is definitely bad! Also got another smallpox vaccination; it didn't react badly, though. Will you send my good Bass moccasins on to me? My other shoes are collapsing. I've just about decided that I can't get to school until Winter Quarter. My Active Duty date isn't until 31 October and Lord knows how long after that till I get to the Separation Center. It will give me a rest to wait and I don't think I could take being discharged and going right up to school late, all in the same week. I take my entrance exams in a couple of weeks so things are looking good. I can't believe that I'm having such a swell time. I suppose something will happen to snaf it up soon, but till then . . .

All my love,
Bug

P.S.: Carmen tells me that Lena is much better and that they are going to discharge her. I'm so glad.

From Dad—Apr. 14, 1946:

I am glad that you approve of my new vocation. I have been at Blake just as long as I care to and I think that the change and lack of pressure will make a new man of me. Not that I am in too bad shape; Johnson assures me that time will turn the trick. I promise to be in top form when you get here. We did a walk this afternoon around Lake Harriet. I need more of them for I am very soft after the winter.

From Mom—Apr. 14, 1946:
The skiing must be wonderful. It's rather amazing to think of your getting to be such an enthusiast when you never did any here. Your friend Scott must be quite a trial. You ought to be able to write a book by now called, "Men I Have No'ed." Only one thing bothers me; please don't drink too much. I know you are free, white and twenty-one but even so—go easy on that. Write as often as you can. You don't know how I look forward to your letters.

16 April 1946

Tuesday

Hello Family,
Gosh, I'm a lazy bum about writing letters. I hope you understand it's not because I don't love you. Can't remember when I last wrote—oh, yes, it was last Tuesday. We went to the Bermans' but Lt. had just gotten a typhoid shot and was feeling lousy so we didn't stay long. Mrs. Berman is going to have Jerry and me over for dinner soon. They are real characters from Brooklyn. Instead, Bob, Dorian, Jerry and I went over to the Chateau and drank, discussed the C-10, sang songs and told dirty jokes. We had a lovely time. Wednesday evening I went to bed at five o'clock and slept like a veritable log to make up for so many nights of gaiety. Thursday Jerry and I went to dinner at a swell seafood place on the road to Tacoma where I had my first French fried onions since Lee's stopped serving them on account of the shortage of fat for the war. Friday Dorian and I went up to the NP Rec Hall and played records on the Magnavox. Just after chow we had a cocktail party in Jerry's office, which is really a glass-enclosed booth right in the main hall. Someone had given him a bottle of Hueblein's Manhattan mix, and the Red Cross gals donated cocktail glasses. There were Larry (a guy who works in OT), Scotty, me, Dorian, and Jerry, and just as we were toasting, in walks Miss Miller so we had a jolly party. Miller isn't a stool pigeon or a prude, she just doesn't know how to handle people.
Saturday morning I went over to the Convalescent Hospital to try to get some ski equipment (didn't succeed). It was a gorgeous day, warm and sunny and little white clouds whizzing around in the sky. The mountains showed up clear, and seemed very close. Flo,

Emma and I walked the five miles back to Section Five. It felt so good to walk out in the country again. That night I went to dinner and to Racy Roberts with Scotty and had a very dull evening, thank you. Although I finally got him to argue with me (half-heartedly at best) he becomes more possessive and more boring every time I see him, so I think I shan't go out with him again. Life is too short to waste on insipid people. Spring is really creeping up on us and the rain is much more infrequent than before. Sunday afternoon Jerry and I went for a long walk around the lakes dressed in sloppy clothes. I felt just like a civilian. In the evening one of the patients and a Red Cross girl came over for dinner. She cooked it and we did all the dirty work. We had fillets (liberated from the mess hall), potatoes fried with onions, pork chops, frozen peas, and "garbage salad" made by me. A pleasant change from mess hall and restaurant food.

There really isn't much news aside from social doings. More kids keep shipping in. We now have about 250 WACs—far overstrength. Our old Duty Sergeant from BGH, whom I loathed, is working in the tool room in OT, which is fine because I can leave early for lunch and can work with patients. I hope she gets varicose veins from running back and forth. Nyah! EC is in Med School now. No new rumors about discharge for the last month which is rather odd. We used to get one every week, about. I'm going to apply for furlough as soon as I find out when EC's two-week vacation between spring and summer quarter comes. Nothing new on U of Chicago; I'm still waiting for the entrance tests. I must rush to Orientation now so goodbye. Hope you are all feeling healthy. My cold has left, thank heaven.

All love,

17 April 1946

Wednesday

Dear Mom and Dad,

In this letter I'm going to tell you off. I wish to register a complaint; namely and to wit: I object to the tone, or rather some of the tones of your letters of late. You sound so crotchety; maybe it's just Minnesota Spring blues or something. But why all the complaints about me not writing? I don't seem to recall writing oftener than once a week except during times of extreme boredom or upheaval, and I think I've been getting off my one a week lately, maybe not till Monday or Tuesday, but you get them, I hope. And also, don't worry about drinking too much. I know it sounds like a lot when enumerated out in a list, but then I can think of some weeks when you seemed to be pretty gay, too. Maybe my young constitution can take it better than you can. I remember only one real binge I went on since I've been here and that was a couple of weeks ago with Scott, and even then I had only four highballs during the evening—it just hit me wrong. OK, that's all.

I am and have been for the last three weeks working very hard in OT. I've been in the tool room by myself which is like working in Dayton's during the Christmas rush. And just this week when we got in a new WAC who could take my place, today she gets a telegram that her father died and takes off on an emergency furlough for three weeks. I hope Challford gets back from hers pretty soon because it's kind of rugged running back and forth in that room all day. The only time I get to sit down is at lunch. This week will be rather irksome. Last night I pulled CQ and had to run from 4:30 till 11:00 chasing down people who had phone calls. Tomorrow night we are restricted to clean all the windows and woodwork. Friday night we wax and buff the floors. All this due to a big White Glove Inspection by the Colonel. You no doubt will be pleased to hear that I'm not going anywhere this weekend except up to Seattle Sunday afternoon to visit a U of Washington professor that Dorian knows. I looked in the PX for Easter cards or presents but couldn't find anything that wasn't insipid or that was worth buying. So the best I can do is wish you a Happy Easter in Polish: "Zyce Cy Wesolego Allelujah," to which you reply, "Zayennie." This I got from a crazy guy who called up last night while I was on CQ. He was on CQ in a dispensary over at North Fort and just wanted to talk so we chatted for about an hour. He also taught me two ways to say "Thank you": "Dzien Kirai," and "Bogzaplacz." Of course, these are pronounced completely differently than they look. This is all for now. Will write you next Monday.

Love,
Annie

P.S.: I'm also on latrine detail this week. I just want you to know I do other things besides just running around having fun.

From Dad—Apr. 21, 1946:

Easter Sunday: That's telling them, Corp. Annie! You WAC NCOs sure know how to dish it out when you have to and that's a fact! A bawling-out in the very best Bosanko tradition, if I do say so as shouldn't. Only you shouldn't have included your poor old pappy. Me, when they reach 21 I ain't got nothing to say unless it costs me money, and then I aim to say plenty. Remember, too, that your Mammy and little brother are both cursed with New England consciences which tend to bother them considerable. You are from my side of the family—a blooming Celt. Be sure that we realize life ain't all beer and skittles and we don't begrudge you a good weekend when you can get one! In the afternoon we went with the Danielsons to look at a farm they are aiming to buy in the Tonka district; nice buildings but too near and expensive. Might have possibilities as suburban real estate before too long.

Clothes just ain't, these days. I looked all over for a new sport coat (regular price $15) and finally ran some to earth at YQ at $40 to $50!! One coat, mind you. I finally dug out one at $25. I am afraid that our economy is due to blow up with a loud bang before too long and am I glad that most of my great wealth is in sound assets and that I have a basic commodity to sell. Also my insides are about 7/8 OK by now. Don has plowed up a big patch by the East Farm and we shall plant before too long.

From Mom—Apr. 22, 1946:

We, too, are having wonderful weather. I had been fortunate enough to get a leg of lamb for Easter dinner; meat has been very scarce here. Thursday afternoon I went to a cocktail party at the Minneapolis Club for the chairmen of the Red Cross Fund Drive—for the really important people who had worked. I, of course, being an important person, was there. My ward got the highest percentage of quota and also most money of any of the wards, so I was well pleased.

Well, I guess I got told off! I won't hound you any more about writing. It's true I get a weekly letter which is all one can expect of a busy person. It's just that I enjoy your letters so much I look forward to them. And I know you don't drink too much. By the time people are my age, or Dad's, we know better how to handle it and what our capacity is. As for you having a good time, you know I'm always glad that you are having fun—the more the merrier. I'm always pleased when you write that you are going out a lot and having dates, so don't imagine I'm criticizing you for that, for I didn't!

Hope you had a nice trip to Seattle. By the way, what sex is Dorian? I can't tell from the name if it is a girl or a man!

> *Loads of love,*
> *Mother*

22 April 1946

Monday

Dearest Family,

I hope you weren't too PO'd at my last letter but I was kind of sore and I just had to get it out of my system. I'm OK now. This barracks is really getting me down. It's brimming with people and you can't get away from all their silly yakking. Here tonight I thought I had escaped into the reading room which is about the size of our downstairs John, and there are five people in here now and more coming in every second, all chatting merrily. Gossip and dull stuff. Ah me, patience is the highest virtue! OT is getting me down too. Miller has me in the tool room all day and it's a damned irritating job. Maybe my five-day pass will rehabilitate things. Also, Challford should be coming back soon, we hope. The discussion now in here centers around the difficulties of holding a man. Dat don't interest me; all I worry about is getting rid of 'em. Yak, yak.

The weekend was most pleasant. Saturday Dorian and I went up to Rainier to the ski meet which was later cancelled because of a blizzard. But we stayed up and skied anyhow. The snow wasn't too good—sort of wet—but we had fun. That night Bob took me to the NCO Club where we had a terrific steak, better than most restaurant ones, and danced and chatted. Sunday afternoon we drove up to Seattle where we joined Dorian and Harkins at this professor's house. What a house! Functional but not stark, with a fantastic view out over Seattle and Lake Washington. It was a gorgeous spring day with sun and good smells and new little leaves and flowers and stuff. We didn't get up there till 5:30 so we stayed for supper, played records and had conversation. There were many people milling around. Later, when the mob thinned out, we had a long session about German Geopolitics (Bob had to give orientation on it today) and ended up discussing comparative government procedures of England and the US, and the Liberal press. It's really fun to be able to talk to people again. Things have worked out pretty well for this weekend after much switching around of plans and working of deals. We are leaving Friday night and won't be back till next Thursday morning, so don't worry if you don't hear from me. I'll try to get off a postcard at the end of the week. The best thing is that it won't cost much. Got to hit the sack now. Hope you are all well and stuff.

> All my love,
> Bug

23 April 1946

Tuesday

Dearest Mom,

Dorian is a *girl*! Graduate of Cal, getting her master's in June. Is a psychiatric social worker; is my big buddy. Much fun person. Most congenial person, except for Carmen, that I've met yet in the Army. I'm taking my test from Chi this afternoon. Wish me luck! I hope you aren't mad anymore at me. I haven't had a drink for two weeks except wine last Sunday.

> All my love,
> Annie

24 April 1946

Wednesday

Hello Family,

Just realized what an absent minded dope I am. I forgot to say muchas gracias for the pants which were much needed, and the hankies which were ditto. I'd been using all my beat-up four-year-old lingerie for dusting the floor, and my supply was somewhat depleted. I have a real sharp idea for a present for you-all, if I can find it. You just got to wait. The weather has been celestial of late. Nice and warm and springy. Scotty and I played two sets of tennis yesterday afternoon. I stink. Then I helped Dorian iron out some of the wording in her thesis. We're going to work tonight and tomorrow and then it will be all done so we can go on pass with clear consciences. It's going to be somewhat rugged hitch-hiking with skis and blanket rolls but we have things worked out pretty well. Here is a funny poem: "Lover's Lament":

You took my love,
You took my heart,
You took my breath
Right from the start.
And I didn't mind,
Please keep these things,
But give me back
My Air Corps wings!

I'm thinking of un-joining the American Legion. I never really knew what I was getting into and I don't think I like some of the things they advocate. Their newspapers are so aggressively back-slappy and booster-clubby that it annoys me. I want to look around before I decide what kind of a Vet's organization I want to be active in. Fine idea to join the White Bear Yacht Club, Dad. They have swell tennis courts, which is nice as there isn't anyplace else near the farm to play. Also nice pool and dances and things. Cynthia B. doesn't like some of the people that belong—"Too snobby," she says. But who cares about them. If you pay your dues and have fun playing tennis you don't have to chum with the snoots. Somewhere in the distance is playing a Glen Miller record. It reminds me of spring in Faribault when we used to lie out on the front steps after school and someone's Vic[trola] upstairs would float music out on the air, and we would be thinking about the JS [Junior-Senior Prom] and Commencement and finals. I'm glad the farm is coming along so well. It must be lovely out there at this time of year.

This morning I went to the dentist. Three cavities and much drilling and hurt. They have popped up since just before Christmas—not good. I am a bad girl: I have started wearing ankle socks with no stockings, mainly because I have no non-runny stockings to wear. I wonder how long it will be before they catch me? Jerry got back from San Fran yesterday, and he's mad because I am going away this weekend and he can't have a date. Men are selfish stinkers. Finally heard from William who is helling around Juarez and doing no work at all as far as I can see. He still hasn't decided where he's going to school. He better watch out or he won't get in anywhere. Did I tell you that Joseph is entitled to put Dr. in front of his name now? He's interning at Northwestern Hospital. Got to go back to the tool room so goodbye. I'll try to get off a postcard during the weekend.

Love,

28 April 1946

Mount Baker Lodge, Heather Inn Dormitories, Sunday

Dearest Family,

Here I am back at the old stand on Sunday night. It's just after chow and I am pleasantly pooped. After pulling many deals, such as getting ski equipment when the Colonel expressly forbade it, and promoting bed-rolls, and getting out of compulsory Company meeting, and getting off the Post out of uniform, we finally got up to Seattle Friday night via a ride from a guy in the EKG lab. We stayed the night at Stuart's—he is the Prof. we visited last Sunday. We each had a double bed to ourselves in their nicely finished-off attic. Also, we had baths! My first since Christmas pass at Grace's.

Saturday morning we popped up at dawn and taxied down to the bus station for the 6:30 to Bellingham, from thence at 10:00 a.m. by a local bus up to Glacier and from there in a station wagon to the Lodge. Up to Glacier it was beautiful spring weather and the scenery is tremendous. Mountains looming up in the distance, glimpses of the Sound, and the valley floor dotted with prosperous-looking farms, meadows and white cherry blooms. There are lots of wild flowers up here, plus many gardens of domesticated spring flowers like hyacinths, fields of tulips and daffodils and daisies. Saturday was warm and sunny so it really was a glorious ride. Above Glacier the mountains set in and as we approached Baker the snow got deeper and the scenery more rugged. Right now it feels like the dead of winter; the snow is twenty feet deep all over. We arrived about noon and skied some after chow. In the evening we sat around the fire drying out gear, and later they showed some ski movies. The main lodge has the restaurant and is very swanky; everything has Peter Hunt designs painted on it.[90] It's full of

---

[90] Peter Hunt was a designer who promoted Pennsylvania Dutch patterns for home decoration.

officers and fairly wealthy ski afficionados. The dorm last night had the younger crowd—namely, high school and slightly older. Very noisy and puppy-ish. They have all gone now and peace descends upon the joint. 'At's what I crave—peace and silence, good chow, some exercise, and more peace. I'm reading Theodore Dreiser's *The Bulwark* and I think he is a cruddy writer and vastly over-rated. But I plow on so I can denounce him with impunity. The dorms are awfully cold, being on the ground floor; the snow comes up above the roof so the buildings are buried except for the chimney. However, we are sleeping on the third deck of the bunks and the sleeping bags are pretty good. They have a piano in the main hall and now that everybody's gone I can get in some playing. Skiing wasn't too good today; wet snow falling since yesterday afternoon and continuing still. We hope it will stop soon. My turns are getting better—I can almost stem now. Got to go for now—must wax my shoes and hit the sack.

From Dad—Apr. 28, 1946:

Here it is past nine of the clock and I am too darned lazy to do you a real letter so you will have to put up with this. It has been a poor week. Wednesday evening I came down with a peach of a cold and was out of the picture till yesterday noon when I came to enough to take your Maw into town for supper and a movie. Today has been very springy and I managed to do a little work; a few screens on, cleaned up the next door lot and put in a few early onions. We are putting in the real garden on the farm and will not have that done till the middle of May which should be about right. I had hoped to get out this weekend, but I did not have the pep. Damn these colds, they sure do take it out of you.

6 May 1946

Monday

Dearest Family,

I don't know how much I can get written this morning because I am incarcerated in the tool room still and yet. We've got a new fellow but he turns out to be a goofball of the first water, so the burden just falls back on good old efficient me. This character has been in the Army about two weeks and as such has no idea about property responsibility, expendable and non-expendable inventory, and stuff like that. He just gives everything blithely away with a happy smile. Which makes it rough on me.

Let's see—I think I last wrote you on Sunday night. Right after I finished the letter we went over to the Inn and danced schottisches and polkas until we were exhausted. Monday morning we awoke to clear blue skies, sun, and fresh snow over everything. We got some swell pictures, I think. We were on one of the junior runs and there was no one but us around. Silence, peace and bright sun. What bliss. We skied a couple of hours and then it began to snow again so we came in and had chow and played rummy till it stopped snowing. Then we went out again, but somehow my balance was off and my self-confidence wasn't too good and I fell and wrenched my knee and ankle. Just then, George (my principal dancing partner of the night before) came out to give us a few pointers, and he made me get back on the horse that threw me. Soon I was doing professional snow plows and stem turns, but the minute I stopped skiing that damn knee got stiff and hurt terribly, and I had to wear an ace bandage. Monday night I was treated with much tender care. I got carried *to* a party, given in one of the cabins by a guy who worked there. We had hot buttered rums and sat around looking at the fire till we were in a stupor, and so home.

You must understand that there is a certain type of person who inhabits a ski lodge. Two types, really. One is the ski bum, usually wealthy, smooth clothes and equipment, who follows the snow around the country from lodge to lodge. Ski bums may have jobs as instructors or some such deal so that they can ski all day. Of such were George, Norm, and Hugh. The other type is the hostely eager beaver with no money, doing everything on a shoe string, cooking his own meals and not taking the tow. That was Dorian and me, only we didn't cook. Tuesday I sat around in front of the fire all day with George dancing attendance on poor, crippled me. We played bridge and gin rummy and cribbage, and in the afternoon I finished *The Bulwark*. That night we had a real cut-throat bridge session and Wednesday we had to come down. Luckily we got a ride all the way to our barracks from George and Norm who were going to Portland. It was a gorgeous day. High up in the mountains the snow was deep and cast blue shadows, and as we dropped down it got more and more spring-like with flowers everywhere. I have never seen such scenery; it leaves me gasping. All the Cascade Range was clear that day—May Day.

In Bellingham we stopped and had a sirloin dinner for $1.50—no inflation there.[91] From Bellingham down we drove along the bluff overlooking the Sound and the islands in the Straits of Georgia. As we got near Seattle, Rainier rose up like an incredible Hollywood backdrop. That mountain is really weird. When you see it, you don't believe it's really there. It always seems to be floating in a pink mist—more like an idea than a mountain. It's most uncanny. In Seattle we stopped to let Norm's girlfriend off. They live in Mercer Island in a house much like the fancy [Lake] Minnetonka kind [upper-class area west of Minneapolis]. After lying in deck chairs on the terrace, watching the sun set and drinking tall, cool drinks, we reluctantly shoved off for Tacoma and El Fort. And so a lovely five days was ended. No Army to bother us a-tall.

Thursday I managed to get out of work all day by having experimental overseas WAC clothing tried on me all morning. I'm a perfect thirty-six they said, but it ain't true. The guy didn't pull the tape measure tight enough—maybe he was bashful! And I had the dentist working on me in the early afternoon. After which I took off and Jerry and I went swimming in his lake. Cold, like Lake Superior, but we did it. I went home and started the *Arch of Triumph* [by Erich Maria Remarque] but fell into bed at an early hour. Friday night Jerry and I went to dinner at the Bermans' in Stillacoom. Before dinner we drove around the little roads by the Sound and smelled lilacs and lilies of the valley and oohed and aahed at the scenery. You just have to come out here. We had a very good dinner—Ev baked zucchini squash with cheese and tomato sauce and celery. Afterwards we sat around recovering from eating too much and then played "Categories," a word game involving much vocabulary, at which I stunk. These people around here are really on the ball and I am but an infinitesimal tadpole in a large ocean. It was a good evening. We got to laughing so loudly that the

---

[91] Prices were not controlled, and the scarcity of items that continued for some years after the war contributed to an inflationary effect, which my parents mentioned in letters of April 21, 1946. Prices in small towns tended to be lower than in the big cities.

landlord popped up and roared "What's wrong?" I guess he thought we were having an orgy or something.

Saturday night we went to a birthday party for a man who is some kind of city official for Tacoma. There were lots of interesting people there—a guy who writes for the *Seattle Times,* a doctor who is with the County Health Board, the Democratic Representative for Washington, a union organizer—all with wives or girlfriends. Much talk and drinking and dancing and gaiety and it didn't break up until 3:30. I stayed the night with the "Birthday Man" and his wife. We slept real late and had a large breakfast while we listened to the Symph. Then we lay out in the back yard and got suntanned and relaxed. For dinner we all piled over to Jerry's and had spaghetti and talked for awhile and then got me back home early to bed, and so, "my week."

I don't know whether or not I can get a furlough. There is a deal that no one can get one if he or she is within ninety days of discharge, and we are pretty positive that something will be done in July about Eighteen Month people. In any case, the thought of sitting up all the way to Minnesota only to come back to be discharged is rather appalling. Besides which we only get twelve days now. After all it won't be long now. There is a rumor going around that some of the Company will be shipped to Texas because we are over-strength so much. I hope I don't get roped in. The next time I pack I want it to be for good. Dorian and I were in luck. While we were gone, Col. Boyce, the head of the WAC Corps, visited the joint and they had big inspections and were restricted over Saturday and Sunday, and everything was horribly GI.

My tests for Chicago weren't bad at all and have been sent off. Now I have to wait for the findings of the Admissions Committee, and I hope I don't show up as a complete moron. Bill is still in Texas when last heard from which was quite some time ago, cuss him. He's having too good a time to write I guess, but I don't really blame him. Can't think of any more news at the moment. I'm sending a bunch of books and letters; you can stuff them away in my room if there's space enough by this time. What a job I'll have, hoeing out my closet when I finally do come home!

All love,

From Dad—May 5, 1946:

Another tough week fighting the laryngitis and not doing so well. My voice quit on Friday and is still gone, but I feel a bit better and managing some fair sleeps. Damnblast *the thing. Spent the day on the farm though it was cool and blowy and am half asleep now as a result. We got in a big mess of spuds, snags of onions (sweet and plain) and will do another mess of things next week. Milking nineteen and everything looks grand. We can hardly wait to move out. Mike drove the tractor and Midge helped round up the cows. Quite a day.*

Piles of love from us all . . .
Pappy

7 May 1946

Tuesday

Dearest Family,

Today has been a good day:

1. I got three extra pairs of nylons due to a foul-up on my clothing record. Hooray for the inefficiency of our Supply Sgt.
2. I gave a pint of blood and thus am eligible for $25 pretty soon through the mail. They [the army] upped the price $15, but we didn't get a shot of whiskey the way we did at BGH—only tomato juice.
3. Although someone walked off with my pen, I have another which is much better—an Esterbrook with a better point and it doesn't leak.
4. I'm going to see *Rebecca* again, it has come back to North Fort.
5. This isn't so good, I'm afraid. I'm going to be roped in on this experimental clothing deal. The most typical varieties of shapes have to wear these pants and boots and other things for ninety days, so I'm told. My name is on the board, along with numerous others, to see the CO tonight, and I tremble. Who wants to wear high boots, wool socks and wool pants in the summertime, I ask you?
6. The weather still holds good. Bob and I drove all around Tacoma last night while he looked for cars to buy and it was lovely. The sunset looked like Texas because the mountains stood out sharp against the red sky. The sparkling Sound and the pine trees were out of character, though.

In my parka with Barb Hawkins
waiting for the bus on our ski trip to Mt Ranier

Jil in the snow at Mt Ranier

Lil, Jess from Texas, & Flo on a three-day
pass to Port Angeles on Puget Sound

Me with Flo, another occupational technician

7. Carmen writes that Lena and Cummings are both getting married, but she doesn't say who to. One by one everyone drops off the tree, but not me. Got too many things to do first.

8. Enclosed find pictures of Mount Baker trip. Dorian and I both look haggy, especially Dorian. When she looks haggy she goes whole hog; when she gets fixed up she looks quite decent. Accompanying notes are on the back. Mount Baker itself is over another peak from the Lodge. You have to ski over Panorama Dome to see it.

Goodbye and all love,
Annie

Surprise for Mom should arrive Saturday.

From Mom—May 8, 1946:

Spring is so far advanced here—lilacs are marvelous. It's been about 85 this week, but too dry. Saturday I went downtown with Dad while he had a throat treatment. He has had such a bad case of laryngitis and it is still bad. He's awfully tired, too. I sure will be glad when school is over. I was interested in your reaction to Theodore Dreiser. I have never cared for his things, even when he was the bright young modern many years ago. Did you by chance read The Egg and I? *Very funny. The authoress is a niece of Jim Sanderson over at the U. I miss you so, Annie. It will be such fun to see you in June; that's not far off now. Hope your furlough works out all right.*

Emergency Leave

12 May to 9 June 1946

[When I got back to the Fort from a weekend pass on the evening of Mother's Day, May 12, the CQ told me the sergeant wanted to see me. Like a kid in school, I immediately thought I'd done something wrong, but that was not the problem. The sergeant asked me to sit down and handed me a telegram that said something like this: "Dad died suddenly early this morning. Please wire if you can get home for funeral Thursday. Love, Mother." I remember feeling stunned and wishing I had someone to hold me while I cried and talked but there was no one. I just walked and walked around the post until bed-check, mulling and grieving.

My memories of the next month consist of blank gaps interspersed with some sharp scenes. The trip home was especially vivid. On Monday I arranged with the Red Cross to get an emergency leave of fourteen days and travel authorization on army planes to hitchhike back to Minneapolis. I wired my mother that I would probably get home in time for the funeral, but I would call her en route when I had a definite arrival time. I have often wondered since then why I did not call home right away, to talk and find out what happened. One reason might be a kind of automatic reaction from depression days and wartime that phone calls were to be used only to announce bad news or specific travel plans. Long-distance lines were not to be used for just conversation. My letters refer to calling home only about three times in the nineteen months I had been away.

Early Tuesday morning my friend Bob drove me to the army air base where I sat on my duffle bag, dressed in my Class-A uniform with skirt and high-heeled pumps, waiting to be allowed on a plane heading east. Finally I was told I could get on a C-47, a small, low-flying plane going to Kansas by way of Great Falls, Montana. The C-47 had no passenger seats, only stretcherlike seats running down each side. When I got on, the benches were filled with enlisted men and officers, and it was indicated that I should sit on the floor. Not only that, but I was told to wear a parachute pack that had thick straps running down between my legs and under my skirt. I was furious, but so cowed by army discipline and officers that I did not complain aloud. I felt that justice was done when almost all of the men became airsick as the plane bounced through air pockets going over the Cascades and the Rockies. They were using the "urp-bags" and looking queasy while I felt all right and had a good head for air motion even though this was only my second flight. Tuesday I sat up all night in a Wichita train station and after a day-long train trip arrived home in Minnesota on Wednesday evening.

At the house a number of people were gathered around my mother, but I remember only my Aunt Nell from Milwaukee. I sat in a chair opposite my mother while she told me that on Saturday night before Mother's Day, a bad spring storm started with heavy snow and high winds. At some point she was aware of my father getting up and going downstairs, presumably to check on the progress of the storm. She heard a thumping noise that she thought was a storm door slamming, but in the morning she found my father collapsed and dead on the kitchen floor. In a tight, controlled voice she said she thought she should tell me that when Dad had the stomach surgery four years before, the diagnosis was cancer, but they decided not to tell my brother and me. I heard this news in a state of numbness, and that is the way the next week went. Everyone was super controlled, not "breaking down," but also not talking much except about unimportant details. The funeral-parlor viewing—a quick visit by my mother, brother, and me—was on Wednesday night, and the closed-casket Masonic funeral was at St. John's the next day.

By the end of the second week at home, which remains a complete blank, my friends persuaded me to accept a blind date to a sorority-fraternity party, where there would be a good crowd because so many fellows were returning from the service. My date was Ken Green, recently home from the navy. He was outgoing and talkative; we found we knew many people in common from the university. Even though he had left for the war before I was enrolled, I had heard of him because of the fame of his piano-playing and the Boogie-Woogie Club that had entertained Dimitri Mitropolous with the notorious ditty Ken had composed, "Beat Me, Dimitri, with a Beethoven Bass." When he heard that I was due back at Fort Lewis in two days, he suggested that I apply for an extension of leave. This had not occurred to me, but I remembered many people in our company getting three weeks' compassionate leave, so I called the local Red Cross and was surprised to receive authorization for two more weeks. This time was spent thawing out with Ken and my friends. I met his father and his mother, a warm-hearted Irish lady who wrapped me in a hug upon first meeting. Ken and I danced, listened to music, "smooched" (as we called it), and talked about our families, the war, religion, philosophy, and Life. Then it was June 9 and time for me to return to the army and for Ken to start summer session in the law school.]

11 June 1946

Tuesday

Dearest Mom and Mike,

Well, here I am back at the old stand and starting things off right by getting out of inspection. Don't worry though; I have legitimate reasons. One being that my bed isn't made up with all the blankets—all the barracks are moved around and I got gypped out of a blanket. Another reason is that my OD uniform is all wrinkled and also I have the wrong kind of patch on, it appears. We are now a part of the Sixth Army under General Stillwell. More darn red tape and junk.

My plane left about ten minutes after I called you, Mom. We had a very nice trip as it was pretty clear by that time and I slept most of the way. This trip I got a meal on the airline. It was real good, served in all kinds of cagey little cups and compartments. I am still extremely tired and pooped in spite of a good night's sleep so this won't be too coherent. Good news for me. Dorian hasn't shipped out after all. The whole deal was called off and I am very glad. Flo was on the list too. That would have really cleaned out my few chums at one swell foop. I got my blood money in the mail today and also my pay check for last month so as soon as I can get to the bank and cash them I will send you a money order. I got lots of letters, probably the last for some time—they always come in spurts. One from Grace which had much the same news as was in yours. A card from Carmen who was having a layover in Chicago and liking it much. Two letters from William and one from Alta who is getting out July first—what a deal that is. I burn every time I think of it. She and another WAVE are going to work or study (I couldn't quite tell which) in Chi this fall and have offered me a share in whatever kind of an apartment they can get. I think I will take them up on it, at least at first, because it would be more congenial than Pappy Berghoffer's upstairs dining room.

I start work tomorrow—don't know what doing because I didn't see Miss Miller. Challford still isn't back, worse luck. She turned into the hospital in Chicago with something wrong with her feet, but that makes more work in the department. Luckily I won't get the tool room foisted off on me because "Mom" Fisher, the WAC from BGH, is firmly entrenched therein and I think she feels it's her domain. Well, she can have it, bless her little heart. Bill writes that he saw an order which stated that for planning purposes the WAC may be assumed to exist until June 30, 1947. So we all have to root for the teenage draft which seems to be the only way I can get out before my two-year stretch is up. I am resigned to my fate, it says here. Dorian is off to Frisco next week for a five-day pass to receive her degree. She is still madly finishing up on the charts for her thesis and I helped her tonight. The PR [Public Relations] Office is going to make quite a big thing of it, and rightly so. It isn't every day a WAC gets her master's; it's just every day they rob Crown Jewels.

Talked to Jerry and find, not so oddly enough, that I am completely over my infatuation for the young man. Chalk it up to experience, sez me. Maybe my mild attack of "love" will immunize me for quite some years, who knows? We are still buddies though. We are planning on starting an AVC (American Veterans Committee) chapter in Lakewood, along with a slew of other people. I'm wanting something to work at to occupy my mind and keep me from going bugs these last few months. Madigan seems so desolate and grim after home. Unbearable Barracks—that's my slogan. Oh well, I won't be bitter and I am determined to make the best of things. I think I'd better stop this before I fall completely off my chair. Will write again in a couple of days and give you the latest on what goes on in OT. Till then, all my love and I hope that the sleep increases now that this wicked girl isn't home to keep you up till all hours. I'm truly sorry I worried you so much, Mom.

> Many hugs and kisses to you
> both,
> Annie

From Mom—June 12, 1946:

I shall be so glad to hear from you and find out what sort of trip you had back. It certainly was a wild night with a high wind and hail. Had a letter from Nell and she wants Mike and me to come over next week. Think we may go for a few days. I am feeling better and think it would be good for us both.

I feel so bad to think how critical I was of you, darling. You know how much I love you and how grand I think you are. It really was only because I have been so dazed and nervous that I wasn't too reasonable. It seemed as if we didn't really talk, but I still couldn't speak of Daddy without breaking down. You must know, however, how much we meant to each other. I never knew a man who was such a good husband as he was. And a father too. He was so tremendously proud of you and Mike.

I must go up and go to bed. Didn't sleep too well last night because I

*had drunk about six cups of tea, and it was as bad as a coffee jag. All my
love, dear, keep your courage up—it won't be long now.*

12 June 1946

Wednesday

Hello Family,

The great news is here at last, we are pretty sure. This morning
the "Horsepital" was abuzz that a TWX had come through that
definitely Twenty (or Twenty-one) Months would be eligible July
first. I never heard of anything getting around so fast in my borned
days. And tonight in Company Meeting, Lt. Brand said that she
had heard verbally from unimpeachable sources that such was
so—Twenty Months, that is. And that orders would be out soon on
it, and we would be notified immediately she hears anything. She
said only about twenty in the Company would be under this. I was
rather surprised; I thought there would be more, but maybe not.
Now that I think of it, most of the kids came in last spring. Oh
happy day, etc., but I don't really dare believe it after what
happened a couple of months ago, and in that case Flo had seen the
TWX with her own two eyes. But here it really seems to be very
much on the level. You will no doubt blow your top, but I am
cooking up a bright little scheme to go down to Texas after
Separation and see Bill. He knows quite a few civilian couples living
thereabouts with whom I could camp, and coach fare is so little I
think it would be a fine idea.

Dear old Miller is back at her old task of giving me the
business, but this time it didn't work. And when I learn for sure
about this discharge deal and have my orders, I will calmly proceed
to give her the business right back. She needn't think she can
intimidate me . . . Work isn't too bad, but guess what? Mom Fisher
got *another* furlough, this time to see her son, and Miller thinks I
should go back in the tool room. But no deal. I will raise one hell
of a stink and ask for a transfer and gripe to the head of Recon
before she can get away with it. Well, enough screaming for now.
I'm helping Dorian with her charts again. This is the last night. The
thesis goes out tomorrow and a great load will be off our chests. I
sweat it out almost as much as she does. Big date with Jerry
tomorrow. Cocktails at Allens', dinner at Lakewood, and thence to

the play he is in. Flo, Harkins, Dorian and I are going down to the Sound on Sunday and have a picnic, and that seems to line up my social doings for the weekend. Although one never knows what happens to plans around here. People change them about three times before finally deciding what the H. they are going to do!

All my love,

16 June 1946

Sunday

Hey, hey people—how come no hear from you? Dope on discharge is true!! After twenty-one months, OUT!! Which for me is the third of July. I don't get in with the first group but I guess three more days won't kill me. You'd better send that large suitcase out so I can pack my stuff around, and include . . . please . . . (1) peach dress; (2) Mom's brown and white pique suit; (3) red skirt with felt flowers; (4) white silk shirt; (5) beige cotton gloves; (6) green coat (if dry-cleaned). I am now trying to work a deal so I can be discharged at Camp Beale in California and get paid travel money. Besides Texas, I am also thinking of swinging up to New York to see Carmen and Dorian before coming back via Chicago. That should get me home sometime in August and then I'll have about a month before school starts. I can swing the deal on my own money by squeezing the pennies and traveling cheap and camping on friends so I won't have to be obligated to anyone.

Today was putrid and rainy, as it has been all week, so we couldn't go to the Sound. Instead we cooked our wieners up on the NP Ward and had an indoor picnic. The dinner party and play Thursday was very fun. Last night was a huge party at Jerry's given by the Bermans for a couple of Lt.s who are being discharged. In the afternoon Jerry and I had two dinners; one at Bermans' and one at Allens'—pretty cagey. When the party was on full swing, Jerry and Bob came back from the play with half the cast and a slew of other people so there was much conversation and dancing and fun. Ev Berman brought over mounds of salami, cheese, salad, olives, and stuff, so we also had a feast. That's about all the news I have at present. Got a letter from Grace and she is anxious to hear from you.

All my love,
Annie

17 June 1946

Monday

Dearest Mom,

Guess where? In the tool room! Yes, Fisher went on furlough today, and Annie's the goat. But only for a couple of afternoons a week, thank heavens. I was glad to get your letter today. The mails must be awfully slow or something. Milwaukee sounds like a good idea; a change of scene and being a guest with no responsibilities should be fun. No more news from here. Last night Dorian and I hitchhiked to Max Frolic's for a seafood dinner which tasted not at all like Army chow. Ugh, what stuff! I eat in the PX often to escape from it and from the chow-lines which are absolutely blocks long. After eating and gabbing over many cups of coffee we hiked partway back, about three miles, before picking up a ride, and the combo of good food, plus exercise, made me sleep like a top. I'm all caught up on sleep now. I do hope you are sleeping better now and not sweating out the dawn hours with the birds. The sun is shining today for a change. It's really pretty chilly here all summer; too cold to go swimming, durn it.

As this is just a scrawl hacked out between tool dispensing, I shall close. All my love, Mom dear, and I am wishing strongly for you that you may conquer your nerves before very long. In this messy world one must accept things philosophically and live on. After all, I feel, in view of the horrible things that have happened to the peoples in Europe and the homes that have been broken up far worse than ours, that we have much to be thankful for. We have so many happy remembrances of fun together that I feel compensated. Of course, you have a much harder job to adjust because your mode of life was disrupted, but I know you will succeed. I'm rooting for you, kid.

Love and many kisses,

P.S.: Packages of books and stuff will start arriving soon. The great day approacheth!!

From Mom—June 16, 1946:

Good to get your letter yesterday and to know the trip wasn't too uncomfortable. By now you should be pretty well rested up. Thursday morning I went down to see Dr. Johnson. He said my blood count was OK, likewise heart and blood pressure, but thinks my nerves and fluttery heart feeling are due to the good old menopause, and gave me a large shot of estrogen, and I'm to come in for them every two or three weeks. I think I feel better already.

We have had another tragedy at Blake. Bill S. died Friday night. Of course everyone has known he has had a bad heart for two years, but even so, it's always a shock. Poor Jeanne. She and Jeanne-Anne had dinner with us today—she's being a pretty good sport. She is taking his body East for burial, with a service here at St. John's tomorrow afternoon. Needless to say, I'm not going.

Mike and the Hodgies and I went to the farm yesterday afternoon. Our garden looks pretty good, only I don't suppose it will get much attention. If it survives and produces anything it will be by good luck more than anything else. Mike and I are going to Milwaukee Wednesday morning on the Hiawatha and will stay until Sunday or Monday next week. Most important of all, we got our meat in Stillwater yesterday. It makes a very fine showing in the deep freeze. Had a good pot roast of it for today's dinner. Miss you lots darling.

From Mom—June 19, 1946:

Hooray, hooray! What wonderful news! We had your letter of Wednesday, yesterday, and your airmail of Sunday came today confirming the rumor. I'm so glad for your sake, for I know it would have been hard to stay in till October. And you can get all lined up for school in the fall. I can't send you my suitcase for, as you know, Mike and I are planning on Colorado and are leaving for Milwaukee. But I am sending you a check to buy yourself a good one. I was thinking of getting that for your birthday in the fall, but you can have it now.

Of course I don't *think much of the idea of your going to Texas—I* think *Bill should come to see* you. *But I suppose you'll do as you please in the matter. Do you think you can afford to use all your money traveling around the country? I should think you'd need it for fall clothes. Do remember that I won't know until fall what sort of an income I'll have for the use of all of us, and we may have to cut down some. I shall help you on your* necessary *educational expenses but the income may not run to travel and luxuries. I suppose this will sound harsh to you, but I feel as if I should point it out to you. If you think you can afford it, I hope you have a good time. But I thought Carmen was going to Florida??? On the whole, I feel better. Nerves still jumpy at times, but improving I think.*

I had to go to court on Monday and down again yesterday for a conference with a man from the bank and a man from McN.'s office. So much detail, it all makes my head reel, but I guess I should let them *worry, and forget about it. It is so swell you are going to be out so soon—I hardly dared hope for it. Lots and lots of love from us both and three loud cheers.*

[This was the last letter of my mother's from this period that I preserved. Several others in June and July were not saved but are referred to in my letters to her.]

21 June 1946

Friday

Dearest Mom,

Finally got your letter in which you acknowledged the great news. The mails sure must be screwed up because so much time went by before I knew that you knew (that I knew that you knew that—etc.). I really believe it now because I signed my application this morning, and should be relieved of duty by next Friday. I am going to Fort Sheridan after all. I decided against swinging any deals and I will let the Army take its happy course. All my plans are still up in the air because I haven't heard from either Carmen or Bill. But of course there is still next week in which to make plans. I counted up all my sheckels and added up what I will get and I figured I can swing this traveling and still have $100 left if I am very frugal and if I continue to wear most of my older clothes next fall.

I feel I'd rather have this experience than have a brand-new outfit to flash around in. It is a question of which is more important. I've saved almost all of this month's salary and also next month's is coming in; also furlough rations and maybe a little bit of Terminal Leave pay. I know we aren't rolling in dough and I want to get some sort of part-time job in the fall. You know I don't like to have to touch you for dough after this long a time, but thanks for the $30 anyway. I guess you'd better forget about the clothes because of leaving next Friday. Just had a brainstorm; send the stuff to Mary B.'s in Chicago and I can whiz in and get it because Fort Sheridan is right near Chicago. Also send me Rachel K.'s address in New York. I will write many letters and tell you all I'm doing and I promise to be home around the first of August.

I trust you are having fun in Milwaukee. I feel that I want to have a little time to be away from things, too, and I hope you understand. Of course I was shocked to hear of Bill S.'s death. Now you have a chance to repay Jeanne for all her goodness to us in our trouble, with the added real sympathy which is beyond people who have not gone through the same experience. Got to rush and shove this in the mail. I've been quite social this week but I haven't got time to tell you about it and still mail this.

All my love, dearest Mom and to Mike,

Also, love to Aunt Nell and everyone.

26 June 1946

Wednesday

Dearest Mom,

Now with the calming prospect of three or four days waiting for the dear Army to move, I think I can write a coherent letter. Up to now, I've been in such a tizzy that I could think of nothing else, but I think I can give you a small account of my activities for the past week or so. At the party a week ago Saturday, I met a very charming fellow, a Lt. in Chem. Warfare, with whom I hit it off rather well. He was on the verge of getting discharged after three and a half years in servitude. Last Monday we both went to a gathering at the Bermans'—lots of good food like smoked turkey, pickled herring, cheese, Russian rye bread and such, and much arguing and talk as is usual at the Bermans'.

Tuesday night I went out to dinner with dear Jerry who, at this late date, has decided he is in love with me. What a silly situation; it all sounds like a *Redbook* story. On Wednesday Bernie received his Ruptured Duck so we went out to celebrate.[92] The only place I knew of was Racy Roberts, the VFW-sponsored bottle club in Tacoma, so we hied ourselves there, only to be greeted with a stern headshake: "No officers!" Frantic flashing of "The Duck" availed nothing. "He's still an officer . . ." Discrimination on the other side for once. So we asked where some other places were and as soon as we got outside, Bernie quickly ripped off all officer insignia and, as he had on OD trousers and battle jacket, he looked like a private. Off we trudged up the hills to the Derby Club and confidently breezed in. Heh! "Officers Only." This didn't floor us, though; we enlisted the aid of a friendly taxi driver who steered us to a road house on the way back to Fort Lewis where we danced to the juke and drank and had a fine time.

Thursday was a gorgeous day, one of the few, and I goofed off early to go for a jeep ride with Bernie and Milt, being driven by a GI who out-ranked me, but he didn't know it because I had on civvie slacks and a blouse. We drove all around the back woods of North Fort which abuts on the Sound. It was a lovely hot summer day and all the mountains were out. Then we came back and played pool and ate dinner at the Officers' Club with a bunch of the boys, I laughing to myself the while because nobody knew I was a WAC. We went to a show and then came back and had a sharp game of cut-throat bridge. Friday we went to a double-feature in Tacoma and then went to the Troubador again and danced. Saturday morning we drove, or rather were driven, into town where we shopped until Bernie's train left. He bought shirts and I got a cute little yellow rayon dress for the unbelievable price of $5.40. Of course it isn't very well made but it's good enough to knock around in this summer. Saturday and Sunday I washed and ironed clothes and read and caught up on my sleep. Monday evening I went over to Bermans' for supper. Last night, Dorian, Jerry and I and a bunch of kids went over to Allens' for an organizational meeting of

---

[92] "Ruptured Duck" was the army slang term for the small eagle insignia issued to people officially discharged from the armed forces.

the local AVC Chapter. I'm planning to join in Chicago but I wanted to hear more about it. It seems to be a liberal and active group that is well worth joining, and the campus chapter at Chicago should be good. After the meeting we adjourned to Max Folics' for beer and much talk. One of the girls lived in Chi about two blocks from Bergie's, and she's giving me the addresses of some of her friends there.

Today started my three-day pass which I extorted from Miss Miller. Slept late this morning and this afternoon Dorian and I went into town. I bought some white shirts for Bernie and two blouses for myself—I wanted several to wear on the train. I'm going to wear my slacks by gum!—no more of this trying to sleep on a coach sitting upright with skirt and pumps. Now I can be a comfortable civilian. Also, I got a bright colored scarf and some political pamphlets Dorian wants me to read. I'm really being pumped full of liberal literature these days—making up for lost time. We had a good Chinese dinner and got caught in a huge downpour while hitching back; I decided to go whole hog and had a swim in the newly opened pool. And that just about covers it.

I still don't know when I leave. The first group leaves tomorrow and I shouldn't be here later than Tuesday, but you never know. I finally heard from both Bill and Carmen. I have a place to stay in El Paso with a Captain and his wife so I am definitely taking off for Texas and will stay four or five days—long enough to get a tan anyway. Then on to New York. Carmen will be either there or in Hartford and Dorian will be out by that time and in New York. Big reunion time. I'm so glad you are enjoying yourself with Aunt Nell. We had fun that time before, didn't we?—except for my attack of GI runs. Hope you get my clothes off to Mary B's, and include my gray suit if you get this in time. Please also get Rachel's address, too. They're turning off the lights now so sack time is indicated.

> With all my love, dearest little
> Mom,

30 June 1946

Sunday

Dearest Mom,

Rotten luck today: I pulled CQ from 7:00 a.m. to 4:30 in the afternoon. I think it's a dirty trick to have such a long shift but such is life in Madigan Madhouse. I am still sitting around sweating out the great day. A kid from personnel said my papers had gone up for approval and that it would take a few days yet—curses. The Sgt. led me astray talking about Friday and stuff. One thing is sure—I'm not going to work any more. If Miller gets curious I'll tell her they're waiting for transportation. Anyway, she's going to San Francisco in a few days so she won't be interested.

Let's see . . . seems I last wrote—my gosh was it Friday? I've been in such a state lately that I don't know which end is up. I know, it was Wednesday. Thursday I went to the Reconditioning picnic at the Officers' Club at American Lake with dear Jerry. We are friends again which is a relief. Friday I felt putrid and lay in bed most of the day and also yesterday. This waiting around is getting on my nerves, but def. Wrote many letters to all my little chums and did much laundry. This afternoon the Allens are giving two big farewell parties for Jerry and I'm invited to both of them and it should be quite jolly and take my mind off the hanging around. What a rotten sentence, but in the midst of this I'm constantly jumping up to answer the phone. Sunday is always a datey day. And that absolutely ties up the news from here.

I'm reading a very interesting book about Old New Orleans called *Gumbo Ya-Ya;* did you ever run across it? Methinks you'd like it much. It was put out as a Federal Writers' Project. I also read Ilka Chase's *In Bed We Cry,* a lovely, trashy novel about crude New Yorkers—such a pleasant relief from politics and Dorian's crusading pamphlets. You gotta have a change of diet some time, sez I. Speaking of politics, did you hear the President last night? I thought he gave quite a good analysis of the price control situation, but a trifle late. I hope to hell they do something about this soon. I got to eat next year and I won't have Uncle Sugar to feed me. Goodbye, Mom dear, and let us hope this waiting doesn't go on much longer. I always seem to be having great farewells and then go on hanging around as an anti-climax. What a deal. All my best love, and I fervently hope you continue to feel better and better.

Much kisses to you and to Mike,

7 July 1946

Saturday

Surprise! I'm still here. Ain't it Awful, Mabel? Tuesday noon my orders finally came out. I'm to be at Separation Center next Thursday, and I'm leaving either Monday or Tuesday. When I groaned and moaned to the First Sgt. she told me that it was due to a lucky snaf-up that I was leaving even that early so I guess I should be thankful. Wednesday I got myself another three-day pass and spent it at the Allens eating, sleeping, reading and riding a bike all around the pretty little side roads. It has been lovely the past few days with sun and warmth. The party last Sunday night was fun—just a social gathering with wonderful hors d'oeuvres and a good punch. Enclosed find a "society" account of it all from the local paper. Monday night, Jerry and I went over to Allens for dinner and stayed with their kids while they went to various meetings.

On Tuesday a mob of us went to an ICC meeting in Tacoma (Independent Citizens' Committee of the Arts, Sciences and Professions). The Bermans, Dorian, Phil (a Red Cross man), me, and a couple of other gals in the Detachment had dinner at an Italian restaurant before the meeting. We had a fine discussion of old Yiddish curses. Dorian and I were the only "goys" in the group so we didn't have much to offer except appreciation. The speakers were most stimulating. The Democratic Representative talked for almost an hour about dirty deals that have cooked in Congress. There was a professor from the U of Washington who gave a brilliant talk on atomic power from which I learned much. And then there were other people who talked about ICC organizing. Enclosed find a brochure.

Jerry got his discharge Tuesday afternoon but he hung around for the ICC meeting after which we went over to Spencers for drinks and conversation, and more inside gossip about Washington. Today I must wash clothes and pack. Tomorrow the Bermans are taking me on a little trip around the Sound, and Monday is the DAY, we hope. I am getting another slight cold, blast it. This climate isn't too good for me, I guess. Oh yes, I'm not going to Texas, I don't think, because I have a deadline to meet Carmen in Hartford, and if I go down to El Paso I'll miss her. My plans are so nebulous.

When you next hear from me I *should* be in Chicago, by gum. So glad you had a good rest in Milwaukee.

All love,

P.S.: Happy Birthday.

[The ICC brochure, entitled "The Job for '46," listed the following issues of legislation that it was supporting: Support of the United Nations Organization; veto power for members of the Security Council; international control of atomic energy; full employment bill for 60,000,000 jobs; extension of price control, which expired June 30; Ellender-Taft-Wagner-Dingell Bill for a national health plan; permanent FEPC (Fair Employment Practices Commission) to end job discrimination; repeal of the poll tax for full franchise in the South; abolition of the House Committee on Un-American Activities; establishment of the National Science Foundation for federal subsidy of scientific research and training; McMahon Bill for government control of atomic energy; Fine Arts Bill for federal sponsorship of art; Unemployment Compensation Bill; federal aid to education; extension of Social Security to cover all workers; Missouri Valley Authority; liberalization of income tax to ease tax in the lower brackets.]

Aftermath

AFTERMATH
NEW YORK
13 July to 8 August 1946

Chicago

15 July 1946

In Chicago at Mary B.'s, Monday

Dearest Mom,

Got your letter today so I'm all up on your plans to go to Colorado and I'll do my best to orient you to mine. Tomorrow I'm going to wash clothes and get packed and I'll leave Wednesday if I can get a seat. Good deal for me: I got a little ticket which entitles me to furlough rates (1½ cents a mile) on trains (coach) to place of induction or anywhere else, and the Army paid us 5 cents a mile to place of induction, so I'll be making it about even to New York. I got $19.75 travel pay and $53.14 in furlough rations, and this month's pay; plus $100 cash for mustering-out pay (another $100 comes next month). Added to which I have $100 saved from my pay. Good, no? I'm sure I won't spend all this dough but it's nice to have a good backlog. I will probably stay in New York till about the twelfth of August when I will come back to Chicago to register at the U. I went down there today and saw the registrar and was informed that the advance registration starts the twelfth, and I can sign up, arrange courses, and stuff. I'll also put my name in for housing. I didn't have time to see Bergie, but I'll write her from New York and see her on my way back. I plan to go to the Vets Administration tomorrow to apply for my tuition because that takes so long to go through. I've had so many errands to run, like getting checks cashed, photostatic copies made of THE PAPER, getting travelers checks, and so on. Tomorrow I'll get my train tickets and then I'm all set. I never did get a good suitcase because, alas and alack, the PX didn't have anything except little satchel things, one of which I bought. I'm leaving my duffel bag with my GI stuff and excess here at Mary B.'s and will express it home when you return. I think you're wise to rent out the little farm house since we won't be back till the end of summer. I agree with all the objections you raised, and we can have fun in town, anyway.

Now for news: Everything went like clockwork on Friday, the twelfth. Physicals, interviews, pay records, clothing check—all on schedule and we even got out an hour and a half early—4:15 it was, and I immediately took off like a bird for Chicago. Ken came in about 8:30 and we went out and celebrated. You are confused about the Greenspot; the pinning was a gag but we like each other and have fun together so why not see each other? He and his friends were coming to Chi and when he heard I would be out and in Chi then naturally we arranged to have a party. His brother and sister-in-law live here and we stayed at their place in South Chicago two nights. Greenie left this morning to go back to school, but we had a swell time. Went to the Art Institute and ate and drank various places, and heard some good, hot music. Tell Mike we heard Lionel Hampton—most groovy. I'm rather due for a good sleep tonight, though. After I wash my hair I shall hit the sack. Mary has been very busy with a special insurance school thing. She told me about seeing you in Milwaukee and it sounded like fun. And I know that Colorado should be refreshing. Goodbye for awhile now, Mom dear.

All my love and hugs and kisses,

New York, New York

23 July 1946

65 University Place, New York, N.Y., Tuesday

Dearest Mom,

It seems that I am doing a lot better on this letter writing business than you are. How about it, hum? I haven't heard anything since that little sad waiting-for-the-train postcard from Des Moines.

I do hope you are enjoying yourself and are having a good visit. Me, I am having a fine time but in the midst of it all I look forward to being calmly at home for a couple of months. Let's see—I covered my Chicago stay pretty thoroughly—now for New York. I got in Thursday morning and found Rachel in a great whirl of packing and excitement. She wrote you about how she was going to Palestine to study. We talked all morning, and she told me all about what she had been doing and how she hated the Army and we had a mutual gripe session—although after awhile I tried to make things brighter because she was getting emotional just remembering it. She really is bitter, and with reasons, too, but nonetheless it is better to forget some things. After lunch she went on errands and I rested because I didn't get too much sleep on the coach. After we went to dinner we walked around in the Village and in Washington Square, and she took me through NYU where she has been going to school. It was a lovely evening but dreadfully hot. When we got back to the hotel, Bernie called and we arranged to meet the next day. He called for me about noon and we rode on an open-top bus all the way from 4th Street to 135th Street on Fifth Avenue and back down to Central Park. The sun was shining and there was a nice breeze and crowds of people and honking taxis and bright store windows and lovely apartment houses. Ah! Tres gai! We had lunch at Essex House (from where I sent you a postcard) and then went to the Museum of Modern Art. For dinner we came back to the Village and met Rachel and a woman she knew at school and we went to a quaint little place. Then Bernie and I walked almost all the way down to Wall Street. We were going to South Ferry, but I got exhausted so we took the subway and then rode the ferry across to Staten Island and back to cool off. It was a lovely ride with all the little lights. The harbor was full of ships and we saw where the Staten Island Ferry Slip [terminal building] was all burned down. After that we went back to Central Park to Tavern-on-the-Green where we danced in the open-air patio. And so ended a beautiful day.

Saturday morning I went to the Temple with Rachel, then we ate at one of the Schrafts, and I took a nap. Later in the afternoon Bernie came over, bringing his cousin who had come over from Palestine three months ago and another fellow who had just arrived. He had joined the Navy there as a Lt. and then they sent him to the States for duty. They talked to Rachel about conditions there. Bernie's mother's family are all in Palestine, so he and the other fellows were able to give her lots of addresses of people to see and who can help her get settled. Then Rachel had to go on some errand, but the rest of us went for a long ride way up into New York State along the Hudson River. It was a terribly hot day and the hills were blue with heat haze. When we got back it finally started to rain and hasn't let up since, blast it. The other guys let us off and we went to see a French movie, after which we sat in a little joint and drank beer, but we decided it was too hot to do anything but just go to bed and collapse. Sunday morning we had breakfast with Rachel's sister Naomi and another woman who wanted Rachel to contact her niece in Jerusalem. The kid's entire family were killed in Poland, and she made her way somehow to Italy and was sent to Palestine where she is in a Children's Settlement. Such a flood of talk she poured out; she was very frantic about it all but I don't blame her. Rachel is going to do her PhD Thesis in social sciences on the adjustment those kids are making. We went over to Naomi's for awhile and chatted, but then went back to the room to shed our clothes and try to cool off. For supper we went to a real Italian joint; at last I find really good spaghetti! Naomi and this other woman were both taking courses at the New School for Social Research and were soon deep in great arguments about relative merits of various profs and such. We returned to the hotel barely in advance of one huge thunderstorm which really rocked the place. It had been raining off and on quite hard but this was a deluge. That evening about 9:00 Bernie and his brother and sister-in-law came for me and we went to Cafe Society Downtown—my first New York night club. They had a good band and a floor show—boogie pianist, a singer, a sharp comic and a rotten ballad singer.

Rachel left yesterday morning early, and I went shopping. Got a Mexican skirt at an outrageous price and a leather Guatemalan purse at a good price and brown dress at a 14th Street dress emporium because I was disgusted at these expensive "shoppes." After doing a big washing, I took off for Hartford where I met Carmen for dinner and much talk. We went over to the home of the family with whom she is staying and talked some more. She had letters from Baggie and some of the other kids from BGH—it was good to hear the old gossip. I stayed at the Y for $1.00. This morning (as yesterday) was heavy rain and me with no raincoat. But Carmen had her Utility Coat and she bought an umbrella so we were OK. We shopped, I bought some good black pumps, went to the Art Museum, ate, and talked until my train left. She's going back up to Maine, but is coming down to N.Y. in a couple of weeks so we will really do the town. It sure was good to see her again. If only for the few worthwhile people I have met, my Army life was not wasted. So . . . here I am now this evening writing belated letters to people. Got a long letter from Ruthie telling of the doings of kids at home. Time to hit the sack. I do hope to hear from you soonly.

All my love to you and Mike,

8 August 1946

New York, New York, Thursday

Chere Mom,

Now I'm the one at fault about writing letters. Of course the reason is that I've been so busy having a good time that I just don't find space for letter writing or more sedentary pursuits. Dorian has been here for over a week, and Jerry is here, and between them and Bernie I am really kept on the go—sight-seeing and play-going and eating and such. I will relate all the fun things I have seen and done when I return. I should get to Chicago on Monday the 12th, and as I said I plan to spend three days registering and arranging my program. I don't think it will take longer than that and then home for a rest and reunion with family. Prepare yourself for some rather shocking news upon my return.

All my love to you and Mike,
Annie

P.S.: Isn't it awful about the polio epidemic? Maybe I should do volunteer hospital work when I get back.

Afterward
1980s

My final letter to my mother mentioned "shocking news." This was a reference to a tentative plan to marry one of the young men whom I had met during the previous year. Forty years later I will leave it a mystery as to which one it was. What actually happened was even more of a surprise, to me as well as to my mother.

I returned to Minneapolis in mid-August after a stop in Chicago to register at the University of Chicago and immediately began getting calls from Ken Green, whom I had met when I was home in May for my father's funeral. Our relationship, which I had thought was on a "good friends and having fun" basis, started becoming more serious; the idea of settling down with someone became more appealing. I felt natural and comfortable with Ken, and we could talk about everything and anything. His verbal wit and humor were especially endearing. He was almost the only man I had ever met who could make me laugh. I did not know what love really was, but we felt right and good together. One night, Ken said in a teasing tone, "Maybe we should get hitched," and I right away replied, "Name the day!" He claimed to be shocked that I took up his suggestion so fast, but we had been moving toward this decision all along.

In September we announced our formal engagement to my mother and his parents, and I wrote a "Dear John" letter to my other friend. I threw out my plans to go to Chicago and instead enrolled at the University of Minnesota, using my GI benefits. My mother was suspicious of Ken and only grudgingly went along with our plans to get married "in such a rush." I thought this was unfair in view of the fact that my mother and father had met in March and married in August. Young people are *so* unreasonable! His parents were delighted, especially his mother who welcomed me warmly as the daughter she always wanted but never had.

During the next month we searched the want-ads desperately for a place to live. Housing of any kind was nearly impossible to find even a year after the war was over, and many of our newly married or returning married veteran friends had to live with their parents. Finally we found a two-room apartment in a dilapidated old mansion that had been divided up into many living spaces. Our space was the former kitchen made into two narrow rooms, with a shared bathroom, three-ring gas burner, and an old-fashioned icebox with an overflowing drip pan—all for the affordable sum of twenty-two dollars a month, no extra charge for the cockroaches. We called it "The Taj Mahole." In the lull before midquarter exams, we were married on October 26 at St. John's Church, with a reception at my family's house. The honeymoon trip was a drive across the Mississippi River to St. Paul, Ken's home town, and two nights at the St. Paul Hotel.

Our wedding gifts were skimpy, but treasured. A friend of my mother's gave us some percale double-bed sheets that were "prewar and only used once." Another family friend gave us a rolling pin and measuring spoons. My sister-in-law's uncle in Chicago knew somebody who knew somebody who had access to some prewar appliances and obtained for us a shiny chrome streamlined toaster that still works perfectly after more than four decades of use. We also received with gratitude a used waffle iron from my father-in-law's business partner.

On Monday we were back to studying, trying to get into the academic routine after years away. The GI Bill paid for all tuition, books, and supplies at the college of one's choice. Each veteran also got a stipend for living expenses, with married male veterans getting an added dependency allowance. Between Ken's and my GI allowances, we got $155 a month from the Veterans Administration. By the end of the month, funds were usually low, so we ate lots of Campbell's soup and invited ourselves to the families for free meals.

We were on a waiting list for a new car, but never made it to the top, and finally bought our first car, a used Studebaker, in 1950. Today's flood of consumer goods in the burgeoning malls still has

Ken + I at our wedding reception

the power to amaze this Great Depression and World War II survivor.

My mother, widowed at age forty-six, began to pull herself together and lead an independent life. After selling cosmetics for a short time, she was offered a job in the fund-raising and public-relations office of a medical foundation in Minneapolis, where she worked until retirement. When we were expecting our first child in 1948, rental housing or apartments were still terribly difficult to find, especially for people with children. We helped Mother sell the house on York Avenue and buy a duplex where Ken and I lived in the lower unit for three years and where she stayed on for many years. The farm was sold in 1951. None of us ever lived on the place, but we went out for picnics in the summers, and we adopted a barn kitty from the tenant farmer.

My brother Michael finished Blake School and, after getting his education degrees from the University of Minnesota, taught junior high school social studies in the Minneapolis suburb where he and Sally, also a teacher, lived and raised three children. My mother in her last years lived in a retirement residence, a little foggy about details in the past but able to remember how wonderful the lilacs smelled the spring she met my father.

In October 1986 Ken and I celebrated our fortieth wedding anniversary with a repeat visit to the St. Paul Hotel. We remembered our forty years of fun and anguish, fighting and loving, raising three baby-boomers in the 1950s suburbs, Ken building a law practice and me returning to school as a psychology graduate student in the 1960s, spending the 1970s as a two-career empty-nest couple reveling in all that space.

Now, in the 1980s, Ken and I are thinking about retirement. We enjoy being with our adult children: son Paul, our two daughters Kate and Martha, and their families, including five grandchildren at last count. When we get together at the cabin on Whitefish Lake, it is what Martha calls a "Real Family Ordeal." Ken is telling jokes, kids are racing around and showing off, and everyone is talking at once and forgetting to take turns.

For millions of Americans who were young in the early 1940s, the war years were like a mountain-climbing adventure before coming out onto the settled adult plateau of the 1950s. We had suddenly left our humdrum lives, our jobs, and schools and were moved all around the vast United States or across the Atlantic and Pacific oceans to lands we had never thought we would see. We did not have to worry about our families and homelands being destroyed while we were off seeing the world. We were learning new skills, meeting new people, eating and drinking exotic substances, and trying out new social roles.

For the many service people whose lives were at risk where bombs and guns were going off, the war was not a cook-out. But for the rest of us, the slight tingle of danger and the unknown gave the kind of excitement that leads today's adventurers to polar expeditions and space exploration. We were all adventurers in those days. Then we grew up, came home, went back to work, and once in a while swapped war stories around the backyard barbecue.

Did the experiences of the war years make a difference in our lives? Was it a wrenching difference causing a move in a new direction? Was it a disruption, a revelation, a negative influence, a growth period? Was it an adventurous interlude to be looked back on with some fondness many decades later? Responses from both men and women would likely include some degree of "all of the above."

Joining the WAC gave me the chance to be more than a spectator in the worldwide upheaval that touched everyone's lives. One of my reasons for joining was that I felt that young single women with no family responsibilities should not be sitting comfortably at home, business as usual, when the fellows our age were being called into service. The WAC did not turn me into a feminist; I had been a feminist since I took an American history course in tenth grade. But my naïve 1940s self thought that women could contribute more to life than housework and babies. It did not occur to me then that there was a large part of humankind that did not want women to contribute and were threatened by the idea of women contributing. Nearly fifty years later, *this* war is still going on. The army itself did not seem like a drastic experience to me, nor do I think it made me into a different person. I had left home at fifteen to attend a rigorous and rule-bound church boarding school where I became used to living with a group of women, lacking privacy and freedom but having a strong sense of bonding. These conditions continued during my two years of college and then in the army.

While war service contributed to my personal growing-up, it indirectly led me into the 1950s backwater of child raising, low income, and the "togetherness" trap. It postponed my educational timetable by two years, and my relatively early marriage did the rest. I truly wanted a close family of more children than my own, where my brother and I were separated by five years, and I did not think I had the option of waiting until my thirties to start that family. My solution was to get the childbearing out of the way early on and then to go back for professional training later when I did not have to pay for child care. By the time Betty Friedan's wonderful book *The Feminine Mystique* came out in 1963, I had already been through the raised-eyebrow barrage of "What's this old lady of thirty-five doing on campus?" and "Why are you going back to school? You don't want to go to *work*, do you?" and "Aren't you ever going to be through writing term papers?"

In most lives there are points of choice, roads not taken, lucky or unlucky encounters; everything makes *some* difference. Looking over your shoulder for "should of's" and "could of's" in your life, unless you can put what you learned to current use, is just an emotional dead end. So I will never regret my "time out" in the army and my share in the great mid-twentieth-century experience of World War II.